Gender and Sociality in Amazonia

Gender and Sociality in Amazonia

How Real People are Made

Cecilia McCallum

Oxford • New York

First published in 2001 by
Berg
Editorial offices:
150 Cowley Road, Oxford, OX4 1JJ, UK
838 Broadway, Third Floor, New York, NY 10003-4812, USA

Berg is an imprint of Oxford International Publishers Ltd.

Library of Congress Cataloging-in-Publication Data
A catalogue record for this book is available from the Library of Congress.

British Library Cataloguing-in-Publication Data
A catalogue record for this book is available from the British Library.

ISBN 1 85973 449 9 (Cloth)

Typeset by JS Typesetting, Wellingborough, Northants.
Printed in the United Kingdom by Biddles Ltd, Guildford and King's Lynn.

Contents

Acknowledgements

Research funds for the fieldwork on which this book is based were generously provided by the Economic and Social Science Research Council of Great Britain, the Nuffield Foundation, and the Leverhulme Foundation, while I was first a doctoral student and then a visiting researcher at the London School of Economics and Political Science. I also thank the Central Research Fund of the University of London; the RAI for a Radcliffe-Brown Memorial Award; and the Museum of Mankind. I was able to finish writing the book while working as a visiting professor at the Federal University of Bahia (UFBA) thanks to support from Capes and CNPq in Brazil. I am also indebted to the Postgraduate Programme in the Social Sciences and the Institute of Collective Health of UFBA, my bases there in the past few years.

Many people have contributed to making this book. My greatest debt of all is to the Cashinahua people, only a few of whom I can mention here. My sincere gratitude to Francisco Lopes, Sueiro, Anisa Sampaio, José Sampaio, Luisa Augusto, Antônia Lopes, Rosa Lopes, José Augusto Pai, José Augusto Filho, Alcina Augusto, Zaira, Montenegro, Edvaldo, Augusto Pinheiro, Mouro, Deulza and Isabel Domingo, Leoncio, Laura, and Grompes. I also thank all those who are not mentioned but who received me with such tremendous hospitality on the Purus, the Curanja and the Jordão rivers.

In Brazil many people helped me immensely at the time of the fieldwork. Ricardo Arndt, Bruna Franchetto, Vanessa Lea, Alcida Ramos, Selma Bara, Joaquim Carvalho, Mouro Almeida, Marlete Oliveira, Mary Alegretti, Ronaldo Oliveira, Vera Sena, Terri Aquino, Nietta Monte, Fátima, Luis Carvalho, Armando, Teresinha, Gema Pivatto, Anselmo Fornechi, Ibrahim Farhat, Rosa Monteiro, Kanaú, Rubinho, Lori Altman, Roberto Zwetsch, Marco Antonio Mendes, Vera Botelho, Padre Paulino, Otarcília and the Josephine Sisters of Manuel Urbano. I thank them all.

I have received help from many friends and colleagues in writing about the Cashinahua. I thank all those who commented critically on my earliest analyses at the thesis-writing seminar at the LSE. My special gratitude goes to my thesis supervisor and friend, Joanna Overing, for all her

Acknowledgements

insights and wisdom. I also thank the examiners of my thesis, Marilyn Strathern and the late Alfred Gell, who gave me the help and the courage needed to go on and transform it to form the basis of this book. Others who have contributed over the years include Eduardo Viveiros de Castro, Christina Toren, Penny Harvey, Elizabeth Silva, Andrew Jones, Thaïs Silva, Stephen Hugh-Jones, Graham Townsley, Philippe Erikson, Christine Hugh-Jones, Maria Phylactou, Bruna Franchetto, Vanessa Lea, Don Kulick, Margaret Willson, Carlos Fausto, Luisa Elvira Belaunde, Elsje Lagrou and Ken Kensinger. Finally, the book would have been impossible to write without many years of help and stimulation from my dear *compadre*, Peter Gow. 'Valeu!'

My sincere thanks go to Kathyrn Earle at Berg for her support of this book and for her understanding as I struggled to finish the manuscript on time. The artist Ailton Lima kindly drew the *kacha* (Figure 12) for me.

I mention those friends and family who helped from the start with special thanks. My father, Mike McCallum, for inspiring me to become a traveller; my late stepfather, John Tatham, and grandmother, Molly Henry; Heather Gibson, Patrick Burke, Ana Paula Souto Maior, Claire Jenkins, Dilwyn Jenkins, Patricia Thorndike, Angela Amorim, Giovanni Silveira and Carlos Montenegro. I feel a special debt of gratitude to my friend and mother-in-law Clarice Costa Teixeira.

I shall find it hard to repay my husband, Edilson Costa Teixeira, and my daughter, Anna Karenina, for so much comprehension and support. I also thank them profoundly for their occasional impatience, a necessary reminder that life is so much more than a book. Above all, I thank my mother, Anne Tatham, to whom I owe everything. I dedicate this book to the three of them.

List of Figures and Tables

Figures

Table

A Note on Orthography

Foreign terms are in italics in the text. The language is indicated afterwards in brackets, unless it is already clear from the preceding text, with the exception of Cashinahua. Thus Portuguese is indicated by (P.); Spanish by (Sp.) and Latin by (Lat.). Cashinahua has an agglutinative structure and words are built up from prefixes, infixes and suffixes. I therefore write verb roots with a hyphen, to indicate that when spoken a suffix is added, for example '*pi-*' (to eat). The Cashinahua orthography adopted here is based upon Susan Montag's dictionary and grammar (1981), slightly adapted for English readers. I substitute 'h' for the 'j' of her dictionary. There are 18 letters in this Cashinahua alphabet, including four vowel symbols. The examples in italics in the following chart are English words, except where indicated. I am grateful to Thaïs Cristofaro Silva for her help in making it. The responsibility for any errors is mine.

a   As in *apple*. Low central oral vowel as in the Cashinahua term *ia* (louse). Also occurs as a low central nasal vowel, as in the Cashinahua term *ian* (lake).

b   As in *bat*. 'm' can sometimes be in free variation with 'b' at the beginning of words. Voiced bilabial stop.

ch As in *church*. Voiceless alveo-palatal affricate.

d   At the beginning of a word, as in *dog*. In the middle of a word it usually becomes a tap, like 't' in the American pronunciation of 'city', and in some orthographies may be written as 'r'. Voiced alveolar tap.

e   This sound has no equivalent in English. It is pronounced with the lips in the position for English 'e' as in *elephant*, but the tongue in the position for 'u' as in *ugly*. High unrounded central vowel.

i   As 'ea' in *pea*, or 'i' in *pip*, or 'e' in *pet*. Allophones [i] and [e] in free variation.

h   As in *hot* or *hat*. Voiced glottal fricative.

k   As in *cat*. Voiceless velar stop.

m   As in *mat*. Sometimes it occurs as 'b' – though the two symbols 'b' and 'm' represent distinct phonemes. Voiced bilabial nasal. It can be in free variation with 'b'.

n   At the beginning of a word or syllable, as in *not*. At the end of a syllable it indicates that the preceding vowel is nasalized. Voiced alveolar nasal.

p   As in *pat* (but slightly more plosive). Voiceless bilabial stop.

s   As in *satin*. Voiceless alveolar fricative.

t   As in *take*. Voiceless alveolar stop.

ts   Like the 'ts' in *its*. Voiceless alveolar affricate.

u   Either as 'u' in *put* or as 'o' in *pot* or *hotel*. High rounded back vowel, with allophones [u] or [o].

v   As 'w' in *water* or *wish*. Sometimes interchangeable with 'u'. Rounded back glide.

x   Represents two sounds. Either 'sh' as in *shadow* or *ash*; or the same sound made with the tip of the tongue turned back. Voiceless alveopalatal fricative. It might occur as a retroflex consonant.

y   As in *yap*. Sometimes interchangeable with 'i'. Unrounded palatal glide.

Introduction

This book is about 'gender' in a double sense. It is a study of gender and sociality as conceived and lived by the Cashinahua, an Amazonian people. It also evaluates recent trends in gender studies in the light of this ethnography. The book reconsiders approaches to sociality in the literature on indigenous Amazonian 'societies', taking inspiration from anthropological work on gender and sociality in other regions. Thus, it is an ethnography of a particular people, a comparative discussion of gender and social life in a specific ethnographic region, and also a dialogue with ideas and theories emerging from other areas of the human sciences within and beyond anthropology.

A fundamental premise of this book is that there is no anthropology that is 'more than' ethnography, no free-flying methodology, no theory to be articulated without the colour, taste and smell of empirical description. All the book's weight – and all its value – derives from the attempt to answer some of the complex questions that Amazonian peoples pose us. These questions speak to a series of issues that anthropology and gender studies in general ceaselessly debate: for example, hierarchy and inequality, sameness and difference, reason and affect, mind and body, materiality and representation. In the pages that follow I show how the Cashinahua themselves stimulate us to confront these issues with their own perspective. As is customary amongst my own kind, I investigate this perspective by borrowing language, inspiration, concepts and analyses, now from Amazonianist colleagues and now from other anthropologists, in a three-way critical dialogue between the Academy, the Indians and myself. Yet, as the new gender studies has taught us, none of these 'persons' are pristine or bounded. Rather, each is partial and fluid. So, if anthropologists can be deemed 'the Academy', they are only so by virtue of their function as in some measure the filters of other dialogues with other peoples, and this was so even before Malinowski 'invented' fieldwork or Mauss 'the Gift'. If the Indians are special and different, their difference is deeply entwined not just with many millennia of barely glimpsed historical change and development, but also with five hundred years of immersion in a history that began as European and mutated into a global one. And if I may be deemed a unique 'self', I must admit to the most diverse influences and embodied experiences that make me, if not a 'partial' being, at least a complex one.

With respect to this book, the most profound aspect of my self that was exercised in its making is the one that the Cashinahua themselves forged, both deliberately and unwittingly, over the two years that I spent amongst them. But other influences also come into play, amongst them the original idealism about indigenous peoples that a classic education in social anthropology did not dispel. This idealism was coloured by the climate of optimistic anti-racism that prevailed in Britain at the time I first journeyed to Brazil to begin fieldwork (1983). The book is undoubtedly marked by it. Anthropology is not a 'neutral' science, but rather a positioned knowledge of peoples who are made part other by the observer's eye, and part kin despite it. Inevitably – and luckily – the idealism was tempered by the discovery that the Cashinahua are human beings like any others, so that if the book is a useful contribution to the struggle against racism, then it is so as an account of another way of being human. It is true that even the most romantic young ethnographer has difficulty in maintaining a Rousseauian perspective in the face of the startling concreteness of life amongst Others. In my case, my first nights in a Cashinahua village were interrupted in the hours before dawn when my hosts tuned in to a particularly aggressive Spanish-language programme of an Evangelical radio station (actually for my benefit, though I did not know it at the time). I wondered how I would get through the next eighteen months or so (perhaps just as much because of the early hour of the broadcast as because of the message it blasted out). But the fact that I had not yet learnt Lévi-Strauss's lesson in *Tristes Tropiques* that authentic savagery is not to be found caused less disillusionment than the discovery that not all Indians are nice people. Some of them, of course, are extremely nice (and so I am able to write this book today). One of the most important lessons I learnt is this: that earthly angels are a figment of the Christian imagination. Another, is that if Rousseau's 'noble savages' do not live in the Americas, the people that do inhabit the forests of that region, like the Cashinahua, are indeed authentic and, as well as human, inheritors of a most original and creative way of thinking and being (which I explore in the chapters that follow).

As a young fieldworker in the 1980s, I also brought another set of preoccupations with me, derived from feminist debates both within and outside anthropology. I wanted to find out more about women's lives in an 'egalitarian society'. I wanted to redress the lack of information on women in anthropological studies. I also wanted to contribute to the debate on patriarchy and gender relations. If when I set out for the field feminists discussed 'sexual inequality' and deconstructed biological reductionism, by my return the declared winner of the fight pitting culture against nature was 'gender'. Few spoke of biology any more, only of its 'construction'. Thus I was safely able to see gender, like kinship, as 'constructed', though this did not solve all the puzzles I saw posed by the Cashinahua ethnography. Soon after my return, though, I acquired a manuscript copy of Marilyn Strathern's *The Gender of the Gift* (1988). It was like manna from heaven. Although many other influences shaped my writings about Amazonia and the Cashinahua, this book was especially important.

Over years of writing and repeated fieldwork trips to Acre (the state where the Brazilian Cashinahua live), I came to acquire a nuanced understanding of the complexity of the relationship between gender and power in their social system. In this book I demonstrate that a binary distinction between 'male' and 'female' structures social life in the Amazonian societies under focus, but that it does not underwrite a power 'structure'. The book's treatment of this issue owes much to those writing about gender in the 1980s and 1990s, many of whom developed Foucauldian approaches to power; but at the same time it is critical of certain tendencies. A chief concern of feminist anthropology in the 1980s was the social and cultural construction of sexuality and gender. Often feminist anthropologists transferred the 1970s concern with 'sexual inequality' and 'universal male domination' into theories that saw power as culturally and socially produced (a production seen as opposed to 'reducible to biological differences'). In the 1990s some postmodern approaches posited 'hegemonic masculinity', constructed in discourse, in the place of patriarchy, built on socio-economic relations between the 'sexes', as the source of men's 'universal domination' in human societies. Yet for a few anthropologists, including many Amazonian specialists, such a presumption did not fit well with the view from 'the ground'. It did not seem correct to posit universal male dominance in all lowland South American societies (Overing 1986b).

These issues are put face-to-face with the Cashinahua ethnography in this book. In the progress of the chapters that follow, it will become clear that neither men nor women consider that men dominate women in Cashinahua communities, though they might say that they are 'larger', or 'stronger' or speak better in public. I explore the reasoning behind such statements, in a discussion of Cashinahua epistemological practices, ontology, cosmology and eschatology as these shape social, economic, political and religious practice, in the first six chapters of the book. These chapters describe the most important aspects of day-to-day life in a local community. As a whole, they make the point that a theory of gender and sociality in Amazonia can only emerge from the perspective of the mundane and the ordinary, before being addressed to the extraordinary and apparently transcendental events and processes that some approaches to gender and social organization prefer to treat. Then, in the last, concluding chapter, I address directly the issues raised by 1970s feminist anthropology, its development in the 1980s, and the later, postmodernist, gender studies. I critique earlier studies of gender and sexuality in Amazonian societies through a re-analysis of so-called 'rituals of sexual antagonism'. I call attention to what Amazonians say about them, for example, that they function as increase rituals. I show how they are concerned ultimately with the production of day-to-day sociality. The rites may be treated as discursive practices that construct and enact specific 'takes' on sexuality, reproduction and alterity, but not as vehicles of 'ideology' or as 'discourse'. I then counterpose indigenous and post-modern views of subjectivity and personhood, representation and embodi-ment, and gender and power, in the context of my analysis of Cashinahua sociality, introducing the view from recent work on 'Amazonian perspect-ivism'. And so I am able to throw into relief some questionable aspects of 'performative gender theory' and related postmodern approaches to gender by demonstrating points of incompatibility with Amazonian ethnography. The conclusion insists that an anthropology sensitive to gender should incorporate indigenous ideas and concepts into the work of theoretical construction. Anthropological theory must humbly trace its own route through, not beyond, ethnography.

Sociality and Social Theory in the Amazonian Context

The book develops a specific view of sociality in Amazonia based on my interpretation of the ethnography. The term 'sociality' itself has gained visibility in contemporary social analysis as part of a move against anthropology's Durkheimian legacy. Its key concepts, anchored in the Society/Individual dichotomy, are seen by many as at best difficult and at worst 'theoretically obsolete' (Ingold 1996). However, 'sociality' is not yet a theoretical concept, but rather a term used in different senses by a variety of analysts. As a concept, its methodological bases are still under construction. It evokes a number of approaches that share in common a rejection of aspects of the Durkheimian heritage, such as the idea that all humans seek to *represent* the social formations in which they live as in some sense 'societies'. These approaches seek alternative lines of analysis more in tune with non-Western philosophies and ontologies, but diverge amongst themselves in important aspects.[1] The concept of sociality I develop in this book is specifically designed for the Amazonian context. Its elaboration is based on the way the Cashinahua practise and talk about social relationships with each other, with foreigners and with non-humans (spirits and animals). There is a strong *formal* aspect to this concept of sociality, for social relationships are organized according to a set of compatible logical systems, including moiety exogamy, preferential endogamy, cross-cousin marriage and an alternate generation namesake system. There are also important affective and moral components to the concept. Thus I stress the local values that inflect social interaction with a moral dimension, in which 'sociality' may be deemed a desired effect of certain transactions, and 'anti-sociality' the effect of others. It may also be said that I use the term sociality with two facets: one side shaped in reaction to Cashinahua social logic; and one side etched in response to new critical approaches in social theory. (It could be added that in a personal archaeology of my own discovery of the potential of the term, Strathern's (1988) discussion of Melanesian forms of sociality was decisive.)

The counterpart of the term 'sociality' in the literature is usually 'the person' (just as 'the individual' is that of 'society'). The present book is no exception. For indigenous Amazonians, persons are made, not born. This is so important in the organization of social life that once it became clear that African models based on the notion of descent do not easily fit these societies, the notion of 'personhood' became a central focus for social theory developed for the region (Overing Kaplan 1977; Seeger *et al.* 1979). In the Cashinahua case, the work that goes into producing themselves as 'Real Persons' (*Huni Kuin*) – their self-denomination – simultaneously produces gender as an embodied capacity for production and reproduction. Gender may be understood as an epistemological condition for social action, one that accumulates in the flesh and bones of proper human beings as either male or female agency. Once I have shown how this is done in some detail, I go on to examine how gender constitutes sociality itself when human agency is exercised within an interdependent set of social relationships. These relationships are organized in gendered configurations. They generate sociality through a series of productive and reproductive transformations in the economic cycle linking predation, work, appropriation, distribution, exchange, circulation and consumption. Alterity is a crucial feature of this cycle. All action is defined in relation to a distinction between same and other, so that social relationships operate along a scale, re-constituting otherness at one end, or transforming it into sameness at the other. As Viveiros de Castro (2001) asserts, kinship is never assumed or given for indigenous Amazonians, but rather constructed (in a phenomenological sense) over time. It is otherness – the social relationship expressed in an idiom of affinity – that is taken as 'given'. The *original* component of sociality, if we follow his reasoning, the base line from which its other components must be painfully created on a daily basis, is the social relation between distinct beings (whether humans, spirits or animals) who are each other's 'potential affines'. I would add that the mundane realization of this potential gives rise to the successful constitution of sociality, and that it always takes a gendered form. In the Cashinahua case, for example, one essential configuration is 'male–male affinity', which allows the transformation of hostile difference into potential sameness. This relationship can only be productive, however, in dynamic interrelation with another: 'male–female affinity'. By this 'relation between relations', other bodies are transformed into 'same' ones. Potential affines may become kin.

This approach to sociality and to kinship is built from one earlier 'processual' approach to social and economic organization in lowland South America and set critically against another. Turner (1979a, 1979b) adapted a model originally developed by Meillassoux (1981) for the Gê-speaking groups of central Brazil. He saw a social hierarchy structured by economic processes. Women were 'exchanged' within 'the system of family relations' in the creation of affinal ties, yet in uxorilocal marriages. Fathers-in-law controlled their sons-in-law through their control of women, via the institution of brideservice. Later Rivière (1984) and others adapted this model for elsewhere in Amazonia.[2] There are a number of difficulties with this approach.[3] One is that it takes gender as a naturally given aspect of male and female bodies, though now it is clear that Amazonians think that human bodies must be fabricated. Another is that male individuals and/or collectivities are deemed inherently social and political and their actions are assumed to revolve around the issue of 'control'. Women are thrown to 'the domestic' and the 'pre-social' (and are also assumed to be objectified values that men 'exchange'). Rivière takes up the distinction between 'brideservice' and 'bridewealth societies' to elaborate his model further. He argues that it is wealth in people, not things, that structures Amazonian social organizations, so that they are best characterized as 'political economies of people'. Like Turner, he emphasizes the importance of labour in the socio-economic process. Notwithstanding the difficulties implied by the model, this emphasis on the value of labour in Amazonian economies is an important insight, and the contrast with Melanesian systems is instructive. Strathern (1985) developed Collier and Rosaldo's (1981) distinction between 'brideservice' and 'bridewealth' societies. She writes:

In brideservice systems, things act as neither gifts nor commodities. . . very specific strategies are being used in the construction of relationships. In Collier and Rosaldo's brideservice systems . . ., relationships are set up by direct transfers of labour, that is, people perform services for one another, including supplying others with the products of hunting and gathering. The social value attached to the exchange of items is derivative from the relationship in question (Strathern 1985:202).

It follows from this, she says (in accord with Sacks 1979), that women in brideservice systems do not become gifts.

In the Cashinahua case, women are not objects to be 'exchanged', but producers and consumers themselves. Persons are the authors of items and substances that are either alienated or consumed. They are no longer proper persons when no longer authors – for example, when they travel or after death. The social value of 'items' lies in the enmeshing between their origin, in a person's authorship, and their destiny, in another's consumption of them. A true person works and makes others consume, thus growing their bodies and strengthening sociality. Bodies themselves must in the end be considered alongside other products made by properly human persons in the constitution of sociality. They too may be consumable, once divested of productive agency – and indeed the bodies of close kin once were consumed (McCallum 1999). The point to be stressed here is that 'Real Persons' are both makers of other bodies and also the accumulated effect of myriad 'consumptions'. This takes the form of embodied memory, so that, as Gow (1989) so brilliantly shows for the Piro, kinship itself is always constituted in a field shaped by memories of being cared for in the past.

In 1991 Gow published his analysis of Piro kinship and economy, developing a processual model of their mutual constitution in the socio-economic cycle linking production, distribution and consumption to reproduction, the making of people. This analysis, based on the study of an indigenous community on the Bajo Urubamba river in Peru, has shaped the approach to socio-economic organization and gender developed in the present book. This means, firstly, that social relationships are treated as in constant motion rather than reified in fixed structures. Secondly, no one relationship is seen as the crux of the system (least of all a 'male–female relation'). The focus of analysis shifts in two directions: away from the shape of the structures we may abstract (virilocal, patrilineal, etc.) and away from the relations between fixed terms (men and women, sons-in-law and fathers-in-law, etc.) to the relations between relationships (male–female affinity in relation to male–male affinity, for example) and to the embodied agency involved in social action itself (male or female human agency, for example). To begin to explain what this means and what it tells us about gender and sociality in Amazonia, it is time to turn to the Cashinahua.

The Cashinahua

Cashinahua people have lived for many centuries in the upper Jurua and Purus area, in the tropical forest region at present divided by the frontier between Peru and Brazil. Flowing from the hilly upper reaches in Peru, these two major tributaries of the Amazon are easily navigated, so that when the first Brazilians searching for rubber trees arrived, in the mid-nineteenth century, they had relatively easy passage. They encountered weak resistance from the many indigenous peoples who lived in the region (Chandless 1866, 1869; Tastevin and Rivet 1921; Tastevin 1925). It was soon dealt with or pre-empted by enslavement in debt-bondage or the practice of organized massacres known as *correrias* (P.). One of the headwaters of the Jurua, the Muru river, and its affluents the Humaitá and the Iboiçu, were home to the ancestors of the present-day Cashinahua when the first settlers arrived just before the turn of the nineteenth century (Figure 1). The first recorded contact, in 1892, heralded dramatic changes in their lives. A century later, their population was scattered across a wide region, ranging from the Brazilian upper Purus, where I did fieldwork, to the Curanja river in Peru, where Ken Kensinger conducted pioneering studies in the 1950s and 1960s, to the Jordão river at the headwaters of the Jurua, which I visited in 1984.

The rubber boom, in full swing in 1892, provided the impetus to the events that so changed Cashinahua people's lives. Many of them died. Others were 'adopted' as workers by *seringalistas* (P.), bosses who controlled rubber production in delimited swathes of the region. Others fled to the headwater regions in Peru. Sometimes decades passed without contact between the scattered groups, who shared the same immediate ancestors. Yet they remembered each other, and sporadic visits usually resulted in marriages and the renewal of kinship links. As a result they still share much in common: the organization of marriage; naming; agricultural and hunting practices; forms of distribution and consumption; cosmology. But differences also emerged. Distinct dialects of *Hancha Kuin*, the Cashinahua language, evolved. Some groups are bilingual in Portuguese (especially the men). The practice of living in communal houses (*malocas* (P.)) fell into disuse, as did funerary endocannibalism. Certain rituals were no longer performed in some areas. And distinct

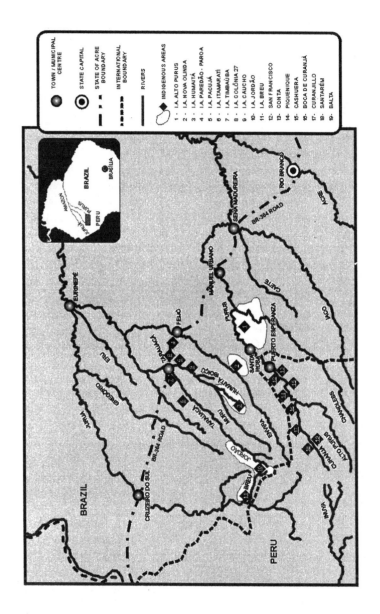

Figure 1. Map of Cashinahua areas in Brazil and Peru (1984)

settlement patterns emerged. These changes reflected differential insertion into the new regional economic systems that accompanied and followed the rubber boom. They were, to a large extent, shaped by the system for financing and controlling the extraction of wild rubber in the Amazonian region that was perfected in the nineteenth century, but which endured and developed until the late twentieth century. This is known as the *aviamento* (P.) or *habilitación* (Sp.) system.[4]

Aviamento is the 'fitting out' or 'supplying' of *seringalistas* (rubber bosses) with equipment and foodstuffs necessary to workers producing rubber by extracting latex from naturally occurring rubber trees. The bosses were lent money or given supplies by large commercial enterprises (originally based in Manaus or Belém). These, in turn, were in debt to international financial institutions. Each boss established dominion over a large area of forest known as a *seringal* ('rubber estate'), brought in men (often fleeing from poverty and droughts in Northeast Brazil) and sent them out to *colocações* ('placements') in the forest to tap latex. He supplied his workers, known as 'clients', on a credit basis. The debt was paid in large balls of smoked latex, but prices were fixed so that it was virtually impossible to pay off the total amount of debt. Many workers were trapped in virtual slavery. Thus the system was in fact a chain of debt reaching from the smallest hamlets in the headwater regions of the Amazon to the major banks of London.

The nineteenth-century Cashinahua lived in excellent rubber-producing territory. For this reason, many of their present-day relatives live at its margins or in areas (like the Peruvian settlements) where rubber suitable for permanent extraction of latex is not found. An important exception are the Cashinahua who live in the Jordão river area, where a high density of rubber trees is to be found. They are descendants of a group taken there as workers by a *seringalista* called Felizardo Cequeira (Aquino 1977). In Peru the intervention of the state and the Summer Institute of Linguistics (a North American missionary organization) in setting up schools, a health clinic and an outlet for the sale of handicrafts and other products led to the growth of one settlement, Balta, of over six hundred residents in the late 1970s (Kensinger 1995). Normally, though, village populations number between fifteen and one hundred. Those who were incorporated into the rubber economy proper as tapper families lived scattered in small settlements several hours apart, the *colocações* at the 'mouths' of rubber paths. Such paths wind through the forest from one tree to about one hundred others, circling back again to the point of origin. Other paths or streams and rivers connected the tappers to the local seat of power, the boss's home and the storehouse for the supplies, sometimes several days travel away (Da Cunha 1966; Bakx 1986). The rivers were lifelines to the outside world.

The world price of rubber collapsed in 1912 and by 1920 the non-indigenous population (now considerably out-numbering the indigenous) was falling, though it stabilized and increased gradually thereafter. A local rural economy developed and the power of the bosses diminished. But the *aviamento* system remained in place and there were a number of smaller booms (especially during the Second World War) and new waves of in-migration, again mainly from Northeast Brazil. After 1970, during the twenty years of military dictatorship (1964–1984), an important development occurred. The military government encouraged the sale of vast swathes of state land, incentivated settlers and built a road in from Southern Brazil. 'Development' policies led to ranching initiatives and above all, land speculation. The old rubber bosses left and land-grabbers moved in, selling illegally claimed land, from which they expelled the tappers, to companies and 'ranchers' – though in fact by 1985 the land cleared for beef represented only a small proportion of the state of Acre. Most ranches were located away from Cashinahua areas. This in fact had a beneficial effect for Cashinahua land claims. Rubber tappers found it difficult to make a living. Many moved out to the towns, whilst the new settlers did not venture far from the areas close to the new roads or the official land settlement projects (Bakx 1986). But in some areas tappers organized trade unions and resisted the ranchers and land-grabbers, led most famously by Chico Mendes.

While the social movement defending tapper rights to a livelihood from the forest emerged, a number of non-governmental and Church–linked organizations stimulated a parallel movement amongst the indigenous peoples. From the 1970s these groups helped indigenous cooperatives obtain funding so that the Cashinahua could bypass intermediaries in the sale of produce and purchase of supplies, thus escaping the debt traps of the *aviamento* system, and also learning to manoeuvre politically in regional and national arenas. During the 1980s the NGOs included the Pro-Indian Commission of Acre (CPI-AC), founded by a local anthropologist and staffed mainly by non-Indians; a local 'Union of Indian Nations' (UNI-Norte); and the Catholic Church's lay 'Missionary Indigenist Council' (CIMI). The activities of these different groups helped the Cashinahua to begin to operate politically at a regional and national level, in defence of land rights, so that by 1999 many of the Indigenous Areas claimed under Brazilian law were registered if not recognized (Monte 2000). The CPI-AC set up an education programme, training indigenous teachers and 'barefoot doctors', and by 1990 UNI-Norte was sending medical teams into some areas, attempting to deal with a health situation so poor that only a major goverment programme covering both indigenous and non-indigenous populations could hope to improve it. The Brazilian National Indian Foundation (FUNAI) had a local branch, which ran the under-financed *Casa do Índio* (Indian's House) in the state capital, Rio Branco. Sick Indians and their relatives lodged here, and FUNAI nurses cared for them in precarious conditions. The turbulent political scenario of the 1980s and 1990s saw the indigenous leaders struggling to obtain land titles, better healthcare and more funding for local economic projects, including, increasingly, the development of sustainable extraction of forest products (Aquino and Iglesias, n.d.). Although rubber may be produced under this new model, withdrawal of government subsidies in the 1980s led to a collapse in its price, so that the Cashinahua, like other Acreanos, continue to search for a viable means of generating a cash income. Unlike many, however, they practise a sophisticated swidden agriculture and gather, hunt and fish an extensive and nutritionally rich variety of foodstuffs, so that if lack of cash means that modern tools of production are sometimes hard to obtain, subsistence itself is not.

The Cashinahua are important players in this scene, as might be expected, for theirs is the largest local indigenous population in Acre (and also on the upper Purus region on the Peruvian side of the border). Their numbers are expanding. In 1985 there were a total of about 2,090 Cashinahua in Acre and about 850 in Peru (McCallum 1989). In 1999 there were about 3,964 in Acre and an estimated 1,500 in Peru (Aquino and Iglesias 1999). During the period 1984–90 I visited a number of Cashinahua villages in both Brazil and Peru, spending a total of two years in the field. Most of this time I lived in one village, Recreio, in the Alto Purus Indigenous Area – the AIAP (*Área Indígena do Alto Purus* (P.)), whose population fluctuated between one hundred and one hundred and fifty people. Most of the residents were close relatives of the Peruvian Cashinahua. Others arrived from Peru just before or during the main stretch of my fieldwork (1984 and 1985). An hour upriver by motorized canoe another large village, Fronteira, was made up mainly of Cashinahua who had settled there some years previously, coming from the Énvira river. All these people called themselves *Huni Kuin* (Real Persons), a term that they may translate as *Índios* (P.), thus extending it to all indigenous peoples (even their downriver neighbours, the Kulina, whom they tend to mistrust and even dislike). Strictly speaking it refers to Panoan-speaking peoples such as the Sharanahua and Yaminahua. The term *Kaxinaua* is a nickname with a possibly derogatory flavour, invented by other Panoans, and sometimes used by the Cashinahua in inter-ethnic situations for

Introduction

convenience's sake. It may be glossed as 'Vampire Bat People'. *Huni Kuin* is conceptually opposed to *Nawa*, 'Foreigner', the term used to refer to non-Indians, who may also be more narrowly specified as *Cariú* (P.). *Cariú* is the local Acreano term used to refer to the regional populations of rubber-tappers and town-dwellers, whose varied phenotypes speak of indigenous, African and European descent. *Cariú* people occupy the opposite side of the Purus river from the AIAP and very occasionally visit the villages. Normally, however, each group keeps to itself. Relations remain peaceful but tense. Hostility may flare up occasionally if Cariú invade Indian land to hunt or fish (McCallum, in press). Local racism holds that the Indians (*Cabodos*) are little better than animals (Aquino 1977). FUNAI had supported the expulsion of some Cariú families from the AIAP in the 1970s, and in 1985 memories of this recent dispropriation were still fresh. But not all Nawa were bad in Cashinahua eyes. 'Good Nawa' like myself were considered useful and at times necessary, helping in encounters with powerful outsiders, bringing and dispensing medicines and other useful knowledge, and (ideally) acting as trading intermediaries. During my stay in Recreio, I engaged in all three, though not as much as my hosts desired. Most of my time, nevertheless, was spent either in humdrum activities such as working in the gardens with the women, helping prepare food, child-minding, handicrafts, fishing and visiting, or else learning Cashinahua, talking with my 'informants', taping, taking photographs and making notes.

Reflections on 'the Cashinahua'

Most of this book is written in the ethnographic present, though often I am writing about events and patterns of living that I experienced a decade ago. I choose this tense in order to underline the fact that the thinking and practices described in the book have historical weight and manifest a certain stability in social and cultural organization. The ethnographic present allows easy communication between this text and other anthropological studies, and allows for economy and elegance of style. In order to make it clear that I write about a historical situation, not a timeless 'culture', I introduce dates or period characterizations in the text when necessary, for example when referring to specific events or eliciting evidence that certain ideas or practices have changed. As well as using the present tense freely, I also adopt the convention of referring to 'the Cashinahua'. I should make it clear that this phrase refers in the first instance to an embodied memory in myself (and in their other ethnographers), rather than to any hypothetical group of people paralysed in the flow of (Euro-American) historical time. This construction, 'the Cashinahua', should be taken extremely seriously, I believe. It originates in memories generated by long-term co-residence with flesh-and-blood individuals, memories constantly renewed by return to the fieldnotes, interview transcripts, texts, tapes, photos and other paraphernalia brought back as 'data', as well as the publications of other anthropologists who write about them and to whom I shall refer throughout the book. If 'the Cashinahua' appear to become a fictionalized personality in the pages of anthropological texts, they do so under the constant pressure exerted by this wealth of real dialogue and experience. Claims to validity rest here.

Notes

1. For discussion of variation in concepts of sociality, see for example McCallum, n.d.; Strathern 1999; Ingold 1987, 1986.
2. Adherents to the political economy of control approach include Mentore 1987; Rosengren 1987; Lorrain 2000.
3. For a critical appreciation, see McCallum 1989; Gow 1991; Lea 1986, 2000; Viveiros de Castro 1986.
4. Cashinahua history is discussed in McCallum 1989; Kensinger 1995; R. Montag 1998; Aquino 1977; Tastevin and Rivet 1921; Tastevin 1926. On the rubber economy and boom see Cardoso and Müller 1978; Bakx 1986; Weinstein 1983; Wagley 1976; Tocantins 1979; Dean 1987.

–1–

Kinship and the Child

Making kin, through procreation, childbirth and childcare, is for the Cashinahua the archetypal process whereby real people are made. As babies are conceived and raised by their parents and other kin, the multiple acts that give them form, substance, strength and knowledge progressively imbue them with personhood and gender. This chapter and the next describe these processes and the structure within which they take place.

Procreation and Pregnancy

The Cashinahua term for making a child is *ba va*, 'to make be created or be born'. *Ba* on its own may be translated as either 'to be born' or 'to be cooked' and this range of meaning is not coincidental, as will become clear in this chapter and the next. Men and women make babies together, by means of the repetitive interaction of the male organ of procreation (the penis) and the female organ (the womb). Thus, if a person is describing a relationship to a half-sibling, s/he might say '*hina betsa, xankin habias*' (another penis, same uterus). For a long time I was puzzled about Cashinahua opinion on the formation and growth of a foetus. Some people told me it was made of blood and others said that God made it, but all concurred on two points, namely that babies are formed through repeated intercourse, and that any man that makes love to the mother whilst she is carrying a child will also be the father of that child. The Yaminahua say that babies are made out of blood and that semen is male blood (Townsley 1988). The Cashinahua also consider semen and blood to be similar, a view that dates back at least to the early twentieth century, as the following section of a myth recorded by Abreu bears witness: 'When the new moon came out two days later, all the women bled. When they had stopped, they became pregnant. The blood coagulated and when the child was born, its body was dark, they say. When the semen coagulated, the child was born white' (Abreu 1941:5402).

Blood (*himi*) is associated with physical energy and strength, qualities that diminish as a person expends this vital fluid in work, sex, or illness.

Blood can be a dangerous substance and should never be eaten. If food is undercooked people exclaim *'Himiki!'* – 'It's bloody!', and refuse it. A man cannot make love to his menstruating wife lest he lose his luck in hunting, nor may any man see a woman other than his wife give birth, for the same reason. A pregnant woman should not see copious quantities of blood, in case she begin to bleed herself. The smell of body fluids is disgusting and in the wrong circumstances dangerous. Parents scold their young children for masturbating, since both semen and vaginal fluids are offensive. *'Itsaki!'* (it stinks), they will say. Thus, men and women should wash well after making love. Traditionally, women made a special ceramic bowl for this purpose.

This does not diminish the Cashinahua appetite for making babies. Isaias told me:

> One has to work a lot, otherwise it takes a long time [for the foetus] to grow. The man who will produce, who wants to make a baby, he drank a lot of *caissuma*. He can only do it after the woman menstruates, before that it's no use. Yes, there is a mixture of blood and semen. One has to take care, one cannot spoil the 'milk' (i.e. semen).[1]

This description brings out several aspects of Cashinahua conception theory that struck me time and again. Firstly, the act of making a baby involves repetitive work. Frequent intercourse makes the vital fluids clot and grow fast. Sex is itself work, making the body hot and sweaty, draining it of energy, and ultimately transforming seemingly inert matter into life itself. Both men and women do this work; there was never any suggestion that female participation in either the sexual act or in procreation is passive, whilst male participation is active. Indeed the standard word for making love is *chutaname*. *Chuta-* means to fornicate, and *-name* is the reciprocal participle. The idea is conveyed that men and women make love to each other reciprocally. This emphasis on mutuality is also found in beliefs about the way that sex can deplete or strengthen a person. I was told that a woman can grow fat and sleek from sex, while a man who has too much sex grows thin and weak. Later on the woman will get worn out from sex and the man will grow strong. There is an 'exchange', a *troca* (P).

Menstruation is desirable because it means that afterwards the woman may become pregnant. The blood is a sign of her fertility. People told me 'She is menstruating as a preparation for becoming pregnant' – *Himi ikiki, bake bikatsi.* (*Bake* signifies 'a child', *bi-* means 'to get', and here the particle *-katsi* can be glossed as either 'in preparation for' or as 'desiring'.)

Women who never bleed are infertile. It is said that their wombs are dry, and that sex is painful for them. In a similar vein, women who never have sex suffer from hard, dry wombs, so that lovemaking is a kind of 'servicing' for women. Although men may abstain from sex for long periods, women should not do without except when they are recovering from birth or menstruating. Such abstinence is unhealthy. But sex during the woman's menstruation would cause too much bleeding, so abstinence at this time is mutually beneficial. Sex not only stimulates the production of semen, it also stimulates the production of blood. Men are thought to open women up with their penises and in the past husbands stimulated first menses in their prepubescent wives. On the other hand, of course, sex also prevents menstruation, and as the blood and semen clot, forming a foetus, continued sex makes the little ball (*tunku*) grow whilst shaping it into human form. In short, sex not only stimulates the production of life-filled substance, it also shapes that substance.

While sex causes the growth and shaping of the foetus, *Diusun* (God) gives life (after *Deus* (P.) or *Dios* (Sp.)). Imbuing life and giving form are closely connected. The process of forming the foetus is called *dami va-*, which means 'to transform', for example in myths where people are 'transformed' into animals and vice versa, or when men take hallucinogens and their visions are 'transformed' one into the other (Kensinger 1973, 1995). The verb *dami-* means 'to transform oneself', for example a caterpillar metamorphosing into a butterfly. The substantive *dami* denotes a drawing or a doll. Consequently, *dami va-* could be taken to mean 'to make an image or representation', an interpretation that substantiates the idea that the transforming work of sex includes shaping the substances that are produced by male and female bodies in interaction. The origin of life itself is other-worldly. But blood and semen are not conceptually opposed to *Diusun's* participation in the process of conception. As amongst the Bororo (Crocker 1985), other-worldly power is an aspect of the vital substances at play, and not an addition to them.

The fluid and permeable separation between living persons and supernatural entities means that sex with spirits in corporeal form may also result in conception, though these babies are malformed or born as twins (*yuxin bake*, 'spirit children'). Deformations can also be produced by eating the wrong kinds of food and by not eating enough of the right kinds of food. Food, like sex, both makes and unmakes bodies. As the informant quoted above explained, a man should drink plenty of *caissuma*, the thick, pale drink made by women from corn, or corn and peanuts, that ideally accompanies every meal. Sweet manioc may also be transformed into a foetus, but the child will be weaker than children formed out of a diet including plenty of *caissuma* (Lagrou 1998). So it is clear that the substances that are taken in orally by both parents are ultimately transformed into the foetus, apparently affecting the quality of the vital fluids that will be so transformed. (Hence the warning to take care lest the 'milk' be spoilt.) Yet more is at stake than 'quality'. Both corn and peanuts are *yuxin* (spirits) and long to be transformed (*dami-*) into human form (Lagrou 1998). The actions of men and women in planting, weeding, harvesting, cooking and consuming these spirit crops make possible the realization of this desire. Matter, including substances such as semen, corn seeds, cooked foods, or human flesh and bones, is inherently transformable. A description of these processes of transformation throws into stark relief the profound integration between the supernatural and material aspects of these substances.

Mutuality between men and women extends to the processes that eventually result in the production of male or female vital fluids. Corn is harvested and *caissuma* is made by women; so men's semen is best produced by female food, as is also the case amongst the Mehinaku (Gregor 1985). Conversely, women's menstrual blood is produced by male agency and by 'male food' (the semen of their partners).

In the early twentieth century the Cashinahua practised extensive dietary restrictions during pregnancy and after childbirth (Abreu 1941). Years of outsiders' criticisms of such restrictions have resulted in a lack of willingness to talk about them, but do not seem to have affected the resilience of associated beliefs. My friends were sometimes willing to tell me about dietary restrictions, however, and I, like other ethnographers, can confirm that they are practised, even if in modified form. It is held that the qualities of certain animals might pass on to the unborn children, whose bodies come to resemble the creatures consumed by their parents (Abreu 1941; Kensinger 1981, 1995; Deshayes and Keifenheim 1982). The restrictions and potential dangers to the child extend into the period of couvade, as elsewhere in Amazonia (Rivière 1974). Crocker emphasizes, in the Bororo case, that the dietary and other postpartum restrictions 'stress, over and over, the direct, mechanical, metonymic danger of these substances and actions for the infant's own delicate *raka* (blood) (1985:67). Rivière argued that dietary prohibitions did not refer to bonds of physical substance between the parent and child, but rather impinged on bonds of a spiritual nature. In the Cashinahua case, such an antinomy between spirit and matter would not apply. A young child is vulnerable to spirit attack from certain animals that its father or another close relative has killed or its mother has eaten. Whilst in the mother's womb such spirit attack deforms the baby, who comes to resemble the animal consumed, rather than its human parent. After birth it will make it fall ill.

Few writers on such matters have stressed the importance of safe foods like *caissuma*, preferring to concentrate on the dangers of restricted game and fish. As a result the value of roots, grains and nuts, often dismissed as 'non-prestige' or 'mere staples', has been understated. Every diet that the Cashinahua undertake, whether for hunting, first menstruation, illness, or couvade, is based on the same ingredients: boiled sweet manioc, banana, corn and peanuts, all foods associated with female gender.

In sum, it is believed that a child is made of both semen and female menstrual blood, substances imbued with vital force that are moulded by the work of sex in a process described as 'transformation' or the creation of shape. The shape of the child is determined by the nature of the blood that goes into its manufacture, and this in turn is determined by the actions of the parents and the kinds of food that they consume before and after birth. Corn Spirit's desire to become human is harnessed to the procreative process. The process is indeed a mechanical one, since substance is made from substance. Yet there is more to it than this, in the sense that supernatural beings are thought to play a part in the production of life itself.

Birth and Growth

Women give birth inside their own houses, in the privacy of their mosquito-nets, with the help of at least one other woman, usually the mother or any close female friend. The woman's husband plays a crucial role. He stands behind her, supporting her under the arms, as she squats (supported by a hammock) or stands whilst delivering the child. This form of delivery emphasizes the dual male–female nature of parenthood. No man other than the father may see the genitals of the mother, or the blood. If he did, she would be ashamed (*dake-*) and the man would be made *yupa*, unlucky in the hunt. After delivery, the cord is cut, the placenta is disposed of on the outskirts of the village and water is heated for washing the baby and the mother. They lie together in the hammock for several days after birth, hidden from public view. Then visitors are permitted to see the child and the mother begins to move around the house. She may not bathe for several weeks, as this would bring illness to her and the child.

In the early twentieth century women gave birth outside the *maloca*, in a walled shelter built on the patio. Once they were cleaned up, they would be taken into the *maloca* to rest for five days. After this:

... the woman gets out of her hammock. She paints herself with genipapo, so as not to have fever, and so does her husband, and the child is painted too, so as not to have fever. The mother does not stray very far. Once the child is darkened [with genipapo] they always become happy. Once the child is born, the woman does not sleep with her husband any more. Only when the child stands and walks, do they sleep together (in the same hammock) again (Abreu 1941:123–6).

In the 1980s in Brazil mothers also blackened the child with genipapo, smearing the juice on to face and body, as well as their own face, hands and feet. Such blackening 'makes the child grow', and will be repeated periodically in the coming years. New mothers will only venture into the gardens with the child when it is about six months old. As women grow older and have more children, they will spend a shorter time away from their usual work in the gardens. Fathers on the other hand both work and hunt throughout, even within a day or so of the child's birth. Couples sleep apart when the mother is cradling a baby, which she does until it is weaned at about a year. The husband usually slings his hammock next to hers inside the same mosquito tent; or, if he has another wife, he sleeps with her. They will only have sex several months after a birth, 'when the bleeding has stopped completely'.

The parents must stimulate the growth of the infant and protect it against potential dangers from outside such as strong sunshine, rain, spirit attack or 'foreigners' illnesses' such as measles, whooping cough or colds. Children are very likely to become ill and die during the first two years of life. (I estimated an infant mortality rate of about 50 per cent). These outside dangers are most easily transmitted by the people with whom the child comes into close contact. This is why the parents, and the mother in particular, should be especially careful. The mother's first meal should consist of boiled bananas. Women do not always adhere to dietary restrictions strictly (I sometimes saw hungry young mothers reprimanded as they were raising some titbit to their mouths) and these are gradually relaxed until the time the baby is weaned. If mother or child becomes ill, then restrictions are observed more closely.

The baby is fed on demand, and milk enables it to grow fat and large. Whatever the mother consumes affects the quality of the milk, and thus the baby's growth, like semen during pregnancy. When it is three or four months old, the mother will begin to prepare boiled plantain mash for the child, and by one year old it will be eating many kinds of solid food. Growth at this stage derives from bland, fat-free foods such as banana, a plant which has no *yuxin* (spirit). Powerful foods associated with spirits are potentially harmful to its health and corporeal growth. Very fatty foods are entirely inappropriate. Potent foods (including most meats and fats) should only be given in reasonable quantities and should be properly cooked to remove all traces of raw blood. Children are reprimanded if they try to satiate themselves, because too much food inhibits their growth.

Just as *Diusun's* intervention is required for the growth of the foetus, a well-controlled spirit input is needed for the child to be able to grow fat and healthy. This is effected by a number of means, among which are regular medicinal baths, steamings and smokings and the judicious use of plant medicines (McCallum 1996a). Occasional applications of genipapo appear to 'fix' the shape made by the hard work of the parents both during pregnancy and afterwards; at the same time genipapo renders the baby invisible to the spirits. The first application is, in a sense, when the child really comes into this world, when its survival seems more secure and when it is given recognition as a real human. At last, a name may be conferred.

Naming

A newborn child receives its 'true name', *kena kuin*, within a week or so of birth. The naming system works according to a principle of 'parallel transmission'. The true name comes from a limited stock of names that are passed down through alternating generations from people in the category of maternal grandmother, in the case of girls, and paternal grandfather, in the case of boys. Frequently a child has the same name as its same-sex siblings as well as its same-sex grandparents of the correct category. All of these people, as well as any other person, Cashinahua or otherwise, who has the same true name, is a namesake, a *xuta*. Each name has an attached set of euphemistic names, used in ritual settings and perhaps (in the past) for reference or as terms of address. Nowadays, Christian names are used freely to talk about others and to address them.

True names place people in specified relationships with every other person who also has a true name. The use of this system defines a specific type of humanity – *Xutanaua* – 'Namesake People'. The other Panoan speakers of the Purus area, such as the Sharanahua (*Xadanaua*) and the Mastanahua (*Mastanaua*), are recognized by the Cashinahua as *Xutanaua*, but the Cariú and the Kulina are not. It is hard to exaggerate the importance of the namesake relationship in everyday life. It crops up frequently in jokes. For example, people tell their cross-cousins: 'Make a dog your namesake!'; or men joke with their female cross-cousins, euphemistically suggesting that they have sex: '*Min kuka dabidinunkave!*' (Let's go and make a namesake of your mother's brother!).

As far as I know, there is no ceremony attached to name-giving. (However, people described the *nixpo pima* initiation ritual, held when a child reaches between seven and twelve years of age, as 'Cashinahua baptism'.) Usually there is little doubt as to the name the child will receive. In the case of a girl, it will be the name of the mother's mother or MMZ, the *chichi*, who is nearly always co-resident in the house or settlement. For a boy, it will be the father's father's or FFB's (the *huchi*'s) name. If co-resident in the settlement, he will be living in a neighbouring house along with a daughter, who quite possibly is married to the child's mother's brother. Although a name does not imbue the child with the identity of his or her eponym, she or he will have a close and lifelong relationship with this person, and such warmth is also extended to all people who have the same name, even complete strangers, as other ethnographers have related (D'Ans n.d.; Kensinger 1995). A girl will most probably spend much of her childhood being looked after by her *chichi*, her maternal grandmother, who is nearly always her eponym. Boys on the other hand live with their *chais* (mother's fathers), rather than their *huchis* (father's fathers), spending more time with the former. I observed many cases of close relationships between co-resident female namesakes, but few between male.

In the first months of its life, the child may be addressed by parents, siblings and co-resident grandparents with its true name. The term for 'to call, summon' and the term for 'to name' are both *kena-*, and the act of calling the child is also the act of naming it. The repeated use of the name makes the name attach to the child, in an embodied sense. The sounds penetrate the ear and are absorbed into the child's body matter. This repetition, practically a name-giving ritual in itself, is a creative act described as 'transformation', *dami vakinan*, which is of course the same phrase that is used about making the foetus through sexual intercourse.

As the child develops, only its parents, and later on its spouse, may address it by its real name without causing offence. Such a use by others is regarded as highly disrespectful. People are reluctant to utter their own names aloud, and become filled with coyness and even embarassment when asked to do so. During my very first encounter with a Cashinahua, I received a true name. I was told my relationship to everyone present, cross-cousin, daughter, and so on, and told their true names. 'Call him *Epan*, Father; Call her *Chipin*, Elder Sister,' my name-giver told me. He added that it was rude to call people by their names, and that Cashinahua habitually use kin appellations. The knowledge of this made me unhappy several weeks later, because the children developed a taste for calling me by my true name. I complained to a friend; but he replied that it did not

Figure 2. Woman with her namesake granddaughter

matter so much. After all, I had as yet newly received the name, and the repeated use would transform me, *dami vakinan*. Later, when I had really 'grown up', when I had learnt to do all the things that Cashinahua persons do, the children should not call me by my true name. So it is clear that this repetition of the name works to attach a baby or stranger to a name, just as repeated coitus works to form a foetus.

Children jokingly insult each other by shouting out their true names. Adults tend to ignore this, unless annoyed by the noise. A true name is very intimate; pronouncing it out loud is like exposing one's genitals, in that it gives one shame (*dake*). Only very close people such as husband and wife may call each other by their true names, which they do at private moments. The act of naming is an admission of sexual or affective intimacy. Parents may call their children by name, whilst they are still small. The physical intimacy of co-residence creates a bond that allows the use of the name. Typically, when I asked a person for his or her true name, I would elicit an evasive response or a lie. Onlookers would then turn to me and say that my interlocutor was lying, because ashamed, and then answer my question for me. In such cases there is no disrespect involved, since everyone has a right and indeed a duty to know other people's names. If the person whose name is not yet known will not answer, then someone else should.

True names define people as potential *Huni Kuin*, True People. Upon meeting a stranger, all that need be asked is his or her name, and upon the basis of previous relationships with people of the same name, a reciprocal kin relationship can be established. To have a true name establishes one as a relative of every other person who also has one, irrespective of genealogical distance. This idea is expressed in Portuguese by the term *família*. I was told by many people that the Cashinahua belong to one family, and are all relatives, *parentes* (P.). In Cashinahua, as in Sharanahua, this idea might be expressed by saying that all Cashinahua are *nukun yuda*, literally 'our body' (Siskind 1973:50). *Nukun yuda* is opposed to *yuda betsa*, 'other body'. Siskind suggests that this is a biologically based metaphor used in the same way that English speakers might say 'blood is thicker than water' and, further, that kinship for the Sharanahua is 'biologically validated, eternally true'. Such would not be true in the Cashinahua case, since kinship is not understood to derive from 'consanguinity' or shared inherited substance. Kinship is constantly fabricated, in the Cashinahua view, just as bodies are, through daily interaction of a moral and social nature, in the many processes that constitute sociality. Names make such sociality possible.

Therefore, though a child acquires a name and thus an aspect of identity from a specific relationship with another person, the possession of the name embodies the possibility of general relationships with other people who are not also true kin, *nabu kuin*. Every person, through his or her true name, can be placed in a specific relationship to ego. The name is thus at once an intimate personal possession, a part of oneself not readily displayed before strangers, and also a means of making strangers kin. It is simultaneously a fundamental aspect of individual identity, and the basis of an indigenous theory of sociality.

Names are associated with the exogamous moieties (Inu/Inani and Dua/ Banu). Each moiety has its own stock of names. A person is automatically identified as being a member of one or the other moiety by his or her name. Kensinger (1984, 1995) describes the Cashinahua 'section system' as composed of four namesake groups. He says that all Cashinahua are members of one of four 'marriage sections' or 'alternating generation namesake groups' – the *xutabaibu*. That is, each person is either *awaba-kebu*, *kanabakebu*, *yawabakebu*, or *dunubakebu*. The first two, 'children of tapir' and 'children of lightning' respectively, are Inu moiety, and the second two, 'children of peccary' and 'children of snake', are Dua moiety (see Figure 3). Affiliation to moiety by name is something that comes

Cashinaua Moieties and Alternate Generation Namesake Groups

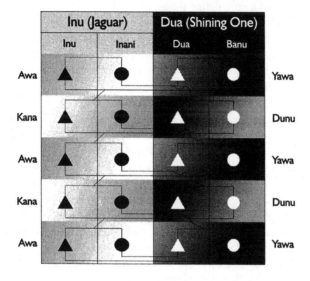

Figure 3. Cashinahua moieties and alternate generation namesake groups

about *de facto* rather than simply as a matter of time-honoured tradition. Although all names are said to belong to one moiety or the other, more than once I recorded cases of people with the same names who belong to different moieties. In these cases their parents had married 'wrong', into the same moiety, or else the people concerned came from different areas, and unrelated families. People consider that their own ascription of relationships between different names is the 'correct' version. For example, I might at first acquaintance with a woman named 'Bimi' begin by addressing her as '*eva*' (mother/daughter). This Bimi might protest, telling me that my name (Chima) had always been a *yaya* (daughter-in-law/mother-in-law) to her name. Thus people conceive of their naming system through the eyes of their own experience: habitual linking of kinship categories to specific names and therefore specific moieties legitimates the connections. But connections do not just extend through lived space and time. Many mythic characters were the original proprietors of certain true names, so the system also forges links to the distant past, to the dead as well as the living.

Names summon up the anonymous past, functioning as signs of people who have been safely forgotten and are therefore thinkable. In this sense names are a component of the body abstractable from the individual kinsperson, who will be longed for and missed upon his or her death. They are attached to and define the body whilst the person lives, but are safely attached to others and repeated into eternity. In traditional funerary endocannibalism, an explicit function of the rites was to detach the name from the corpse (McCallum 1996b, 1999). Dependence on the recyclability of detachable names for the continuity of human life itself is a subject of exegesis by some Cashinahua thinkers, and it is on this topic that a theory of sociality is partially articulated. Pancho, for example, in explaining naming to me, said that names are like seeds. Once planted they germinate and grow, flower and reproduce seeds. The seeds are kept, dried, and planted again, and the names go on. In this way the *Huni Kuin* 'never end'. At stake here is a conceptual contrast between corporeal impermanence and non-corporeal permanence, between bodiless eternity and bodily transitivity. The names solve the vital problem of linking the two. True names are not mere signs for specific individualities, attached to particular bodies, but rather stand for specific relationships, which are themselves always repeated throughout all time. This is a theory of sociality, then, but not of 'society' conceived as a sum of separate individuals.[2] I think that my informant was telling me that the names make possible the eternal reproduction of Cashinahua kinds of relationships. But how deep his metaphor goes may only be appreciated by looking further at the semantic connections that follow from his analysis.

True names are associated with one of a person's several *yuxin* (a term sometimes glossed by informants with the Portuguese *alma* (soul), the *bedu yuxin*. *Bedu* means both eye and seed, and this *yuxin* is indeed said to be seated in the eye, from whence it flies out at death in the form of a bird or beetle on a journey to everlasting life in heaven. If names are also metaphoric seeds, then they must be linked to this immortal aspect of a person's living body (the 'eye soul'), which plays a crucial part in the gestation and maintenance of life. Eye souls are present from the start of life, but but like names they do not guarantee the status of complete humanity. Cashinahua children have incomplete souls until around the time of initiation, but as they grow up, they gradually develop the complementary 'body soul', *yuda yuxin*, that allows them to mature into properly human adults. This progressive building up is comparable to the planting, growth, maturation and hardening of corn, an analogy made by the Huni Kuin and extensively developed in the *Nixpu Pima* rites, when true names are fixed securely into the child's body. The names, then may be a dynamic aspect of the individual, but they are by no means his or her complete identity, and they are a necessary but not a sufficient requisite for being human. While names do embody a theory of a cyclical reproduction of relationships, then, they do not embody a theory of the cyclical reproduction of persons. If a woman eventually becomes like her elder namesake, this is made to happen, with time and much patient teaching, and does not come about when she is named as a baby. The child's body is given form, protected and made to grow by the endless labour and care of the parents. Its ability to act for itself is an essential prerequisite to its ability to learn those conscious skills that it needs to be a real person, to be able to care for others. Most often, these are taught by the woman for whom the girl has been named, the *chichi*, or by the boy's *chai*, his namesake's brother-in-law. The child is made into a social being not by the name itself, but by the relationship that it makes possible.

Babies are also given a Christian name, *navan kena* ('foreigner's name'). Parents try to find a Christian name unique in the region, and might invite non-relatives to name their child, thereby initiating a *compadrazgo* (Sp.) relationship between parents and godparents.[3] When a Catholic priest passes by he will baptize the child and issue a birth certificate. The child receives its parents' surnames in the Brazilian fashion, mother's first followed by father's. (In Peru the father's surname precedes the mother's.) A person's individuality is represented by her or his Christian name and surname, and these also indicate his or her place in the civilized modern world. *Xenipabu* ('old ones') did not have *navan kena*, and this is one facet of the distinction drawn by Real People between themselves and their forebears. The system that hinges on the true names, on the other hand, signals continuity with the past.

Named children and foreigners must be worked upon, transformed, both by repeated use of the true name and by practical pedagogy. Only when a child has mastered concrete skills, verbal and physical, may the potentiality of social being contained in the naming system be fully realized.

Kinship

It is for the child to learn to engage in the social relationships that the true name makes possible. These are circumscribed by kinship. Cashinahua kinship and marriage are structured by the exogamous moiety system and by the preference for local endogamy and bilateral cross-cousin marriage. Formally, the 'structure' of the kin terminology is that of a Kariera system (see Figure 4). Kensinger, pioneer analyst of Cashinahua kinship, distinguishes at this level of abstraction four 'marriage sections' defined by alternating generation links and each composed of two groups (male or female) of namesakes and their same-sex siblings (Kensinger 1984). Rather than concentrating on the formal characteristics of this interlinked set of terminological systems, residence patterns and marriage practices, I consider here the way these are lived and understood by the Cashinahua themselves.[4]

The Cashinahua idea of *nabu kuin* corresponds to the notion of bilateral kindred. The *nabu kuin* are Ego's cognatically reckoned relations, to the level of two ascending and descending generations. Since the Cashinahua favour bilateral cross-cousin marriage at the first degree, this kindred includes both kin and affinal kin. The concept *nabu* corresponds to Piaroa *chuwaruwang* or Kalapalo *otomo*.[5] As in these cases, it is an 'ordinal' not an absolute concept, a matter of degree rather than inclusion or exclusion (Basso 1973). Certain people are sometimes classified as *nabu*, and sometimes as *yuda betsa*, 'another family', depending on context and the purposes of the speaker. Although the idea *nabu* may be explained in genealogical terms, as including all the ascending and descending 'consanguineal' relatives of Ego, it is not conceived as a corporate group by the Cashinahua themselves.[6] Kinship is thought of as constantly created and recreated, both through corporeal transactions from body to body and by asymmetrical prestations of food and goods.

The idea of *nabu kuin*, real kin, sums up for the Cashinahua a world of affection, warmth and caring to which all aspire. People say of a person 's/he is my real X' – '*en X kuin*', distinguishing him or her from more distant or classificatory relations. These true kin are differentiated from others who are also genealogically linked, but only distantly, *nantakea* ('distant, far'). All of these people are *nabu*, or *parentes* (P.), 'relatives', but only the close kin have a legitimate right to affection, and a legitimate duty to give it. This notional circle of people is extended at times to include all Cashinahua under the rubric 'relatives', as when I was told '*Somos tudo família'(P.)* – 'We are all family'. It also contracts. In a dour mood people in one settlement might deny relatedness with neighbours in another, especially in comparisons between Cashinahua raised in Peru versus those from Brazil. One visitor to Recreio from Peru, for example, commented to me that the people of Fronteira are 'another race' (*otra raza* (Sp.)).

The phrase *Huni Kuin* denotes Cashinahua people, but may refer to all indigenous peoples, as a gloss in Cashinahua of the Portuguese term *indio*. *Yuda* ('body') may be used to describe a group of people and is often translated into Portuguese as *tribo* ('tribe'). Although both *yuda* and *Huni Kuin* suggest the idea of common bonds of kinship, they are not kinship terms. *Família* (P.) and *nabu* conjure up a concept of kinship

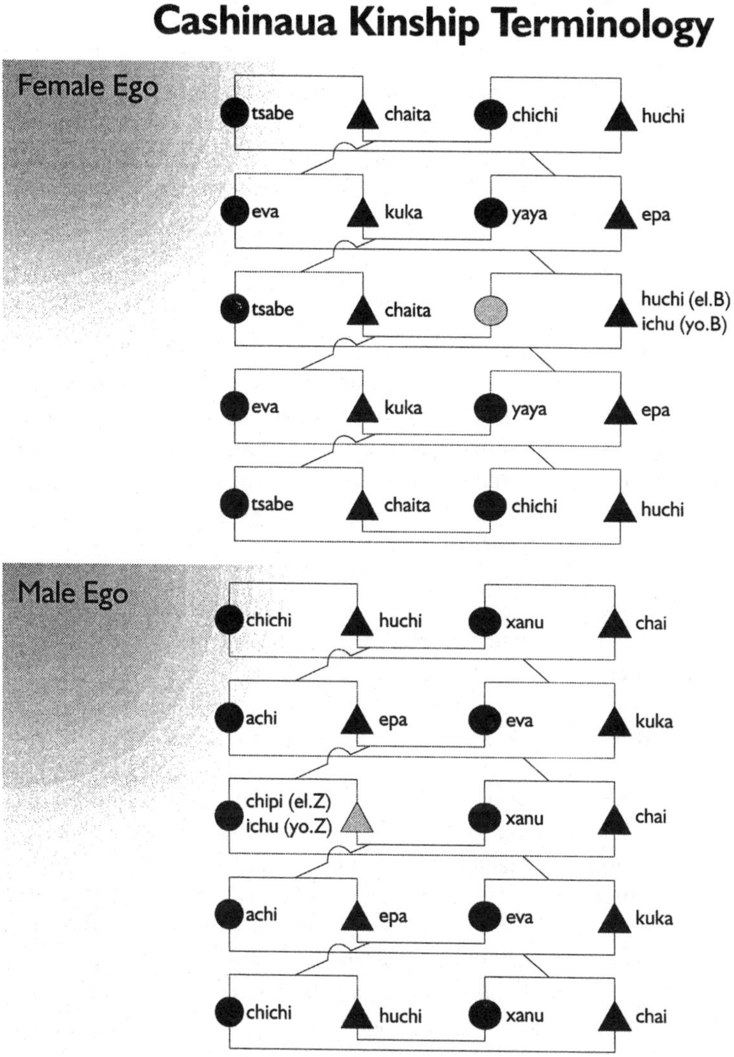

Cashinaua Kinship Terminology

Female Ego

tsabe	chaita	chichi	huchi
eva	kuka	yaya	epa
tsabe	chaita		huchi (el.B) ichu (yo.B)
eva	kuka	yaya	epa
tsabe	chaita	chichi	huchi

Male Ego

chichi	huchi	xanu	chai
achi	epa	eva	kuka
chipi (el.Z) ichu (yo.Z)		xanu	chai
achi	epa	eva	kuka
chichi	huchi	xanu	chai

Figure 4. Cashinahua kinship terminology

as centred around a living group of people who are both genealogically related and share names and the adherence to the namesake system. Thus the Kulina, who neither have a namesake system nor speak a Panoan language, are only referred to as *nukun nabu* with irony, whereas the Yaminahua can legitimately be referred to as such.

People say they 'long for' (*manu-*) their kin: brothers and sisters, parallel and cross-cousins, mother, fathers, namesakes, grandparents and all their maternal and paternal uncles and aunts. Village endogamy springs from this desire, rather than obedience of any 'residence rule' that an anthropologist may posit. Cross-sex siblings attempt to marry their children to each other's offspring, so that the family may stay together. For the Cashinahua real affines are first and foremost kin. Only where no potential marriage partner is available or willing do people seek out distant relatives or unrelated people as affines. Marriage is not seen as a strategy for making alliances with strangers, so much as one for making bonds with kin closer, as is common among Lowland peoples who combine a two-section Dravidian-type terminology with a preference for endogamy (Overing Kaplan 1977). The Cashinahua share this attitude to strangers, and indeed their Kariera-type terminology can be interpreted as a two-section system (Hornborg 1988; Kensinger 1995). It should be noted that despite a preference for endogamy, each settlement is not a self-contained unit. Many marriages are contracted between people who are only distantly related, though generally in the correct moiety relation to each other.

Speaking of Others, Speaking to Others

The kin terms shown in Figure 3 may be used for both address and reference. The figure shows that the terms used for people in the same relative position in ascending generations are also used for people in the same relative position in descending generations. A principle of reciprocality informs reference usage between persons of the same sex. For example, my daughter is my *eva* (female speaker), and my mother is also my *eva*. I refer to both as such, and they refer to me as such. They are also, of course, each other's namesakes. In every case of reciprocal reference usage in adjacent generations, there is a corresponding namesake relation in alternate generations. One's children are referred to by the same term as one's same-sex parent and one's opposite-sex parent-in-law, *kuka* (S/MB) and *eva* (D/M) for a woman, and *epa* (S/F) and *achi* (D/FZ) for a man; one's children's spouses are referred to by the same term as one's opposite-sex parent and same-sex parent-in-law, *eva* (M/

ZD) and *kuka* (MB/ZS) for a man, *yaya* (FZ/BD) and *epa* (F/BS) for a woman. These people, to whom one refers by the same term, belong to the same 'alternate generation namesake groups' (Kensinger 1995). The figure shows how one's grandparents are referred to by the same terms as one's children's children in the same relative position. Thus the top line reads the same as the bottom line. Each of these people belong to a category that ideally includes one set of names, and people of these categories could be *xuta*, the younger named after the elder generation. The replication becomes clearest in the case of the reference terms for cross-cousin. For a woman, her potential husband and cross-cousin is her *chaita*. This term also refers to her MF and her son's son. For a man, his potential wife and cross-cousin is his *xanu*, which also refers to his FM and his DD. All of these people belong to the same 'alternating generation namesake group'.

The essential meaning of most relation terms could be said to be confined to the ascending generation. An *eva* is first of all a mother; the daughter whom a woman addresses as *eva* is in fact her *eva xuta*, her mother's namesake, and the daughter-in-law whom a man addresses as *eva* is in fact his mother's namesake, his *eva xuta*. Nevertheless some terms are used more frequently to refer to people of the same generation, especially *tsabe* and *chai*, as if the essential meaning is in fact sister-in-law and brother-in-law (cross-cousin) respectively, instead of FM (female ego) and MF (male ego). Those people who may be addressed by the same term belong to the same moiety as well as the same alternating generation namesake category. The moiety named Inu (male) or Inani (female) marries into the Dua (male) or Banu (female). The Cashinahua emphasize moiety membership rather than membership in a 'namesake group'. Men say that moiety membership is inherited from the father. Therefore sons of Inu men are also Inu, and daughters are Inani; and sons of Dua men are Dua and daughters Banu. Children therefore belong, ideally, to the opposite moiety to that of their mother. Thus an Inani/Inu child has a Banu mother; and a Dua/Banu child has an Inani mother. Membership is therefore apparently in accordance with a principle of patrifiliation (Kensinger 1985). Where there is no complication, in terms of 'moiety wrong' marriages for example, the premise of patrifiliation holds true. However, the ascription of a supposed 'patrifilial' aspect turns out to be misleading (D'Ans, n.d.; McCallum 1989; Kensinger 1995; Hornborg, n.d.).This becomes clear in the light of cases of mismatches or multiple paternity. From the perspective of alternate generations it is also possible to think of 'membership' bilaterally; women may be thought of as inheriting their moiety affiliation from their namesake grandparent.

In cases of difficulty either maternal or paternal lines may be used to find an appropriate namesake. Moiety affiliation is therefore not only a matter of 'consanguineal' link via a principle of filiation. Links created through the naming system are also important, and sometimes take precedence.

Our clearest evidence that the Cashinahua think of the naming system as separate from filiation comes from their naming of strangers. True names place strangers on a path towards becoming kin – and hence Real People – if they learn to behave like Cashinahua, live together with them, marry them, and speak their language. In the past, captured Yaminahua women were adopted in this way, though such exogamy became rare by the 1980s.

Great importance is placed upon people who are 'real kin', *nabu kuin*, actual relations. *Enabu*, literally 'my relatives', defines the group of people with whom a person should live. The bond with e*nabu* is strong, whatever the name relationship or the moiety affiliation; when distant or dead the physical sensation of their absence is decribed as *manu-* ('to feel longing, to miss'). This emotion can provoke illness in the pining relative, who might become too despondent to work or move (McCallum 1996a). *Nabu kuin* who are subject to appeals by visiting kin to abandon their settlements and gardens to live together in the same village often justify moving as a solution to the distress brought on by such longing (whatever the other political or economic reasons for the move). The Cashinahua feel that close kin should care for each other and have a right to expect such care. Conversely, unrelated people owe each other nothing. Caring for foreigners is tantamount to making them kin, and kin who refuse to co-reside and to work with and share with their own kin are tantamount to strangers (see Chapter 4).

In order to become adult, a child needs to know the set of relation terms presented in Figure 3 and Table 1. People learn by beginning with co-resident kin and affines and later by expanding usage to include all people with real names. All Cashinahua and foreigners who possess real names are addressed and referred to most of the time by kinship terms or by moiety name. Moiety itself is from this perspective a notion subsumed under that of kinship; belonging to a Cashinahua moiety means being part of the Cashinahua 'family', and children learn this understanding of sociality by beginning with their own family. Only afterwards do they learn to use the same terms (with subtle variations depending on context and intended effect) for their classificatory relatives.

A child's co-resident parents, siblings, and maternal grandparents care most closely for him or her when small. They are at the centre of the infant's world. The kin to whom a child is closest are, firstly, its parents, *ibu*, a term that also signifies 'owner'. The concept encompasses both possession and legitimate authority, and is central to Cashinahua economics and politics. Gendered usages in the domain of kinship also have implications for these (as discussed below in Chapters 4 and 5) and the person signified by *ibu* shifts according to gendered contexts. If talking to a woman, reference to *min ibu*, 'your parent', indicates the mother, unless the context points to the father. Similarily, a man's *ibu* is his father unless otherwise indicated. Therefore children are more closely associated with their same-sex parents.

Siblings are extremely important in a child's life, and become more so as it learns to walk and is put to sleep in its own hammock in the same mosquito-tent with all its pre-adult brothers and sisters (Kensinger 1985, 1995). Siblings of the same sex are referred to as *betsa*. This term means 'other' or 'another', so *en betsa* is literally 'another me'. Cross-sex siblings, *pui*, sleep together until the boys reach adolescence and are given their own nets. Sexually active youths ought not to remain sleeping so

Table 1. Cashinahua Kin Terminology

ADDRESS AND REFERENCE TERMS

Female Speaker		Male Speaker	
Tsabe	FM, MFZ, MBD, FZD, ZL, SD, DSW	*Chai*	MF, FMB, MBS, FZS, BL, DS, SSL
Chaita	MF, FMB, FZS, MBS, BL, SS, DDW	*Xanu*	MBD, FZD, FM, MFZ, ZL, DD, SDL
Huchi	El.B, FF, MMB, DS	*Huchi*	El.B, FF, MMB, SS, DDH
Chichi	MM, FFZ, DD, SDL	*Chichi*	MM
Eva	M, D	*Eva*	M, ZD, DL
Kuka	MB, FL, S	*Kuka*	MB, FL, ZS
Yaya	FZ, MFZD, BD, DL	*Achi*	FZ, ML, MFZD, D
Epa	F, BS, SL	*Epa*	F, S
Chipi	el. Z	*Chipi*	el. Z
Ichu	yo. Z , yo. B	*Ichu*	yo. Z, yo. B

REFERENCE TERMS	
Aniva	Adopted child or adoptive parent
Pui	cross-sex sibling
Betsa	same-sex sibling
Dai	co-wife
Bake	child
Baba	grandchild
Xuta	namesake
Dais	son-in-law, or a man's parents-in-law
Babavan	daughter-in-law, or a woman's parents in-law

close to their sisters. Girls stay in the same tent with their younger siblings until marriage. Unmarried boys are thus distanced from their kin, while unmarried girls stay close to them. In terms of sleeping arrangements, as in other contexts, women are more closely associated with the 'inside' and men with the 'outside'.

People frequently address their real parents by the Portuguese terms *mamãe* (mother) and *papai* (father). The Cashinahua terms *evan* and *epan* may also be used.[7] Real MZs are called *evan*, though they may be addressed as *titia* (P.), a Cariú term. The child will be called by its *kena kuin* during the first years, or alternatively by the appropriate relation term, thus facilitating gradual learning of relationships. As the child begins to be able to talk and to identify relationships correctly, people begin to use its Christian name as a term of address. Parents use this name or the appropriate relation term (*achin* or *epan*, male speaker to daughter and son; *evan* and *kukan*, female speaker).[8]

Brothers and sisters, when children, call each other by Christian name. After adolescence, the elder addresses the younger by Christian name, and the younger addresses the elder as *chipin*, elder sister, or *huchin*, elder brother. These terms are quite affectionate, as well as being respectful. Sometimes the younger sibling is addressed as such – *ichun* – and this usage is more common after adulthood. When the brothers and sisters grow up, considerable respect must be shown and Christian names are no longer used. Younger namesake siblings are addressed as *xutan*, and reply with *chipin*, or *huchin*. The most frequent term of address used by elder people to call their younger siblings, or indeed any younger adult, is the moiety name. The use of this term denotes a relationship of seniority. It is the way I most frequently heard people address their juniors, with the exception of parents their children.

As the child grows its universe of action expands. Little children between about five and ten spend much of the day with others playing in or around the village. These children address each other by Christian name, and the whole group is addressed collectively as *naban*, 'kids'. Little girls join in; but by about seven they begin to help their elder sisters or mothers with various tasks around the house or in the gardens. Often they have a baby sibling to care for, though where there is no girl available little boys are asked to do this too.

Girls spend most time with their *chichi* (MM), maternal aunts, mother and eldest sisters. At this age their adult male cross-cousins might begin to joke with them. The people in this category are referred to as their *bene*, husbands, and the girls are their *ain*, wives. Age difference is less important between these cross-cousins than it is between siblings, and the terms *xanun* and *chaitan* are used in address whatever the disparity, rather than the moiety names.

Boys with married sisters grow up in a close relation to their co-resident brother-in-law. The two hunt together, work together, and crack jokes at each other's expense. This is their *chai*, classificatory or actual cross-cousin, whose sister they might marry. Men have very informal and sometimes close relationships with their brothers-in-law, who are addressed as *chain*, or as *cunhado* (P.) or its derivative *cunha*, which has a slangy flavour. Similarily, parallel cousins can be addressed as *primo* (P.), especially on more informal occasions. Elder and middle-aged men address their younger parallel cousins or cross-cousins by moiety name, though there is a tendency to address cross-cousins as *chain* whatever their age. *Chain* is the term used to address strange men, either those whose true name is unknown, or non-Cashinahua Panoan-speakers. Some Kulina have also learnt to use the term, and it is well known to Brazilians who work with indigenous peoples in Acre (McCallum 1997).

Like the boys, adolescent girls might spend time with their same-sex cross-cousin, their *tsabe*, although the two are unlikely to be co-resident in the same house. They could become friends, *haibu*, and spend time accompanying each other to the gardens, on fishing expeditions, or sitting indoors making up their faces, sewing and so on. Although they call each other by Christian name even at this stage, they might begin to call each other *cunhada* (P.). Similarily parallel cousins address each other as *prima* (P.) on occasion. Once the girls have married they tend to use the Cashinahua term *tsaben* more often. Sometimes real sisters-in-law are also linked by a relation of *compadrazgo*, and if this is the case *comade* is always used. However, men prefer to choose *compadres* from outside the village or amongst friendly non-Cashinahua (McCallum 1989).

Young men, upon marriage, move to their wife's house, where they respectfully address their mother-in-law as *achin*; she responds with the young man's moiety name. Although this is a respect relationship and sex or sexual joking between the two is unthinkable, the mother-in-law cares for him like a son. She cooks for him, picks his lice, sews his clothes, or weaves him a hammock. As a sign of affection she will address him as *epan* (F, BS). Her husband addresses him by his moiety name, and is addressed as *kukan*. This relationship is respectful, but also friendly. The young married man works on his father-in-law's projects, such as house-building and garden-making.

Women address their parents-in-law (ideally their paternal aunt and maternal uncle) as *yayan* and *kukan*, and are addressed by their moiety name, or else as *yayan* and *evan*. The closeness of this relationship depends upon a number of factors. If by chance a girl lives virilocally, she will be treated almost as a daughter, just as a son-in-law is treated as a son. Nevertheless, she should respect her parents-in-law, and her relation with her *kuka* will be especially formal.

Potential spouses (ideally cross-cousins) call each other *xanun* and *chaitan*. If one of them marries someone else, they can still continue to use these terms, but as time passes they might begin to avoid the opportunities for sexual encounters and sexual joking that such usage implies, and the elder person uses the younger's moiety name as a vocative more and more. Husband and wife no longer use *xanu* and *chaita*. They call each other *ba* (emphatic *baka*), though only after several years of marriage. This word also means friend, and is employed for strangers of either sex. I was told that when I arrived at a strange settlement, I should call out upon arrival: '*Ba*, I have arrived! Do you have genipapo paint? Fetch it so that you may paint me!'

I rarely heard this term used in this way. D'Ans, however, was addressed as such by the people of Balta, until the night he was named, when they switched *en masse* to calling him by appropriate kin terms (D'Ans, n.d.). The term *ba* is therefore both a means of implying difference and a means of indicating warmth and affection. Unhappily married teenagers never address their spouses as *ba*. Couples in an established relationship, who can call each other by true name, may refer to each other as *en ain*, my wife, and *en bene*, my husband. Co-wives sometimes refer to each other as *dai* ('co-wife').

Grandchildren, referred to as *baba*, are addressed affectionately by real name when very small and after that by Christian name or the appropriate kin term. Grandparents are affectionate to all their grand-children, but especially so towards their namesakes, whom they favour when giving food and presents, and to whom they owe special services. The children address their grandparents with the appropriate kin term. People may address their younger namesakes as *xutan*.

The systematic application of kin terms is practically impossible because of incorrect marriages, for example to classificatory siblings. If everyone were to use kinship terms as terms of address, the result would be the endless stressing of the disharmony between practice and theory. Complex linguistic strategies can reduce the importance for day-to-day living of such inconsistencies (Kensinger 1995). Among these, the use of the moiety name as a term of address is important. Moiety names used in address serve two purposes. Firstly, they are an indicator of age difference, and the associated relations are of a hierarchical nature. Secondly, and in contrast, they override the implication of seniority

Figure 5. Man in a hammock with his grandchild

contained in kin terminology used between elder and younger kin (such as *chipi / ichun* or *chichi / xuta*). Therefore, the use of a moiety name as a term of address performs two opposite functions (McCallum 1989). From this pragmatic point-of-view, moiety is *both* an egalitarian *and* a hierarchical principle of social organization.

Besides denoting age difference, a moiety appellation serves to homogenize younger adults into the four classes defined by the moiety names, Inu and Inani, Dua and Banu, whatever the relationships between them, and between them and their elders. Only the most senior people remain differentiated by the consistent application of specific kinship terminology. This has the effect of emphasizing the specificity of people in the parental generations (those of the original names), and the homogeneity of people who are their junior siblings, their offspring or their offspring's contemporaries (those named after their elders). This effect is important in terms of political philosophy and practice. It means that young adults are categorized as the 'children' of their elders, and places them in a relationship of authority and obedience.

Children themselves, however, are only addressed by moiety name when they reach adolescence. There is a sense in which moieties are most appropriately made up of strong and productive adults, so that the old are beyond moiety as a social category, already in the class of 'ancestor', whereas the young have not yet been fully integrated into moiety. Indeed, old people are often referred to as *xenipabu*, which may be glossed as 'old one' or 'forebear'. *Xenipabu* refers to the recent adult dead, as well as to mythic characters, to Sun, Moon and certain stars.

There are many ways of talking about others or addressing people, and many subtleties of usage barely hinted at here. The speaker might, for example, wish to stress a particular relationship. Thus, if two people related as siblings are talking, and the speaker refers to a younger cross-cousin, wishing to stress relative seniority, s/he will say 'our (moiety name)'. Alternatively, the same speaker might wish to stress another aspect of the relationship, such as potential affinity, in which case s/he will say 'our spouse'. Terms of reference or address thus may shift depending on intent and situation. As a child matures, she or he will become more and more capable of manipulating the linguistic terms available, in Cashinahua, Spanish or Portuguese, in accordance with personal requirements.

Once a child knows how to address and how to refer to its kin, it is considered to be a potential social being, though not yet a fully adult one. In this chapter I have given a brief description of the kinship knowledge that the child needs, and in so doing have provided a glimpse into the social world of the Cashinahua. Although children by the age of seven have learnt the basic linguistic data that they need for social interaction, they must still be transformed, by the active intervention of adults, into adults and full persons themselves. The first stage in the final production of growth in immature people is the initiation ritual *nixpo pima*, which is the subject of the next chapter.

Notes

1. Interview with Isaias and his wife Francisca , on the Jordão river, 1985.
2. In other words, this idea would not fit with any crude Durkheimian vision of 'society' composed of 'individuals'. See the discussion in the Introduction.
3. For a recent discussion of *compadrazgo* in indigenous Amazonia see Gow (1991). The most important relationship in this institution is between the parents and godparents of the child, to which more weight is given than that between the child and its godparents.
4. For greater depth of discussion from a formal perspective see Kensinger 1984, 1995.

5. See Kaplan (1975) on the Piaroa; Basso (1973) on the Kalapalo.
6. See Overing Kaplan (1977) on this point.
7. Kin terms used in reference are nasalized when used as a vocative. This is represented in the orthography by the addition of an '*n*'. Portuguese terms are not so nasalized.
8. Unmarried girls may be addressed as *moça* (P.), 'girl' or 'virgin', most of all by their mothers. Little boys are addressed as *rapazinho* (P.), 'little fellow'.

–2–

Creating Gender

Over the years, children are made to grow from infants who only consume to adults who produce in their own right. A set of rites known as *Nixpo Pima* mark the period in life when this should occur and play an important part in imbuing a child with the capacity to produce. Held for children of both sexes between the ages of about seven and eleven, when adult dentition has replaced milk teeth, *Nixpo Pima* opens a new phase in growth, delineating the point when children begin to be moulded by their kin into male and female persons. It is the formal start of gender differentiation.

Nixpo Pima

This month-long ritual complex is described by informants as *Batismo Kaxinauá* (P.), 'Cashinahua Baptism', just as it was at the start of the twentieth century (Abreu 1941). Its most salient function is the definitive attachment of children to their names, which triggers a maturation that is at once intellectual and corporeal. There is an intimate connection between the physical embodiment of the names and the creation of gender difference in the children's bodies. Indeed, the same techniques simultaneously give rise to both. I hesitate to describe *Nixpo Pima* as a 'rite of passage' or as 'initiation', for fear of creating the impression that it causes a sudden transition from one status to another, or enables the 'initiates' to acquire membership in some sort of closed group of gendered adults. For this reason, I follow the Cashinahua themselves in using the term 'baptism', with the proviso that in what follows, the term 'baptism' should be understood, from their perspective, as a set of ritual techniques that impinge upon the body and endow it with the capacity to be social. I prefer 'neophyte' to 'initiate', because the former suggests participation in a process of learning, whereas the latter implies a more abrupt entry into a new status.

Girls and boys are baptized together. In extant descriptions of the rites the neophytes are referred to simply as *bakebu*, 'children'; and indeed in daily linguistic usage young children are also treated as belonging to the same category, without gender distinction. If necessary, gender may be indicated in the terms *ainbu bake,* 'woman child', and *huni bake,* 'man child'. Only after the time of baptism do girls and boys begin to work at gender-specific tasks, in the company of their elders, and are referred to as *chipax,* 'unmarried girl', or *beduna,* 'young man'.

Pre-contact Cashinahua held that children who had not passed through *Nixpo Pima* would die (Abreu 1941). People no longer make this claim, for the good reason that for lack of chant-leaders there are many children who remain unbaptized and who have suffered no ill effects. Where one is available, the rites should be held every four years or so, during the rainy season in late December or early January. This time of year is *xekitian,* 'corn time', the season for the festival celebrating the harvest of the green corn. Although I participated in the corn harvest of 1984, there was no baptism that year, so I did not witness the rites. Therefore an earlier analysis could only be based on informants' descriptions, on my recordings of *Nixpo Pima* songs and on Abreu (McCallum 1989). However, Kensinger participated in a baptism held in Peru in 1964 and Lagrou in one held in Brazil in 1993, so happily I am able to modify my earlier interpretation in the light of their descriptions and analyses (Kensinger, n.d., 1995; Lagrou 1998).[1]

The baptism's key bodily intervention is the blackening of the neophytes' teeth. *Nixpo* (Sp. *cordoncillo*) is a forest plant which, if chewed, covers the teeth in a shiny, pitch-black layer that is said to harden them and protect them against decay. The stalk is broken off and its end is stabbed against the teeth until the desired effect is achieved. Several stalks, much spitting, and a certain amount of patience are required. This is described as 'eating *nixpo*' (*nixpo pi-*) and *nixpo pima-* means 'to cause to eat nixpo'. Adults 'eat' it from time to time, in order to protect their teeth and as part of body decorations for the *Kachanaua* increase rites (see Chapters 6 and 7). Children are not allowed to eat it until they have been baptized, for otherwise they would sicken and die.

The proceedings begin with a set of nocturnal invocations, known as *pakadin,* sung by the male and female chant-leaders with a chorus from the children's parents. The series is chanted over three nights, as the singers dance rhythmically around a fire made up of burning logs fetched from all the hearths in the village, lit on the patio in front of the house where eventually the neophytes will be confined. These chants invite important spirits and deities of both moieties to the village: the Inka, the original owner of fire, is asked to bring his fire to the village; the harpy eagle, Inka's messenger and a brilliant hunter, is asked to come and pass his skills to the children, as are the *Hidi,* ancestral giants, consummate hunters and gardeners; the sky-blue *xane*, a bird renowned for its intelligence and its leadership capacities, is also summoned (Lagrou 1998). Many of the names sung in these chants are *kena kuin*, 'true names'. As the lengthy process of baptism thus begins, the neophytes keep to their hammocks in their own houses, safe from the dangers attendant upon the imminent presence of the spirit guests. On the fourth day, the Inkas and other spirit visitors arrive and a new sequence of *pakadin* songs known as *metsabuabu*, 'successful workers and hunters', begins.[2] Naming continues as the visitors, who are invoked as jaguars, impart their qualities to the onlookers. At this stage the first of several daytime rituals is held, involving much bawdy joking and mock fighting between men and women, between male and female cross-cousins and between male cross-cousins (Kensinger n.d., 1995; Lagrou 1998). Some of these games may be seen by the children, but they must return to their hammocks when the Inka 'kills' the *bichu* stork, a key player at this stage (Lagrou 1998). In the next few days the men carve the stools upon which the neophytes will sit at the next stage of the baptism, and again the chant-leader sings the appropriate songs and directs the expedition to the forest to the chosen tree from whose buttresses the fathers will shape them. The stools, known as *kena* (which also means 'name'), are carved from a living giant *xunu* or *sapupema* (P.) tree, famed in Amazonia for its perfect dome of foliage and for these buttresses, which stand taller than a man. The strokes of the machetes are like the strokes of a man's penis as he shapes a foetus. The *xunu* is at once home to powerful deities, a way station of the human eye *yuxin*, perhaps headed for heaven, and above all a powerful *yuxin* in its own right, respected for its wisdom, its perfect form, its design, its strength and its lengthy lifespan (Lagrou 1998). These qualities are also to be passed to the neophytes, as they sit upon the *kena*, whose form and painting reproduce the human body (ibid.).

As the stools are being finished, the Inka visitors depart again for the sky, and the danger to the neophytes abates somewhat (Lagrou 1998). Once the stools are safely washed, painted and hung up at home, preparations begin for a *Kachanaua*, involving a collective hunt and the naming of the garden products. According to my informant, the men of one moiety should disappear into the forest for up to ten days on a prolonged hunting expedition. They return loaded down with smoked meat. The men of the other moiety should come back from a long fishing trip at a lake with smoked fish and caiman. Meat and fish are to be gifts for their *chai*s. Each moiety gives in its turn, one in the morning, the other in the evening. At nightfall an all-night dance begins, during which men and women together name (*kena-*) cultivated plants. As they sing, they circle a hollowed-out tree-trunk, which symbolizes both a womb, and the first space in which the Cashinahua were created. Above it are hung manioc tubers and bananas.

The songs concentrate on naming the different 'families' of corn, referred to as *xeki keneya* (corn with design), *Inkan xeki* (Inka's corn), and so on (McCallum 1989; Lagrou 1998). While the men hunt or fish, the women prepare fresh corn *caissuma*. The naming songs chanted during the various phases of this ritual metaphorically compare the ladle with a penis and the drink with semen (Lagrou 1998). Once again corn *caissuma* will be transformed into a person, as it was during gestation, and the perennial desire of the corn *yuxin* to become human will be satisfied. The perfect corn for this task is that known as *xeki keneya*, 'corn with design', a variety that has black grains speckled among the yellow ones. This is the corn that ate *nixpo* in mythic times, so demonstrating its longing to turn human (Lagrou 1998). Once the corn *caissuma* is ready, the children can be directly acted upon.

They are bathed with medicinal plants, painted with genipapo with special designs, and brought to the chant-leaders' house, where hammocks are strung for them. The men begin to dance and sing on the patio outside, around the fire, whilst the women settle in for a night of rocking the hammocks and singing *kawa*. This term refers to a culinary technique common in this part of Amazonia, where small fish and crustaceans, wild mushrooms and other gathered foods are wrapped in leaves and gently barbecued. The implications are clear: The children are being cooked in their hammocks, just as semen is 'cooked' in a mother's womb. The children must lie stiff and straight in their hammocks. If they were to fidget or move, a poisonous snake would bite them. If they lie twisted, they will grow up crooked and bent (Lagrou 1998). The neophytes must stay in their hammocks for several days, rising only to participate in the test of running and jumping known as *ixchubain* ('jumping along'). When they get up, for whatever reason, they should look only at the ground, and if they glance at the light or at the forest they will be doomed.

At dawn on this first day, everyone is called to the leaders' house. Here, the neophytes are given *caissuma* made from green corn (*xeki pachi*), but no other food. After this the 'jumping along', *ixchubain*, begins. Women pull the girls along, and men pull the boys. Whilst the girls are made to run, the boys rest on the *kena*, and vice versa. All day the adults force the children to run about the village, refusing to let them flag. This is very unpleasant, and many children begin to cry and complain, but they are not allowed to stop. Those children who fall are the ones who will die young. Even though they are very thirsty, they are not allowed water, only *caissuma*. At sunset they are allowed to stop, and the men again perform *pakadin* on the patio, whilst the women sing *kawa* and rock the supposedly ramrod stiff children in their hammocks. This daytime running and nightime singing and rocking continue for three days, and several other ritual sequences are interspersed, including a ritual planting of corn (see Lagrou 1998).

Another session of sexual joking and mock battles involves young women simulating ejaculation (by shelling corn on to the ground) in mockery of the young men, whilst the latter shoot mini-arrows at the women's skirts (Kensinger 1995). At dawn of the final day of this stage, the neophtyes are given *nixpo*. In the past this was when their earlobes, nasal septums, nostrils and lower lips were pierced; but this practice was abandoned in the 1930s in Brazil and around 1965 in Peru. The parents and parents-in-law then perform *dawai pakadin* on the patio. This was described to me as a 'kind of carnival' involving *chais*, *xanus*, *chaitas*, and *tsabes*. Men and women of one moiety throw mud at the men and women of the other, and vice versa. The men dance thrusting their uncovered buttocks towards their *chais*, a gesture known as *puinkimei*, and one that has fixed itself in the memories of witnesses, so that in the descriptions I gathered it epitomized the sessions of sexual joking and games.

During this time the neophytes are not allowed to eat any meat, salt or sweet foods, nor may they drink water – restrictions that apply on all occasions when people are more vulnerable to the spirits, as at first menstruation, during the acquisition of the ability to hunt, during illness or initiation as a chant-leader, and pre- and post-partum. The children are only allowed to drink corn *caissuma*. One interpretation for this restriction remits us to the cannibal logic of death (McCallum 1999). Vegetable substance is uninteresting to cannibal *yuxin*, so perhaps, being made literally of corn, the children become uninteresting to the hungry Inka spirits. Even so, the process is still very dangerous. Thus the children must not move at all, and they must stay ramrod-straight all night, like a corpse, so that snakes (the physical manifestation of *yuxin*) do not bite them (and cause their souls to be taken off by the Inkas).

After they are given *nixpo*, the dietary restrictions should continue and the children should stay in seclusion for a week, until their teeth 'are healed' (*sarado* (P.)), as one man told me. At the end of this period they are fed with a little meat, but must vomit it up. Then they are painted black with genipapo to protect them and allowed out of seclusion. A collective fish-poisoning expedition is organized, and the first real meal that they are allowed includes fish, not meat. After this they can slowly begin to eat other kinds of prohibited foods and meat again. Baptism is complete.

Nixpo Pima is the first step in the pedagogic process whereby girl and boy children are taught the knowledge needed in order to be able to engage in adult social interaction. It prepares the child for the corporeal engagements with the spirits that it will have to undertake during these lessons in order to become adult. By doing so it does not cut the child off from one 'natural' or pre-social phase and insert it into another, 'social' phase. In no sense does the child suddenly change into a social being; this is something that happens gradually as s/he grows. However the association between names and *Nixpo Pima* sustains the increasing social ability of the child. Names represent the possibility of sociality, and their attachment gives a boost to the increasing ability of the child to produce as well as consume, or, in other words, to be a social being.

Names are eternal. They are endlessly repeated despite the death of the bodies to which they are attached. They are like the seeds of corn, I was told, and as long as there are people with true names, the *Huni Kuin* will never end. It is especially appropriate that in the songs corn is linked with the Inkas, who are immortal, whose world is unchanging and perfectly ordered, and who are the cause of human death (McCallum in press). Corn is thus a perfect metaphor for unchanging order, as my informant suggested. In the songs, the singer repeats names and then the names of corn, and so on, thus suggesting an association between names and eternal Inka corn.

Corn reproduces cyclically, just as the relationships names make possible do, but it can only do so by passing through a world where its body grows and dies. Hard seeds are stored in the eaves of people's houses, so that, when the season comes round, they may be planted and the life of the plant-body may be reinitiated. Just like human beings, corn has a hard and a soft aspect. As semi-immortal seed, it shows its Inu moiety aspect. But its own eternity is only assured by human agency, vital for bringing it to life annually. Corn is therefore also associated with the Dua, the moiety of heat, corporeal growth and decay, of transient life in this world, as well as with Inu. *Xeki keneya*, the yellow 'corn with design' speckled with black, seems to symbolize this double quality, just as the pale-skinned neophyte with her or his black teeth and patterned face and body brings together the two moieties, or indeed, as a newborn child makes evident the generative power of this conjunction.[3]

The songs thus describe the creation of life, associated with Dua, from the stuff of death, associated with the Inkas and with Inu. It is the relationship between the two principles that is important, that is, the endless circulation between the living and the dead invoked in the ritual, within which transit the growing children are placed. Out of the ensuing dialectic, their growth is produced. The words of the songs penetrate the children's bodies in a physical sense, transferring many powers and qualities to them along with the names. Not only the words but also the corn itself is transformed substantially into the neophytes' bodies. Once again, Lagrou's ethnography clarifies this point beautifully: children who consume much corn have strong bones and grow fast and tall; children who are fed principally on sweet manioc have fragile bone structures and grow slowly. Hardening the teeth, which are the visible endpoint of the bone structure, completes the process begun in *kawa*, when the skeleton was 'cooked' firm and straight. As she says, *Nixpo Pima* moulds the children in a complete sense, reaching bones through the teeth and flesh through the skin.

When the children are given *nixpo* to 'eat', the corn has just begun to be harvested, and is still green, soft and sweet. But within a week or so it hardens on its stalks, and men and women must plan to harvest it all and bring it to the houses for storage. As the corn hardens, so the effect of the ritual 'takes' for the children and they begin to be able to eat meat again. Their reinforced bones have been 'cooked' and hardened by their parents' actions. The black comes off their teeth, and the design off their skins, but the teeth are hard and protected from decay. This time is then especially appropriate for the children to be named and given some permanence within the world of adulthood.

The symbolic linking of teeth hardening in the body and grains of corn hardening on the cob appears to play a role in making safe carnivorous desire. Adult teeth are said to have a 'tooth soul' (*xeta yuxin*), and the operations performed on the teeth could be said to fix this *yuxin* in place. The capacities of hardened teeth are those of a predator, not those of prey. If the children, through becoming eaters of *nixpo*, therefore become more fully human, they also come to resemble the immortal Inkas, the jaguar and the harpy eagle, who are eaters of meat. It is tempting to think that the tooth *yuxin* is fundamental to this end.[4]

The Cashinahua, like other Panoan-speakers, once practised endocannibalism. The body of the deceased was boiled, the flesh eaten by his or her kin, and the bones baked, pounded up and consumed mixed in with corn *caissuma*, or with a soup made from green bananas and game. The bones were ground, like hard corn, in a woman's rocker mill. Thus there is a further association between hard corn, the teeth and (by extension) the skeleton, the most enduring part of the corpse. At death, there was a return, a circulation between dead and living, enacted through the literal consumption of both the soft and the hard parts of the body. Pudicho Torres, headman of Balta in the 1970s, explained to the SIL missionaries that by these means the name was finally detached from the deceased, thus allowing his or her soul to make the journey to the land of the dead (Montag, Montag and Torres 1975). The clothing of immortality can only be borrowed in this life, not appropriated.

Thus *Nixpo Pima* marks a stage in growing up, and finalizes it, so to speak, by the firm attachment of the name. It also prepares the way for the next stage, by making the child temporarily into 'one of the eternal', one of the eaters of *nixpo*, and therefore a *juni kuin*, a real human being. No longer easy prey for the Inka spirits that are so hungry for human flesh, the children are ready for further encounters with the world of *yuxin*, necessary if they are to become full men and women.

Gender as Embodied Knowledge

Nixpo Pima marks the first step in the deliberate creation of gendered difference between boys and girls. After it, the visible differences between girls and boys will increasingly be linked to internalized gender differentiation, as the budding adolescents are taught the productive skills associated with male and female gender. Boys are made by their kin to grow into *bedunabu* ('young men'), imbued with male agency; and girls into *chipaxbu* ('young women'), imbued with female agency. The production of gender is thus linked closely to the economic process, so that only producing adults are completely gendered. What is more, only gendered adults are complete persons. Male and female agency are kinds of human agency (as men and women are kinds of human beings), and the relationship is one of complementary opposition within economic and social processes.

The opposition is reflected in the way that agency is formally acquired. Women's learning takes place, socially and geographically, on the 'inside', while men's learning often involves relationships with beings and spaces linked to the 'outside'. Women learn in a relation of kinship, from their MM (*chichi*), their own namesakes; men learn in a relation of affinal kinship, from their MF (*chai*), their brother-in-law's namesake. Women learn in a predominantly conscious mental state, whilst men learn both in a conscious state and, through hallucinogens, in an altered state of consciousness. Both also learn in dreams, when their bodies are unconscious to the everyday world. Finally, men learn by moving away from the village, travelling in the forest and the city whilst both conscious and otherwise, whereas women learn when relatively immobile, staying, for example, in their *chichi*'s house.

The spaces that the adolescents inhabit, the words they hear, the sights they see and the substances with which they come into contact, all these shape and penetrate their beings as embodied knowledge. The capacity to act is founded on the deposited memory of these experiences and actions past, that adhere to or penetrate the different organs of the body. The Cashinahua describe this as 'the whole body knows' (Kensinger 1995; McCallum 1996a, 1990). The way that the body is made to know, therefore, is the self-same process in which gender is produced.

There is a certain division of labour in the work of producing 'Real Persons'. Maternal grandparents produce gendered differentiation in bodies that the child's parents have produced by correct feeding. Whilst an infant is growing, it is the parent's relation with its body that is all-important. Grandparents assume greater responsibility for the corporeal production of adulthood in adolescents. Namesake grandmothers preside over the first menstruation seclusion of girls and prepare their bodies for learning female skills such as weaving, while maternal grandfathers preside over the production of male bodies suited to work in the gardens, hunt in the forest and fish in the river. The experiences and actions that engrain memory and skills into the young bodies work upon or through the children's various *yuxin* ('souls'), so that the adults who accompany and guide the adolescents at this time may be said to be gendering them in body and in soul.

The acquisition of knowledge requires a relationship between the two major 'souls' of a human body: the eye *yuxin*, also known as 'true *yuxin*', and the 'body soul' (*yuda yuxin*). This latter *yuxin* 'contains' all the knowledge and memories that a person acquires through life. A child's body *yuxin* is weak and unskilled, developing through life until it becomes powerful and, after death, dangerous to the living. The eye *yuxin* and the dream *yuxin* allow a person to see, but knowledge itself is accrued within the *yuda yuxin*. This is where wakeful knowledge and progressive memory are concentrated, as in the Yaminahua *diawaka* (Townsley 1988). It is the seat of consciousness, thought, and will – the aspects of a person that guide interaction with the living. In contrast, the eye *yuxin* is that aspect of a person that interacts with the dead and with other *yuxin* such as the forest spirits. Whilst it is wandering the body lies dormant, unconscious, and unable to speak, but on its return, when consciousness is restored, the body *yuxin* may have been fortified by the experiences of the true *yuxin*. A remembered dream augments incorporated knowledge.

Such memory may be induced by preparing the body, through fasting, the taking of emetics and the use of other medicines; or it may be induced by enhancing a person's ability to see (*uin-*) and to understand or hear (*ninka-*). Vision is an important ability for those who are learning, and hunters and weavers sometimes prepare herbal eye drops so that they can see clearly. Most pedagogy involves the pupil watching the actions of the teacher, rather than listening to explanations. Anyone wishing to learn, whether anthropologist or child, is admonished to watch and imitate. And during dreams and hallucinatory visions people are said to travel and 'see', thereby getting knowledge. When a sleeper awakes, it is customary to ask 'Did you dream?' as a polite morning greeting. Dreams might foretell some future event. Sometimes, they are simple journeys to other places. Similarily, visions induced by drugs might predict the future or simply reveal facts about other places and their inhabitants. But while ordinary waking vision and the visions of the dream *yuxin* are important forms of acquiring knowledge for all, only men should learn through drugs. Women learn principally whilst they are awake.

Body *yuxin*s can only be the repositories of gendered knowledge, then, through the activity of the eye *yuxin* and of the eye. For boys, however, the visions of the eye *yuxin* are relatively more important than they are for girls. This is because men, in order to produce, require a more extensive knowledge of distant places than women need. Also, and equally importantly, this is related to the courage that men need in order to be able to withstand the danger abounding in those places. I now turn to the processes whereby adolescents incoporate these two complementary forms of human agency.

Female Agency

The Cashinahua are famous for their woven textiles, which are produced using techniques similar to Andean ones, but designs characteristic of Lowland traditions (Dwyer 1975). Girls first learn to spin cotton when they are seven or eight years old (Figure 6). As a girl approaches puberty she spends more and more of her time spinning. The resulting balls of yarn are used by her mother or elder sisters to make hammocks and shoulder bags. Around puberty she begins to learn how to weave cotton cloth, baskets (*chichan* and *kakan*) and mats (*pixin*). Learning to weave design into these baskets and above all the cloth is relatively difficult, requiring concentration, endurance and a good memory. To do so, a girl must observe dietary restrictions, and her *chichi* treats her with herbal eye drops that help her to remember clearly and easily. In a private ritual the teacher sings *pakadin* and washes her with infusions of plants that help her to concentrate. The business at hand is serious, for at stake is not just the ability to make beautiful artefacts for husbands, children and

Figure 6. Learning to spin cotton

other kin, or for the market, but also the embodied capacity to generate 'real' identity. Women often told me that design (*kene*) is the Cashinahua form of writing (also *kene*) and considered it unnecessary to learn to read and write themselves. To be considered a 'real woman' a girl ought ideally to know how to weave designs. Skilled weavers are rare and much praised by others, in much the same way that certain men are noted for their ability at hunting.

So girls lucky enough to have such a teacher spend long hours watching the needle as it is threaded in and out of the warp. When each row is complete, the weaver inserts a design marker stick at the reverse side of the crossed warp strings, so that two lines of weft can be completed in one line of weaving. Then the weaving batten is used to push the marker stick back before it is pulled out, the weft thread is pulled through and another line of design is marked. When the marker sticks impede the continued progression of the design, the cloth is taken down and reversed, and the pupil sits down to pull the weft through and pull out the sticks as each reverse pattern thread is pulled through. After thus making several shoulder bags, the girl begins to insert the pattern itself, while her teacher sits beside her watching for errors and telling her the number of lines of warp to pass the weft thread over, and the number to pass it under. The girl must learn three or four complete sets of these numbers in order to qualify for the high accolade of *ainbu keneya*, 'woman with design'.

Though women are above all mistresses of design, and men of the hunt, the other-worldly origin of their skills is identical. On the Jordão I heard the following story: 'The boa taught the old woman to weave design into the things that she wore. Her skirts were all coloured and patterned like the boa itself. A little boy shot arrows at the snake, out of mischievousness. Annoyed, she told the child that he must never kill her, and then took him out into the forest to teach him to hunt, and then left.' It is to this original gift that *nixpo pima* songs refer, as the singers ask for the bestowal of specific named designs on the girls (McCallum 1989; Lagrou 1998).

Women use the same motifs to paint faces, bodies and to a lesser extent pottery. A girl's pots and pans represent one of the skills that she should acquire in order to become a real woman, *ainbu kuin*: cooking. Girls are taught to cook by their mothers and elder sisters, whom they spend many years helping before they may cook in their own right (after marriage and the first child). Young girls are bad cooks, and cannot be trusted to carry out an entire process from harvest to serving carefully and skilfully. It is difficult to boil manioc just right, or to toast corn or peanuts an even brown without burning the grains (as I discovered during my own apprenticeship). When a girl can do this, she is praised thus: 'Now you are a real woman, you know how to cook properly – *min bava unanki*.' A bad woman, by contrast, is *bavauma*, 'without cooking', too lazy or sloppy to prepare food properly. Such a woman grinds her corn roughly, and fails to keep dirt and fibres out of her food. Worse still, she does not cook the meat and fish that her men give her enough, leaving traces of dangerous raw blood in the meals she serves (*bama*, 'uncooked').

The term for 'cooked' is *ba*, which in verb form means 'to create', 'to procreate' and 'to be born'. Cooking food (*bava-*) is analogous to making babies. Similarly, pots are analogous to wombs. Women are responsible, then, for transforming raw substance (meat, fish, vegetables) into cooked and edible substance, just as they are responsible for transforming raw semen into 'cooked' babies in their wombs. Furthermore, the mythic hollow where the primordial creation and transformation took place is also analogous to a womb. In a version collected in Peru, the first people were created in a hole in a tree; and in the transcription the term used for this hole (*xankin*) is that normally used to refer to a womb (Ministério de Educación 1980).

First menses marks the point when a woman becomes able to create, when her womb matures into the organ that allows her to transform her own and her partner's 'blood' into a new human form. Caused originally by the mythic figure Moon, the first collective menstruation was followed by 'all the women becoming pregnant' (Abreu 1941). First menses occasions a small ritual, involving a period of semi-seclusion and dieting. At this time, a girl must stay close to home and work on her newly acquired skills, under the tutelage of her maternal grandmother, for menstrual blood is offensive to the forest and river spirits. The smell draws the attention of the spirits to the presence of human beings, alerting them to possible danger and causing them to interfere in their activities. One reason, then, that a girl must stay at home is to protect her from these spirits, who would be angry at her intrusion into their domain. Menstrual blood, like other bodily substances, links humans to spirits, because it makes the separation between human domain and spirit domain begin to break down. Its smell 'makes a path' from one domain to the other and makes normally invisible humans visible to the spirits. This is why men may not sleep with menstruating women, for they become bad hunters as a result. The blood clings to them and they may only be rid of it through dieting.

In short, female agency involves the ability to produce a variety of objects, to paint and weave design and to transform raw substances into 'cooked' or processed things and people. These are termed *kuin*, 'real', by the Cashinahua, and contrasted with artefacts and persons produced by other groups or entities, such as foreigners or spirits. For example, women should be able to make real hammocks, real pots, real design, real food, and, of course, Real People. Women thus stand at the centre of the production of what constitutes Cashinahua cultural and social identity, rather than at the periphery (as has been suggested for other lowland peoples such as the Gê).[5]

During their apprenticeship the girls must master certain female qualities that they will require all their producing lives. They must learn to be patient and to be still, to be able to sit at home for days on end weaving and spinning. At this time they begin to acquire the corporeal softness and the rounded shape that characterizes feminine bodies and that a first pregnancy will bring to perfect completion. Men and women admire teenage girls for plump and beautiful bodies. During their first menses semi-seclusion, girls drink quantities of *caissuma*, which is described as *xea dau*, 'fattening medicine' (translated rather freely by my informants as 'vitamins'). At this age sex also helps a girl grow and round out. Women like to emphasize their plumpness, using long strands of white beads that they wind tightly around their wrists, ankles and calves, marking gentle curves into the flesh. And though youths also drink much *caissuma*, they grow bigger, harder and more muscular than the girls. This is said to be because their adult bodies are produced differently from women's.

Male Agency

As is common elsewhere in lowland South America, sex is thought to inhibit male growth a little at this stage, and to help female growth, so that while young female adolescents might marry safely, boys often have to wait until they are nearing their twenties. But young men do have affairs, and I never heard adults criticize them for thereby endangering their growth in the way Mehinaku parents do (Gregor 1977). At the age when girls first menstruate, boys are taught formally to hunt and to work in the gardens. Much of the practical knowledge that these activities require is already mastered at this stage. Boys accompany their elder siblings, brothers-in-law, fathers, MBs or MFs on expeditions into the forest from the time they can walk fast enough. Certain kinds of work and hunting magic that are beneficial at this later stage are ideally performed for the boy by his *chai*, his MF, in a series of private rituals. For example, a *kampun* frog's skin, which has emetic properties, is used to induce vomiting to clean out the body. Good hunters neither smell nor sweat as they move through the forest, and are said to be 'cool'. (Menstruating women, in contrast, are both smelly 'like fish' and 'hot'.) Dietary restrictions and the use of eye drops help boys to become *dekeya*, 'with tracking skills'.

By 1985 hunters devoted less time to dieting and to hunting magic than used to be the case, and certain practices appeared to have been abandoned altogether. When the middle-aged hunters of Recreio were young, they were initiated into the hunt via a prolonged diet. They began by using the frog skin to induce vomiting and then killing a *yubexeni* boa to eat its tongue. Then for about thirty days they were allowed to eat neither sweet nor salty foods and no meat at all. The transmitted abilities of the snake *yuxin* helped them to kill a large game animal afterwards. Similar periods of dieting, usually of shorter duration, help restore a hunter's skill if he has been consistently unlucky. A bad hunter might have been invaded by 'a foreign substance, called *yupa*, which can only be removed by his undergoing a month-long fast, abstinence from sex, and, finally, a purification ritual' (Kensinger 1995:17).

Boys thus initially learn to hunt by observing dietary prohibitions that help form their bodies, like girls during their first menses. But the male diet moves into an active phase when the boy goes out to hunt specific animals in the forest, unlike the girls, who continue to 'study' at home in their MM's houses. Ideally, the boy is guided by his MF (*chai*) in his attempts to kill specific animals, as well as in his diet. In contrast to girls, he will also attempt to absorb the tracking and killing skills of the snake into his body, thereby making himself *menki*, a good hunter. As well as all this, he will also begin to take the hallucinogen *nixi pae* seriously at this time. In hallucinogen-induced visions, or in their dreams, Cashinahua men try to 'establish cordial relationships with spirit beings encountered . . . The spirit familiars and pets gained in this way protect and assist the hunter' (Kensinger 1981:170).

This relationship with spirits is very different from a shaman's relationship. A shaman is unable to hunt because the game animals appear to him as human beings and friends. If he were to kill and consume one of the animals that are categorized as *yuxin*, like jaguars, the spirit would find him and make him ill. The shaman looses his ability to make distinctions between domains, or states of consciousness, so that enemies are like kin, humans like enemies, victims like friends. A hunter, in contrast, has no such problems of classification. There is no muddying of the boundaries between spirit world and waking world. In his vision, an animal is just an animal, and may be killed. Although with his repertoire of calls he can trick the animal to come to him, he then firmly delineates the difference between himself and the creature by killing it instead of befriending it, as his seductive calls led it to believe he would. Seduction, in human relations, leads to affection and procreation; in relations between men and prey, it leads to murder and death. This association between hunting and seduction is made explicitly by Cashinahua men. For example, Kensinger (1995) cites an informant who likened the penis of an impotent man to a 'broken arrow'. Penises are like arrows in another way too, for sex can cause women to bleed. If human beings were really to seduce the animals, then (so the myths warn) the consequences would be dangerous. Women, being when they menstruate more visible to spirits than men, are in greater danger from spirit attack, involving seduction or possible rape by male spirits and jealousy from female spirits (Kensinger 1981). Like shamans, they are bad hunters, because they cannot always keep the boundaries clear.

Hunting skills and information as to the location of game are obtained partly through daytime vision (looking and remembering) and partly through 'dreamtime' vision, via the wanderings of his dream *yuxin*, which may be understood as an aspect of the eye *yuxin*. When the drug-taker awakes, he can remember his visions, thus transposing the knowledge obtained in the world of spirits into his conscious repertoire, stored in his 'body *yuxin*'.

Men also seek other kinds of information besides hunting hints using *nixi pae*. In Recreio on the Brazilian Purus there were no sessions during my stay, but a few men would sometimes travel to Fronteira to take the

Figure 7. Boy fishing

drug in the regular Saturday night sessions. They told me that they 'tripped' to the sound of a guitar or a battery-operated record player, describing their visions as 'Indian cinema' (*cinema de caboclo* (P.)), during which they travelled to cities such as São Paulo and other faraway places. Similar uses of the vine are reported for the Yaminahua, the Sharanahua, and the Cashinahua of the Jordão.[6] And in the 1990s Lagrou reported a revival of *nixi pae* taking among the inhabitants of Recreio (Lagrou 1991). Kensinger (1973, 1995) describes a *nixi pae* drinking session in Peru in the 1960s, and it seems fair to affirm that it follows the basic form of the quest for knowledge of all these groups and periods. His description goes thus: After darkness fell the men congregated where the drug was stored and helped themselves, chanting over the brew before they drank to ask for good visions. Then they sat beside a fire on stools or logs. Soon the visions began and each sang his own chant, or sat next to someone who knew how to sing. They swayed their bodies to the rhythm and conversed with the spirits of the drug. Most people maintained physical contact with the men next to them, to help overcome terror. Only the most experienced and strongest sat alone. Kensinger stresses that the search for knowledge itself, accomplished through the wandering of the person's dream *yuxin*, is a highly individual affair.

The men said they experienced transformation (*dami va-*) as rapid motion, visions changing from one to another. They saw snakes, jaguars, spirits, trees, lakes with anacondas and alligators, villages of all kinds of people, traders and their merchandise, and gardens. Such visions might have been warnings of things to come, or information about illness caused by sorcery. Men travelled to faraway places and learned about them. Some years later, also in Peru, Deshayes and Keifenheim (1982) were told that when men die their *yuxin kuin* must make a difficult and dangerous journey to the land of the dead in the sky, during which demons (*yuxibu*) try to eat their souls. Another purpose for taking *nixi pae* was preparation for this ultimate journey, to learn skill and courage in interaction with spirit beings.

Thus men learn bravery through taking the drug, a quality that they will also need during their lifetime as hunters, traders and (in the past) warriors. Women do not need this skill, since they neither hunt nor kill (though women say that facing childbirth requires more courage than any man could muster). When women die, they are not faced with the same difficulties along the path to heaven. Adult men are said to be 'shot' by the weapon spirit of the mythic being Nawa or Inka (their *chai*, brother-in-law) when they die. Women are not shot by this being; instead, their kin (*nabu*) come to fetch them away to the land of the dead (McCallum

1996b). Thus, just as adult men are produced by affinal kin, and women by kin, so too male death may be said to be brought about by affinity, and female death by kinship.

During their productive lives, men must learn to be strong and fierce, though many say that they, like women, are not brave enough to take the drug. Since women do not require such qualities, they normally neither smoke, drink, nor take *nixi pae*, all activities that induce *paen*, 'drunkenness'. If a woman wishes to try one of these stimulants, however, she may. I met one Recreio woman who had taken *nixi pae* in order to 'see' her parents, who lived on the Jordão, and whom she had last seen fifteen years before.

In a drugged state and in dreams men and women can interact safely with spirits, as long as the boundaries between domains remain. As I have said, in a waking state menstruating women both attract and repel the physical manifestation of spirits. Men only do so in this state when temporarily contaminated with bodily substances, or ill or dying. But male shamans do attract *yuxin*, and in this they are like bleeding women. Women also have a secondary association with blood that reinforces their unsuitability as hunters, for they are responsible for the transformation of raw meat into cooked food. Women butcher most game, distribute the raw meat to female kin and give cooked meat to male and female kin and to visitors. Good cooks cannot, it seems to me, be good hunters. Conversely, good hunters cannot be good cooks. Thus men need female agency if they are to consume the products of their hunting, just as women need male agency if they are to be able to produce a complete meal. If too much of one domain passes into another (if men deal too much in blood, or women too much in the spirit world) then gendered agency is blocked, and men become *yupa*, unlucky in hunting, whilst women lose their ability to make human babies. They might give birth to twins (*yuxin bake*, spirit children) or deformed monsters. Men destroy possible kinship links with the spirits, whereas women and shamans unwittingly attract them. Women (and good shamans) should protect and engender kinship, but only in the human domain. To do this, like men they must learn how to protect and strengthen their corporeal, cultural, and moral skills. So it is because of the opposed but complementary natures of produced male and female agency that the formal training of youths and young women takes the form that it does. The next stage in their young lives will be the real test of the apprenticeship, when marriage forces them to fetch, work, play and make love in earnest.

Marriage

Adult marriage is the relationship that sustains the economic system. The Cashinahua conception of marriage emphasizes male–female cooperation and complementarity; assumes a good marriage to be an affectionate and lifelong partnership; and enshrines it as the only relationship that allows men and women to be complete persons. First marriages could be arranged for a child by its parents or elder siblings. In the past a couple were ideally raised together until old enough to marry or, alternatively, until the girl reached ten or eleven years and was deemed old enough to sleep with her older husband. Even now, there are cases of child-brides, but on the whole contemporary Cashinahua disapprove of this practice. The girl suffers too much from giving birth at so young an age, they say. Marriages are usually arranged when a girl is about fourteen or fifteen, and a youth between seventeen and twenty-five.

The preferred marriage is between actual cross-cousins, and a fair number of first marriages are in this category.[7] Marriage is nearly always moiety-exogamous. Indeed it is often said that moieties serve to identify marriage partners for one's children. There is a tendency to arrange or approve marriages between a woman and her MB, who falls within the correct moiety category but not the correct generational category. Pre-existing links to affines should be and are constantly reduplicated, both in the same generation and in subsequent generations. In this way, Cashinahua marriage practice resembles marriage practice linked to a Dravidian-type terminology (Kaplan 1975). Such replication of affinal links allows people to marry endogamously within a community and therefore remain with their close kin afterwards; and such is the general ambition of most men and women. Living with kin is considered to be the most harmonious and feasible form of residence. Kin are ideally willing to share with each other, to avoid conflict, and abhor interpersonal coercion. 'Correct' marriages also result in children of the correct category in terms of parents' and grandparents' relationships and names, so that the system can continue in the second descending generation. Most parents and children seem to find a way for a first marriage to be agreeable to both sides, and if it is not, divorce soon results. However, this ideal of close marriage may well produce conflict and drama between parents and children, and other kin involved in unsuccessful marriages. When adolescents are made to marry against their will, this may lead to behaviour that directly contravenes the non-coercive kin ethic.

In 1984 I played a part in one such case. The young couple were cross-cousins. Her mother was his FZ, and her father his MB. These two parents married them as soon as she reached first menses. Unusually, it was she who moved in with him, sharing a hammock with him in his father's house. During the first year I spent in Recreio they never spoke to each other and only spoke about each other in a derogatory way. From time to time they fought, and she would 'run away' to her mother's house (and once to mine). Then her mother and father-in-law would join together in lecturing the couple on the need to stay together. They would stress to the sullen pair that they were well suited to each other, there was 'no one else', and that they should stop quarrelling and start settling down to married life. This always struck me as strange, since there were at least a dozen unmarried adolescents in nearby Fronteira. The parents preferred to strengthen their in-family ties, rather than initiate new affinal links. This preference resulted in a pair of unhappy teenagers, until finally the reluctant bride, now pregnant, went home to her mother definitively.

In this case post-marital residence was virilocal, but in most cases it is uxorilocal. In Recreio in the 1980s several of the young grooms had come from Peru to live with their bride's family. Some of these youths were unable to resist their longing to be with their own families, and subsequently went home. In some cases the bride's distaste for her man leads to his departure. In other cases the marriage takes and the two teenagers enter into the spirit of their relationship with enthusiasm. They work, hunt and fish with energy if not much skill, and are often to be seen going off together into the forest or the gardens. When relaxing at home, they spend much time flirting and tussling, sharing a daytime hammock, and cracking explicit sexual jokes at each other's expense.

The Cashinahua style of humour is markedly sexual. There are several standard jokes that never fail to draw a laugh. They usually refer to male or female productive activities, and especially to hunting. For example, a man sitting in his hammock drinking *caissuma* calls over to his cross-cousin where she is sitting on a mat with other women. He speaks in a pleading, joking tone, 'Hey *Xanun*, come drink *caissuma*! Get nice and juicy!' (Women do not normally share bowls of *caissuma* with men unless at informal moments.) She retorts 'I won't get juicy, you are useless at hunting!', which the listeners find hilarious. In the another typical exchange, a woman demands publicly that her husband 'kill a deer' for her, pointing out that she is starving for meat. He replies that he will go out tomorrow, but she should accompany him 'to carry the catch because it will be so heavy'. Again, the innuendo is that once in the forest they will have sex. She retorts *"En kamaki, min yupaki"*, 'I won't go, you are *yupa* (a bad hunter)' and the audience roars with laughter. In another case, a man calls his cross-cousin to 'take another banana' from his bunch (*mani betsa bive*) and she replies 'you have no banana' (*min maniumaki*). The couples are 'joking' with each other, *kaxe-*, a type of banter that hinges on sexual innuendo and open ribaldry. This is a skill that adults master progressively, so that old women and men are often the best and loudest jokers. The young are more reticent, tending to blush and keep silent if an older cross-cousin aims a joke at them. Old men sometimes mutter such a joke to their child *xanu*s, thus 'teaching them' how to *kaxe-*. Men also *kaxe-* their brothers-in-law and male cross-cousins (*chai*) in this way, and women (to a lesser extent) their sisters-in-law and female cross-cousins (*tsabe*).

Despite this humour, the Cashinahua feel that marriage and sex are very serious matters, and prefer that adolescents only have sex within a marital relationship, because sex leads to children. A young woman should not have to bring up children on her own. Because all adolescents have sex, they should be married. However, the adolescents often try to put off the official recognition of a love affair by keeping it secret. They know that unless their affair is 'incestuous' or otherwise disagreeable to their parents they will be made to marry and therefore to begin working harder than a single teenager.

Marriage is a simple affair. The boy moves his possessions into the girl's house, and begins sleeping in the same hammock with her. She should carry his hammock for him. After the first night they are considered married, a condition which is referred to as 'with husband', *beneya*, or 'with wife', *ainya*. Subsequently a special meeting will be arranged so that the adults can formally set the teenage union on the right tracks. The couple sits together in the centre of the room, apart from the groups of men and women. Male and female leaders, parents, and other elder relatives or members of the community take it in turns to speak, lecturing the couple on their married duties towards each other. The form of moralizing speech, standard 'teaching oratory', is used in all public speeches (McCallum 1990). I recorded one, which I summarize as follows:

> You, Son, must work hard for your wife, and look after her. You must make a garden, build a house, cut rubber and buy the necessities with the proceeds. You must always hunt and and fish provide her with the meat. You, Daughter-in-law, must work hard at home spinning and weaving, cooking and looking after your husband. You must always fetch manioc from the garden, so that there is always food. You must sew and wash the clothes. In this way each of you will be a good spouse.

Sex and marriage are circumscribed by a particularily strong set of moral values. In a sense, marriage is the most serious business in a person's life, as the following story made clear to me: Two adolescents, sisters-in-law to each other, were rumoured to have been making love to a young married man who was *epa* to one (MMBS) and *kuka* to the other (FMBS). The father of one, who was the other's father-in-law, was told the gossip, and he summoned them to him. In a tone of repressed fury, he said: '*Achin!* You are my daughter and must listen to me. I always teach you, and you never listen. You must respect me. You must not make love with your "father". He is your *chichi*'s BS. It's bad, very bad. You must not make love with men, you are not yet married. You are a woman, you must work hard at women's tasks, work hard and listen to your *eva*. Do not go near your uncle again. Thank God, I am a Believer (*Crente* (P.)), but I am very angry. I could kill him, just like that. So do not go near him, you must work hard and respect me.' He then delivered a milder version of the same lecture to his daughter-in-law. Neither girl lifted her voice in reply, but sat sulking instead. When he had finished, his wife spoke in a similar manner, making the same points in a quiet voice. The girls sometimes intervened with their opinion, but mostly sat and listened. The following morning, the daughter-in-law's mother (his sister) came to the house and spoke sternly to the two girls in the same manner. To her daughter she said: 'You must work hard, listen to me when I teach you, help your mother-in-law, and not make love to any man but my *dais* (son-in-law).' This story illustrates how men and women share the same views about marriage. Indeed, in all the marriage speeches I heard I did not come across differing male and female views. Women, though, are more sympathetic to the problems experienced by young women, as the two miscreant daughters well knew.

Nowadays, marriage is described as the only proper place for sex. Affairs should be kept secret. In the past, people were said to be more relaxed about love affairs. Worse than a discovered affair is a discovered incestuous one, as the story suggests. The girl who made love to her 'father' (her MMBS) was far more severely reprimanded by male and female speakers than her sister-in-law, who had made love to her *kuka*, a member of the opposite moiety and potentially marriageable. Her only real crime had been adultery.

Despite this moralistic attitude to category-correct sex and marriage, when all is said and done, the Cashinahua feel that the important thing is how a marriage itself is conducted. Even if, for some reason, people of the wrong category marry, the mistake will be 'forgotten' with time. My misunderstanding of marriage was corrected by a visitor from Balta, in Peru. He said:

People get married wrong (*chaka*). Someone created an Inu marries the same kind of woman (an Inani) or likewise a Duabake marries a Banu. When such a wrong marriage is made, they always mess up the naming. But they go ahead and give it a name anyway, even when they marry wrong. That is how God ordered it should happen. Since the first days of creation, people have married wrong. They still do it.

I then asked 'Is it bad?' and somewhat testily he retorted:

No, no, it's not bad, it's good! That's the way it is. God made it like that since Adam and Eve. Living, living . . . Look, an intelligent man doesn't marry the wrong kind of woman. He marries his true wife (*ain kayabi*) and he always stays married to her. An intelligent man, one with knowledge, that is how they procreate (*ba-*). Marrying one's true wife and marrying one's wrong wife (*ainya chaka*) are both done in the same way: treating her well, looking after her, not abandoning her and moving on to another woman, like the ancestors did. A stupid man, and there are many still about, will treat her badly, and hunt wrong, work wrong, make love wrong.

In the next chapter I discuss the duties of husband and wife, of adult men and women, to which this informant referred. These activities form the real substance of the relationship, whatever the categorical position of each spouse before marriage. Marriage is primarily a productive relationship. Couples are concerned with the creation of life as parents, as grandparents and as members of a community of kinspeople. The opposition between male and female as it is expressed within the relationship of marriage underlies the ability a couple has to produce. Couples who are successfully married call to each other using the term *Ba*, which is devoid of kinship connotations. Couples who have grown together into a good marriage, show their friendly affection for each other by the use of the term *Ba*. Its use brings to attention the ideal distance between man and woman, suggesting that they are like friendly strangers, thus overlaying their sharing of common kindreds with a kind of lie. The moieties also work in this way, serving to delineate affinal distinctions within the circle of *nabu kuin*. It is very appropriate, then, that men call their wives' brothers *chai*, for this term used as an adjective also means 'far away'.

It is tempting to think that the term *Ba* ('spouse') is derived from the verb *ba-*, 'to be born; to get created; to be cooked', since the marriage relationship is the most creative and economically productive one known to the Cashinahua. In the next chapter I discuss how this works both in theory and in practice.

Notes

1. Kensinger kindly made his manuscript available to me and to Lagrou. Her thesis provides the most complete account to date of *nixpo pima*, including an analysis of a number of important songs, an eyewitness description of different components of the ritual complex, and a sophisticated interpretation of its implications for Cashinahua ontology and cosmology in the light of key related myths. Lagrou (1997) is an English version of Lagrou (1998).

2. In the mythology, as in *Nixpo Pima*, the deity 'Inka' and the spirit people known as 'the Inkas' are both present. Their relationship is discussed in McCallum (in press).

3. Lagrou (1997, 1998) include a sophisticated interpretation of Cashinahua dualism.

4. Indigenous Amazonians in general consider that teeth concentrate other-worldly powers, so the attention that the Cashinahua pay to their own teeth is hardly surprising. The literature most often discusses teeth of dead enemies and predators, however, not teeth in living human bodies.

5. See for example Maybury-Lewis (1979). By contrast, C. Hugh-Jones (1979) documented the symbolic and economic centrality of female production in northwest Amazonia.

6. On the Yaminahua use of *nixi pae*, see Townsley (1988); on the Sharanahua use, Siskind (1973); and on that of the Cashinahua of the Jordão, Aquino (1977).

7. For a genealogical analysis of marriage on the Brazilian Purus between 1983 and 1985 see McCallum (1989).

–3–

Producing Sociality

Sociality is carved out in the daily round, in a series of economic processes that are at once material, conceptual and signifying (Descola 1994). The series includes a variety of forms of production and appropriation of products, their distribution, circulation, consumption and transformation. Gender difference at home, among Real People themselves, provides the central dynamic to these processes, as it does elsewhere in Amazonia.[1] It may be said to be the driving force for the production of sociality itself. Although much of a Cashinahua person's life is spent working, eating, or resting together with members of her or his own sex, everything that is done makes possible and is only made possible by the complementary work or production of an opposite-sex partner. One may sum up the gender dynamic in the following formula: Social and economic production is made possible by male agency in dealing directly with the spirits and foreigners; and by female agency in mediating the transformation of the products of such encounters. Women control the circulation of food between houses and between settlements. They control the cooking of food and its transformation from poisonous to nourishing. Similarly, they transform babies from dangerous body substance to prototype human being. Men, for their part, fetch things from afar. They bring back game and fish from forest and river, manufactured items and foreign knowledge from the city. The ultimate if fragile product of men's and women's joint work ought to be the growing community of living co-resident kin.

From a Human Point of View

This community exists at the interstices of many other worlds that for their part, taking an insider's viewpoint, may each be seen as a working social system. Game animals, fish spirits, Inkas or outsiders such as the Cariú, each of these beings inhabit a particular world that has its own social logic, its own meanings, customs and *raison d'être*. A peculiarity of this understanding of 'nature' and 'supernature' is that each of these beings sees itself as human. These principles are part of the phenomenon now known as 'Amazonian perspectivism'.[2] For a Cashinahua person, it is possible to imagine oneself into the skin of such beings, to take their perspective on the cosmos and conjure up the understandings and meanings afforded from within these alien social environments. Innumerable stories and myths provide ample evidence of such feats of the imagination. They also describe what happens when perspectives really shift. This invariably happens through the body of the person involved. When the boundaries of foreign social systems extend out to capture wandering humans, their bodies sicken, mutate or die. They lose the only point of view that is properly human and transform into another form of being, just as babies do in their mother's wombs if adversely affected by external influences, or children do during *Nixpo Pima* if the rules are not carefully observed. Lima (1995, 1996) discusses the workings of Amazonian perspectivism using data from her research among the Juruna of the Alto Xingu, and argues that as a philosophy it should be distinguished from cultural relativism, since nothing in this understanding of the world corresponds to the conceptual opposition between Nature and Culture, a point on which Amazonianists now concur.[3] The same goes for the Cashinahua, whose thinking and practice fit perfectly the 'perspectivist' frame first outlined by Lima and Viveiros de Castro. Yet one comment is important here. If their 'perspectivism' may properly be described as philosophical, it also serves as a sociological basis for acting in a concrete world. In this sense social action and the concepts that infuse it are never value-free. Cashinahua perspectivism is situated in the moral and emotional field of their own appreciation of sociality. More than this, our understanding of it should be firmly located in the recognition of the way it is lived as a daily experience. The 'human point of view' is not understandable in terms of formal logic or the mathematics of philosophical speculation alone. Our analysis may indeed reveal a formidable logical basis to social thought and action, but this is less than half the story.

Amazonian perspectivism as it is lived precludes much generosity of spirit in relation to the points of view of other beings. Yet it would be unfair to accuse the Cashinahua or other indigenous Americans of ethnocentrism, for 'otherness' is not seen as an essential attribute of bodies or as an inescapable physical condition. Other beings may be made into humans or kin or vice versa. This is not to say that alterity is rendered impotent or that differences are fuzzy. Moiety is after all the basic organizing principle of social life, along with gender. Yet, having raised dualism to an art form, the Cashinahua live it in the spirit of an apparent gradualism, where boundaries may be shifted or crossed even as they must always be re-erected (Lagrou 1998). The difficulties of transformation are not underestimated. Making others into kin takes time and much work, in the same way as making children into gendered humans. The bodies of living beings carry this social history of their own making as memory, so that kinship may be said to be memory itself (Gow 1991). Sociality, then, is not a neutral state, nor does the term refer in my usage to the product of social interaction of whatever kind. Rather, its meaning is doubly inflected by the present ethnography: Firstly, with the moral loading given all social relations by the Cashinahua themselves, a loading that expresses the 'human point of view'; and secondly by the epistemological conditions for action, as based on the embodiment of knowledge, skills, emotions and gender itself. This said, the use of the term adopted here is compatible with the project defended by Marilyn Strathern and Christina Toren in the Manchester debate of 1989, as it is summed up by Tim Ingold: 'Their plea is for an alternative conceptual vocabulary, anchored on the concept of "sociality", that would enable us to express the way in which particular persons both come into being through relationships and forge them anew, without relegating both personhood and relationship to a domain of reified abstraction – epitomized by the concept of society' (Ingold 1996:57–8).

It is in the light of these comments on sociality and the human point of view that I turn to the Cashinahua way of discussing these issues. I begin with a lesson I received on the origins and ideal form of a man's working life and of the moral logic behind it. Elias, my teacher, was a resident of Recreio since his arrival, during the late 1970s, with a large group of kin and affines from the Curanja in Peru. At the time of our conversation (1984) he was in his mid-forties, and should have been at the height of his productive powers; but he was afflicted by ill health brought on by sadness at the recent death of his eldest son. His household depended on the productive activities of his son-in-law, wife and daughters, so Elias sometimes had time to sit and answer my questions. I asked him to tell me how the *xenipabu* ('old ones') hunted and then to compare their ways with modern practice. He began by telling me how young men used to kill a boa constrictor, eat its tongue and subsequently observe a diet, lasting a month, during which they abstained from meat. After this, they would slowly begin to eat all kinds of meat again; and then, he continued:

They would hunt for a peccary and once it was killed they took it home and gave it to their wife and fed their children and their parents. Then they would work the day through, and another day, three in all, and then they would go again. They say that this time they would kill a deer. That is the way to become *menki*, a good hunter. To make one have the quality of a hard worker – to be *dayakapa* – is done in the same way. Once the knowledge has been acquired and you have already killed game, you go off to work. Having done this and made a garden and burnt it, you can begin to plant. The first thing to plant is banana, and then, next to this, manioc. Then you must weed. One cannot get vegetables in the midst of an overgrown mess. If you try to harvest in that sort of situation, snakes always bite you. That is the way to do it, that is the way our *xenipabu* have always done it, through working.

When you diet, you can work, and when the work has been done, all through one day, on the next you can go hunting, so that our relatives may eat. But you may not eat yourself, until a month has passed. When you begin to eat again, 'swallowing the snake', you start by hunting a rat; and once that has been done, it is proper to kill big game, deer and peccary.[4] Giant Snake, the big boa, is a skilled hunter. A skilled hunter and at the same time you work [*sic*]. Working, you become a hard worker. Once you have touched a snake you draw out work, the quality of a hard worker. In exactly the same way you become a skilled hunter, a *menki* hunter. That is how they all do it, our old ones, that is what they do. God, whom we call *Diusun*, gave them this order in those ancient times, he ordered them thus: 'This one having been made skilful shall be transformed into a hard worker. This one having been made skilful shall by these means be enabled with the ability to shoot game successfully for evermore.' After he did this, it was done everywhere by our forebears, who first acquired the knowledge and then went hunting. This done, everywhere they were always able to eat.

Elias believed in the old-fashioned values according to which a man should hunt one day, and on the next work hard in his garden in order to be able to feed his family. Like others, he held that modern Cashinahua men should follow this pattern, as is evident in the manner in which he slipped between past and present as he talked. In this view, the essence of a good and proper man is one who is both *menki*, a skilled hunter, and at the same time *dayakapa*, a hard worker. Male work, characterized by hard physical labour, is closely linked with the ability to hunt successfully, and indeed the knowledge needed to do the one thing is acquired at the same time as the knowledge needed to do the other. A man should live his days in a cycle of *daya*, work, and *yuinaka tsakai*, hunting, balancing one activity against the other, planting root vegetables and other crops for his wife to harvest and bringing back game from the forest for her to cook. According to the moral view, then, such a person is a proper man. Such a prodigy is likely to become a *xanen ibu* – a 'true leader', characterized by his ability to feed his people. Such a figure calls out each day to the men to come and eat in his house, and his wife, who is *ainbu xanen ibu*, 'leader of the women', calls out to her female co-residents likewise. In Elias's words:

Men used to leave at dawn without eating in order to go hunting. Once they had woken up they would set out after the game animals – peccary, armadillo, deer, jungle turkey, spider monkey, howler monkey. If they killed a tapir they would leave it there whole, come home, return [for help] to bring it back and only then they would drink *caissuma* and sweet plantain drink, and finally eat boiled manioc and banana; having set out hungry and come back hungry, hunting. When we return home from such an expedition, we may not eat alone. The way to eat is to call to each other. Calling is like this: we call to our elder brother, we call to our mother's brother, we call to our father, we call to our brother-in-law. Calling, by ritualized shouting: '*Heeeiii!* Come together that we may eat! *Pinun bukanven! Heeeeiiii!*' In this way you could become a leader. Feeding people is becoming a leader, whereas a miserly man, who eats alone, can never become a leader, a *xanen ibu*. That is how our old ones used to become leaders, that is how it was done everywhere. Those leaders were *menki*, good hunters. There was another kind of leader, ones who knew powerful prayers [*deveya*, 'with prayer'], and we call them *Chana* [oropendola] leaders.[5]

People who knew no chants could be leaders too, by feeding people as I have described. 'Come together to this place that we may eat!' they used to say; and they would come from far, from very far, and they would come walking from a distant place to visit us, and it would be impossible to be sad. 'Cho! Come here beside me, quickly!', and they would be happy and in high spirits. Once they have thus been invited in [with the stylized greeting] we tell our wife 'Hurry! Our so-and-so has arrived! Quickly give them food!' The way to eat properly is to serve manioc, and green banana, and meat, to them, and listen to them, and talk to them. That is the way it was done in the old days, by the ancient ones. They used to have two and three leaders in a single village, among our ancestors who lived in the headwaters, on the high ground. One would be a *Chana* leader; one would be a leader who worked hard and hunted well, called a Real Leader, a *xanen ibu kaya*: one who sat at the centre.

Men were not the only leaders. Women were also leaders. Here [i.e. in Recreio], no one has become a leader yet among the women. There isn't one. There is always a male leader. Amongst our forebears who lived up there in the headwater region the leader's wife would become a leader and she would make them get food reciprocally. She would call: 'Let us go together [to the garden] and get food! Younger sister! Sister-in-law! Paternal Aunt! Mother! Elder Sister! Let us set out to fetch food! For our husbands have gone far [out hunting in the forest], so let us all go now!' When she had said this, and they had gone and brought back the food, they used to cook. And at dawn as well they would call to each other, our ancestors, and they would eat.

Elias was talking about the past, yet he was also describing the present. His brother Pancho, *xanen ibu* of Recreio in the 1980s, invariably began the day by calling out the formal invitation to all men to eat with him, the drawn-out ritual shout echoing across the village. Such a call contrasts with the silent signals and almost inaudible invitations that lesser people send across the cleared ground between each house when they have something to share. In the evenings, if there was anything to eat in his house, or if he was in a buoyant mood, he would call out again: 'Brother! Father! Uncle! Come all of you and eat! Let us drink *caissuma* and eat manioc!' When they came, Pancho's wife played the part of female leader, serving her food to her male guests. Yet all men and women are like 'leaders' when they are able to extend such hospitality. The notion 'leader' is a summation and intensification of the notion of adult person. A fine man should be able to feed all those with whom he lives and works; and a fine woman likewise. And of course, neither can behave as leader without the other's help. But before I describe the productive activities that allow such behaviour, it is necessary to give some further thought to the environment in which they take place.

The World and its Inhabitants

The Cashinahua think of the world around them as a source of things that they desire. From the forest come game, wild fruits and nuts, medicines, drugs and decorations, and the raw materials that they use to make all kinds of tools and houses. From the river come fish, crustaceans and water. From the city come manufactured goods, exotic foods, fuel and other consumables, and the raw materials needed for making various tools, clothes, and mosquito nets. Humans engage in a variety of different kinds of social relations with the beings that inhabit these spaces, relations that largely correspond to different forms of predation and exchange and that are constitutive of alterity. To clarify the basic contours of these interactions, it is simplest to begin by way of contrast, with an idealized vision of social interaction at home.

The social world and the constitution of identity begin in the *mae* or 'settlement'. This space is inhabited principally by human beings who are *nabu kuin*, 'real kin', and the relations between them ought both to define and, as they take their daily course, to create sociality. Inside the *mae* the different dwellings surround the leaders' house, which (as Elias emphasized) stands at its centre. All around, the gardens separate the *mae* from the forest and its constant encroachment. It is this space that stands for the implicit concept that I attribute to the Cashinahua and term 'the inside', following Rivière's (1969) use of the terms 'inside' and 'outside' to describe the Trio's mode of linking social, political and physical space. My own use of this concept is drawn from the Cashinahua precept that kinship and humanity are both constantly in process of becoming and also thoroughly interlocked. Proper behaviour towards kin is behaviour that both defines what it is to be human, and creates humanity. The inside is the space where kinship and humanity are precariously locked together. Here kin engage in social relations that ideally break free from calculated exchange or pitiless predation and obey a spirit of unselfish and peaceful generosity. Social relations in the inside should be conducive to a state of amicable sociability – but of course they rarely are entirely so. However, in an ideal vision such as that Elias propounded in describing his forefathers' mode of living, the social relations characterizing the inside that figure largest involve one-way flows of goods and services, as when a *xanen ibu* feeds and looks after his followers. But more than this, they are also characterized as the productive and reproductive interaction between men and women, epitomized by the relation between *xanen ibu* and *ainbu xanen ibu*. Thus 'male–female affinity' constitutes the socio-geographical space of the inside.

Interactions with the denizens of the outside, on the other hand, are characterized by 'male affinity', an expression that captures a number of mutual features of social relations with the Other: Seduction, with its dialectic of attraction and avoidance and (in the case of encounters with strangers, animal predators or game animals) its constant menace of violence; Humour and the ever-present possibility of domestication; Repulsion (as when Cashinahua neglect to offer food to visitors); Trickery (as when a trader cheats on his prices); Predation (when a hunter kills his prey, or the Inka's weapon spirit deprives a man of his true soul); and, above all, the demarcation of difference. The outside (like the inside) is not so much a term denoting a fixed physical space, then, as a concept referring to certain forms of relationship that constitute morally informed spaces of interaction. And it should be emphasized that while this interpretation of the spatial aspects of the play of alterity and identity is compatible with recent analyses proffered with respect to other Amazonian societies, it differs in its emphasis on the moral weighting given to types of social action.[6]

In everyday parlance the Cashinahua do indeed tend to associate types of people with distinct geographical zones corresponding to 'outside' and 'inside'. They themselves are true human beings at one extreme of a continuum of humanity inhabiting this level of the cosmos. Wild Indians and *Nawa* (non-Indians) are at the other end. In terms of space, the latter are located downriver (in the city) and the former upriver (in the headwater regions), and the Cashinahua in the middle. Thus spatial referents for the outside are also extended in linear form along the river. This in turn connects the lived world to the other realms of the outside, such as the sky, the underworld, the deep forest and the depths of the rivers and lakes. The term 'outside' therefore refers to a number of different regions and spaces, inhabited by other humans, and also animals, deities, demons and spirits, which are contrasted to the domain of the *Huni Kuin*.

It would be incorrect to offer a graphic representation of these spaces. The cosmos is not conceived as absolute or fixed. What is more, individual understandings and descriptions vary considerably, as one expects in Amazonia (Descola 1994; Leeds 1974). People also express doubt about their own understanding of cosmology, and the contours of the universe may be subject to debate. What is not in doubt, nonetheless, is the basic distinction between inside and outside, for this is lived on a daily basis as an experience common to all.

The spatial opposition 'inside/outside' is linked to a temporal one between eternal and linear time. The former is the time zone of the dead, the latter of the living. Eternal time is an aspect of all concrete things, places and people, manifest in the *yuxin* that inhabit them; but it also has its proper separate place above and below the earth. This present condition originated in mythic time. During the early phase of mythic time there was a conjunction of the world – now the place of linear time and mortal beings – with eternal time and space. The present world with all its beings and things began to take shape out of this undifferentiated condition, and the myths tell how many species were created and made distinct from human beings during this next period (Abreu 1941; D'Ans 1975, 1991). History began when immortality was lost to humanity, and the eternal beings, such as *yuxin*, Gods and demons, were spatially and visually separated from the mortal ones, such as animals, plants and people (McCallum in press). Linear time is therefore characteristic of history, taking place in the context of mortality, process and change. Therefore one may characterize the inside as located in linear historical time, and as separate from the mythic time of the 'old ones'.

For the Cashinahua history and linear time are closely associated with the social spaces located along the river. The headwater regions are the home of 'wild Indians' or *brabos* (P.), who are said to be like the savage ancestors of the living Cashinahua. The downriver regions are the home of the Whites and of city people. They are associated with the future, with progress as well as with danger. Spaces along the river may be used in this logic to denote the Cashinahua understanding of their own place in linear time. If the inside is at the centre of a concentric spatial arrangement, a bubble within a world of outside, it is also located temporally at a point in linear time represented by the river.

If we abstract Cashinahua cosmology from a reading of the myths they tell their children, then the river links the inside and the outside, and the living and the dead, the mortal and the immortal. At the beginning and end of the river lie the passages to the afterlife. The beginning of the river is a land of huge slopes and mountains (although few Cashinahua have ever seen a real mountain). At the end of the river the water turns to clay (and in one account this probably happens in the state of Ceará, original homeplace of many Cariú immigrants to Acre). There lies the 'root of the sky', pictured as a vast tree, leading up into heaven (D'Ans 1975). Heaven, the land of the dead, is the domain of immortality. Seen from below it is the sky, a world in itself, with forests, rivers and villages of the spirits of the dead. It may be reached along the rainbow. The land of the dead may also be reached through holes in the ground which lead to the underworld (or, for converts to Christianity, 'hell') – closely associated with the deep pools of the river and lakes where demons and deities (*yuxibu*) reside. As well as the dead, various mythic ancestors (*xenipabu*) live in the sky, seen from below as stars and as the moon. Beneath the sky is the layer of the clouds, and then a realm of 'pure wind'. The next level of the cosmos is the earth, and beneath it is 'pure *jene*' (liquid, river). This cosmos, as throughout Amazonia, links space and time in a fluid fashion. Faraway places are the home of mythic characters, the dead, and the disembodied. The far reaches of this earth are the first stages of another cosmic level and the beginning of a distinct temporal domain.

The Cashinahua themselves use their extensive mythological corpus to teach cosmology and history to interested outsiders. But knowledge of the universe is also constructed out of personal experience. Notions of space and time are more than abstract concepts whose logical ordering may be revealed by an intelligent anthropologist in sifting through myth, ritual and descriptions of remembered historical events. Individuals gather knowledge of places and beings in the cosmos as they engage in social relations constitutive of the inside or the outside on a day-to-day basis. The cosmos is not just 'learnt' as passed down wisdom in the form of discourse. It is also lived and embodied as experience, both within and at the margins of the process of producing sociality. For example, out-of-body experiences provide the opportunity to garner knowledge and powers from outside the properly social domain that may be useful upon return to it. During sleep people travel to the other realms of the outside.

In their dream state they see normal phenomena, such as trees, animals, river water or clouds, as spirit houses, spirits in human form, solid earth or celestial trees. On return to a waking state the sights are retained as memory of dreams. Drugs, extreme fright or illness may also induce such visions, and they are known to be the 'reality' of the dead. Those who have nearly died can describe their journeys along the rainbow or down through holes in the ground to these other layers of the cosmos. As does every Cashinahua child, I heard a number of tales of such near-death experiences, during which the unconscious person's soul visited the dead and saw how they lived. My informants emphasized that in the afterlife the dead spend their time 'living' by partying, playing and engaging in rituals. Without pain or suffering of any sort, they are said neither to eat nor to have sexual relations. This state is described as 'no more history', and as 'no more dying' (McCallum 1999).

Knowledge of the outside is also accumulated in ordinary waking experiences. These may either be in the form of simple inter-corporeal experiences such as between a hunter and his prey; or else they may involve brushes with spirits and demons themselves. Since tangible beings are composed of spiritual *yuxin* aspects invisible to the waking eye, such encounters may happen at any moment, though certain places, such as deep pools in the river, or certain times, such as dusk, are more conducive to them. Living persons may encounter spirits in the village at night, in the gardens and forest even by day. Most encounters with spirits are with the generic category *yuxin*, ghostly beings of human form that are more or less dangerous depending upon the circumstances of the encounter. At night when normal vision is obstructed by the dark, *yuxin*s invade the space around the living, becoming audible and almost visible as humans. They are like European ghosts, though shyer and less powerful, since a lighted lamp, or a shut bedroom door, can usually keep them from disturbing the sleeping bodies of the living. People may also chance upon the *yuxibu*, fierce and powerful deities, monsters or demons, who have an appetite for human souls and may appear to the awake either as animals or as monsters. Some of these *yuxibu* live deep in the lakes and river pools, or high in certain trees (Abreu 1941). Unlike the *yuxin*, they never appear in human form, but rather, when the physical and mental state of the human observer is conducive, they appear as monsters. Normally, they too are 'just animals' (*só bicho'* (P.)), albeit often very large and frightening examples of the particular species.[7]

A Cashinahua hunter seeks to avoid spirits and demons in the forest or along the river. Direct interaction with *yuxibu* or *yuxin* is devastating to a man's hunting skills. Thus shamans (*yuxian*) are the worst hunters, for they are no longer able to make the distinction between inside and outside that is necessary for predation. He (or, more rarely, she) sees what should properly be the outside as inside, as a human world where social communication is conducive to friendship. The idiom of affinity, in this breakdown between orders, is extended to its logical conclusion: the animals are no longer terminological affines, but rather affinal kin, like the shaman's own human *chais*. The shaman may consider practising sexual relations with the male animal's sisters. And indeed many myths tell of the disastrous consequences of a breakdown in the separation between domains through the 'realization' of affinity in sex with beings from outside the human social world.

The relationship between inside and outside is properly one of male affinity, but not male–female affinity. Male outsiders are addressed as *chain* (brother-in-law); female outsiders, however, are not addressed as *xanun* (female marriageable cross cousin) by men. To treat such a being as an affine would be detrimental to the integrity of the inside. As wives, female foreigners would take men away from the Cashinahua and transform them into foreign 'insiders'. By keeping affinity male, the Cashinahua protect the boundaries of their own sociality and yet acquire the things that they need from outside to reproduce their own social life.

Cashinahua social organization ensures this protection through endogamy. In ritual, the male aspect of affinal relations with the forest spirits is stressed as a prelude to the integration of outsiders (represented by one moiety and then the other) into the inside, as Chapter 7 details. In hunting, men employ seductive techniques to lure game animals and birds to them, as elsewhere in Amazonia; but then the hunter destroys the chances of friendship and the creation of inter-species sociality by killing the animal. Male affinity is thus two-faced: either a man can end by cohabiting with the being he addresses as 'brother-in-law' and loving the latter's sister, or he can kill him. This logic extends from animal–human social interaction to that between humans. Relations between humans always contain the possibility of affinity fulfilled in heterosexual activity and kinship. But equally, human beings are always dangerous, always potential enemies and, like game animals, might become the object of male violence. Then what is produced is no longer 'sociality', but what one might describe as its opposite – 'anti-sociality'.

Production

A central tenet of the production of Cashinahua sociality is the imperative to act generously to kin, counter-balanced by the freedom to be mean to strangers. Generosity and miserliness are the personal acts that make or unmake proper social bonds. Being miserly with close kin is tantamount to making them strangers. Being generous with strangers signals a willingness to transform them into kin. In the first case social relations conform to the patterns of 'anti-sociality' and in the second to those that produce sociality. This is quite clear to the Cashinahua, who see each other sanguinely as swinging constantly between behaviour appropriate to outsiders and that proper to insiders. This is described in terms of moral attributes of the person. For example, in discussing one man whose actions I had questioned, his nephew told me 'My uncle is like that: one part of him is good and generous, the other half is mean and bad.' And this same uncle gave his own moral ambiguity a historical and also an evangelical Christian twist. He explained to me that in the past he had murdered many people. But now that he was a proper believer, he had left to one side his earlier ways. However, he also pointed out that when he was angry he might become murderous again.

The ability to be generous depends upon the capacity of a person to produce. Personal responsibilities for mutual kin and co-resident affines provide the moral motivation of production. The Cashinahua phrase for 'making oneself responsible for a person' is *dua va-*, which also means 'to help, to satisfy a desire, to treat well, to look after, to domesticate'. Thus a person might say 'She always treats me well (*Ea dua vamiski*), giving me manioc, making me drink *caissuma* and feeding me all kinds of food.' The phrase *dua va-* sums up the way that kin should treat each other, and implies not only generosity and kindness, but also a notion of service, of response to legitimate desire. Non-kin, like the Yaminahua, do not deserve any kindness unless they are in a position to act as if they were real kin. Need is legitimated by kinship. Treating someone well is tantamount to making them kin. The highly valued quality of being *duapa*, 'generous', 'kind', is the opposite of being *yauxi*, 'miserly'. It is etymologically related to *dua va-*, and indeed kin are expected to be generous to each other, and miserly towards strangers. It should be noted that the same phrase for 'to look after'/ 'to act as responsible for' also means 'to domesticate the young of wild animals'. This conflation of meanings indicates the active nature of being *duapa*. Feeding well and looking after is a process that makes someone or some animal closer, more like oneself, kin. The same transformation can also be performed upon strangers. That is, by the act of feeding and treating well, a Cashinahua person begins a process of denying – or indeed changing – the alien character of strangers. In fact, all welcome visitors are treated with generosity, pressed with gifts and fed and fed again. Conversely, to treat a kinsperson or co-resident in a miserly fashion begins a process of denying kinship. To act ungenerously is more than a symbolic statement of alienation, however. It is also produces it. For now it should be remembered that in a sense all work leads to domestication, and all domestication makes kin.

Work (*daya*) is distinguished from fetching activities such as hunting. *Daya* involves either backbreaking sweaty tasks like digging in the garden, or finicky but demanding ones such as cleaning, beating, spinning and weaving cotton. The idea of *daya* suggests repetitive physical effort and patience. The knowledge and corporeal ability to perform all productive activities are acquired rather than innate, as are strong and healthy bodies. The product of most work – food – is the substance that sustains life and promotes growth. However, the wear and tear of daily toil is thought to weaken a person's body progressively, so that in the end old age and finally death result. Everybody is capable of strength, but men are thought to be stronger than women. In fact, they need such physical prowess in order to endure their daily work round.

Men's Work

Early each morning, just after dawn when people are still lazing in their hammocks or emerging to sit blinking on the verandas of their houses, women take down their cotton to beat, and diligent men take up their hoes and weed the *terreiros* (P.): cleared ground around their houses. A conscientious worker can be told by the impeccable state of his *terreiro*, its boundary marked by a neat ridge of earth and dried weeds that he has scraped off the surface. This provides space for the house's chickens to feed themselves. Occasionally, a woman will take a broom to the ground to clear up the debris that accumulates there; but she will only weed it if her husband is too lazy or ill to do so. Other men, especially the young and strong, take up their axes and set off in search of firewood for kindling the morning fire. As the sun rises the sound of the beating of cotton is replaced by the thud of axe against log, and the women put away their baskets and begin the task of making breakfast. After the meal, while the women pick up their weaving, or set out to the gardens, men turn to any number of pre-arranged activities in the settlement or in the forest, often part of an all-male work group. On some days men stay at home to work on small tasks, such as making tools.[8]

Men maintain the spaces within which their women work and bring back forest products for them to process. They confront the forest directly in the creation and maintenance of domestic space. They make and weed gardens, slash paths through village and forest, dig wells, and construct houses. Whereas women's work is basically the same the year round, men change activities depending on the season. Men's work is seen as physically more exhausting than women's, but also less repetitive. Men may work alone, in pairs or in larger work groups. One man can carry out house construction alone, in which case it takes at least several months. Other men help in certain tasks that require at least two workers, such as carrying the lengths of *paxiúba* (P.), a tough palm wood used for the floor. Houses are built in the Cariú style, but tend to be larger than neighbouring Cariú houses and with fewer walls. In the older houses the sleeping room is usually partitioned off, separating the kitchen area with its clay hearth from the living area. A properly furnished house has shelves in the kitchen area, usually boards suspended by fibres from the roof. Platforms are built up from the ground at the edge of the kitchen area. These *girau* (P.) are an important feature of Cariú and some Cashinahua houses. They serve a variety of purposes, acting as washing up stands, storage areas, and sunning platforms for seeded cotton, salted fish and so on. Men say that they build houses and these kitchens for their wives, and they are regarded as primarily female spaces. But the ownership of gardens and houses is not clearly attached to either the woman or the man. The owner 'changes' according to discursive context.

Men usually arrange cooperative workdays for achieving the main tasks of house construction, fetching the poles, or the thatching, and putting up the frame and the roof. This form of communal work is also organized for many other of the heavy jobs that men do: clearing an *estrada* (rubber path) or an overgrown garden; felling the forest for gardens; canoe-burning. These are all tasks that many perform on behalf of one man and in his name. This collective labour without immediate product or benefit to the man's helpers is typical of the organization of male work. The *ibu* or 'owner' of the house or garden is responsible, on these occasions, for feeding the work-party. Ideally he should make a large kill a few days before the work is to be done. Alternatively, he may persuade his wife to make corn *caissuma* or manioc beer, and she will cooperate in providing the rest of the *daya piti* (work food). People expect to be fed beforehand, so that often the sun is high before they set to work. However, in the summer, when there is much heavy work to be done, such formalities might be forgotten.

Most collective male labour takes place during the dry season (April–October). Between the months of April and October men and women working together plant the beaches with peanuts and watermelon. Male collective groups cut and plant new ridge gardens at this time, and clear the rubber paths and prepare them for the summer season of tapping;

and some years they also clear the paths demarcating Indian land. These tasks are intercalated. During May men begin to clear the *estradas*. Groups ideally go out several times a week until they are all cleared. It should be possible to start rubber-tapping and *caucho* tree felling at this time. During the same period men go in smaller groups to clear light undergrowth at places chosen for new ridge gardens or *bai*. A collective work party fells the larger trees, if possible between July and September These are left a few weeks or so to dry out before being burnt. If the burning does not go well then a further week must be spent in *coivara* (P.), burning off the stumps and branches that did not catch fire, so as to leave the ground fit for planting before the arrival of the first rains in about October.

Planting the new ridge gardens is the responsibility of men, usually working on their own, though a wife may help her husband (Kensinger 1975). Manioc and corn are the main crops, and they are planted mixed together. A variety of other vegetables and fruit are also considered important – sweet potato, papaya, banana, yams, rice, pineapple, sugar cane. The most important non-edible crops are cotton and fish-poison. By the time the bulk of the planting is completed, the watermelon season is over and the peanut crop has been harvested from the beach gardens. There is a lull in agricultural work until the corn ripens in December and January, during which time the men can devote themselves to rubber collection. However, the most assiduous workers never abandon the gardens for long. Apart from weeding the new gardens so that the newly planted crops can survive, the older gardens must be tended, and in particular the banana plantations must be cleared of undergrowth and augmented. All these tasks are the responsibility of men. Women only clear undergrowth for short periods while they are harvesting.

It is often easier to mobilize the help of a few other men to perform agricultural tasks. In smaller settlements the adult men, who are often brothers-in-law to each other, cooperate, but there is no hard and fast rule about who helps whom. Brothers, cousins, fathers, uncles and so on might form part of a smaller work group. In Fronteira, where the largest sibling group and leading kin group of the village counted seven adult brothers, affines tended to help each other in smaller work parties. On the other hand, in one *seringal* on the Jordão eleven brothers living dispersed in several *colocaçoes* cooperated with each other during the period of peak agricultural activity, while their father spent his time hunting for them. Even unrelated men may cooperate if they are co-resident. In time such unrelated neighbours will usually form affinal ties, or enter into a *compadrazgo* relationship. It is not actual or classificatory kinship that generates cooperation and sharing, then. Living together means working together, too. For this reason any visitor is requested to help in some collective venture that has been planned during the time of their stay. Thus arrangements are flexible, and depend on the help available.

Small cooperative male work groups that habitually work together are always co-resident in the same house or small settlement; hence a common relationship between co-workers is that of son-in-law and father-in-law. In many cases the young men, newly married and uxorilocally resident, find themselves working hard for the first time in their lives. This labour has many of the characteristics of 'brideservice'. However, the son-in-law does not necessarily withdraw from the household having successfully secured his marriage and performed the requisite term of 'service'; if the marriage is successful he may stay on 'for life'. Those sons-in-law who stay on become fully independent adults and are not in a subordinate relationship to their father-in-law. Young men are never ordered directly to perform major tasks, only minor ones. Instead, they are expected to volunteer themselves when the father-in-law is considering some activity, or to work and hunt on their own initiative. Young grooms who feel that the burden of responsibility placed upon them is too much are free to leave and often do. Elders frequently become dependent on younger people for their subsistence and that of their own youngest children.

In the mid-1980s men could acquire industrially manufactured goods and consumables by selling or exchanging rubber. If a man or adolescent was allocated one of the *estradas* in a village meeting, he could tap rubber two or three times a week from about April to January, although in practice few men were so diligent. The Cashinahua considered the production of rubber a secondary activity, unlike their Cariú neighbours, and though some men boasted about their capacity to produce, it was rare for more than fifty kilos to be made by one man during a season. This figure varies considerably from settlement to settlement and between individuals, but overall Cashinahua men are poor *seringueiros*. In the view of Cariú tappers a man should work six days a week and produce one ton of rubber each season. In areas where there was no rubber to be tapped, men and especially the newly married worked as *caucheiros*, or as lumbermen, or engaged in wage labour on a daily basis for the Cariú bosses. (Women refused to work for outsiders, although I came across two women who had worked briefly as domestic servants).

Tapping, hunting and fishing are usually solitary activities. Whereas women work alone at home and collectively in the garden, men work collectively in both garden and village, but produce alone in the forest. The most valued form of individual production is hunting or *yuinaka tsaka kai* (going to kill game), an activity described at length by Kensinger (1995) and Deshayes (1986). Men go 'walking' or *ni-* in the forest, searching for game animals to kill for their wives and mothers-in-law. Hunting, like fishing, involves not work, but rather searching and fetching. It does not make a man sweat as work does, and hunters are said to come back from the forest cool. Men hunt alone, setting out early in the morning and returning at dusk. After a day's work, when there is no meat or fish in the house, they might walk out for a few hours hunting or cast-net fishing in the late afternoons. Collective hunts set out of the village together but split up once the hunters are out of earshot of the village, except in the case of sighting a band of peccary, in which case the man who spots it signals to the rest and they join him in pursuit. Sometimes women accompany their husbands on hunts, ostensibly to carry the game home for them, but also to make love in private. On extended hunting-camping trips, which last up to a week (though in the past they lasted longer), a woman might go along to do the cooking and the work of preserving the game by smoke-roasting. Men also perform this task. As always, the division between male and female work is not subject to strict rules or 'taboos', and each gender may perform tasks normally allotted to the other as occasion arises.

Women's Work

Women work most of the time in the settlement and in the gardens. Women sometimes go out into the forest, but their principal place of production is the inside. Women are responsible for keeping the house and patio clean of debris by sweeping them and for washing clothes and hammocks. They also butcher small game animals and fish and complete the butchering of large game animals. Women gather fruit and nuts and fish small streams, either with other women and elder children, or with their husbands and co-resident family. Such activities should provide no more than a supplement to the diet, and are of no great interest when meat is plentifully available. However, some women bring home proportionately more fish than their husbands or other male members of the household, and female fishing expeditions should not be underestimated. Visiting is also a source of food. Women visit the houses of other settlements from time to time and can expect to return home with their baskets laden with gifts of food. Such visiting is an important source of subsistence food for new settlers and those whose gardens have failed (McCallum 1998).

The principal female tasks are cotton work and the harvesting and cooking of food. Women harvest manioc and banana two or three times a week the year round. They also harvest a seasonal crop of corn once a year, at the height of the rainy season, and peanut twice a year. The main peanut harvest is at the end of the dry season in September or October. The style of harvesting is the same for both seasonal and perennial vegetables. However, the start of the seasonal harvest is marked by a more ceremonial approach, involving a collective harvest followed by a collective meal hosted by the woman in whose garden the harvest was made. Once the seasonal crops have fully matured, they are brought for storage in the rafters of the owners' houses; the task of preparing the bunches is the men's.

Women spend about five or six days a month engaged in semi-ceremonial collective harvesting. Proportionally more trips are spent harvesting with one companion in their own garden. These trips are much faster, and do not involve polite hanging around, or preliminary collective meals. Yet harvesting is ideally carried out in group expeditions. It is important to realize that the work process from beginning to end, whether on a collective or an individual expedition, is carried out by one woman, or in the name of one woman. Generally the people who help a woman are her younger dependants, daughters or siblings, girls who have not yet acquired responsibility for work of their own. These helpers are identified with the owner (see below). Most commonly of all the helper is her daughter. Mothers also help their adult daughters. Everything that a woman harvests belongs to her, no matter in whose garden she obtained it.

Women harvest both in their own and in other people's gardens. Early in the morning one woman invites others to harvest in her garden, and a group is formed, sometimes comprising most of the women of the village. They gather informally in someone's house on their way out of the village. The expedition from beginning to end proceeds in an informal and lively atmosphere, which masks the strict etiquette shaping the expedition. For example, if any woman wants to stop on the way to check her nearby garden for ripe fruit, the others must wait patiently for her. There is no attempt to save time, and a harvest that takes one woman in the company of her child at most two hours to accomplish, takes her four or five during a collective expedition. Efficiency is not an objective, then. The entire process of digging up, preparing, packing and carrying one woman's load of manioc home is carried out by her (and perhaps a junior helper) alone. A helper does not appropriate any of the manioc. Adult women rarely do another's work for her, preferring to sit and chat while she completes her preparations for the return home. The owner of the garden might make a gift of banana or papaya to a particular woman during the expedition.

Figure 8. Women engaged in semi-ceremonial collective harvesting

The recipient will harvest it herself. Such presents are only made to women, usually to visitors who are spending a few weeks or months in the village. When all the baskets are packed and ready, the group sets off back home.

The group separates upon arrival, and each woman goes to her own house and hearth, where she cooks the manioc or bananas in preparation for her husband's return from hunting or working. On days when she is free from other tasks, and especially before a special occasion like the arrival of visitors or a festival, a woman also prepares *caissuma*. This drink, made from corn, or corn and peanuts, constitutes one of the three essential elements of a proper meal – the other two of which are either boiled manioc or green banana, and either meat or fish. Cashinahua cuisine includes a number of unusual recipes (in the standard Amazonian repertoire), for example, green plantains in roast peanut sauce, or grated palm-heart and fish soup. The most common root vegetable dish is certainly sweet manioc prepared in a sauce of its own leaves and left to cook slowly over the fire until soft.[9]

Women manufacture cotton goods, especially shoulder bags and hammocks, and baskets used for storage of small objects and pottery, though the importance of this latter craft has diminished since the introduction of aluminium ware. Cotton work is women's work *par excellence*, and cotton continues to be an important crop. Women beat out the cotton in the early mornings, and then sit teasing out the cotton and spinning at night. Once they have enough balls of thread they dye them and prepare to weave. A large hammock takes about two weeks of work to weave – longer if it has a complicated woven pattern . A shoulder bag takes one or two days at most.

The hammocks and bags are used by the Cashinahua, although most people in Recreio during the 1980s slept in cheaper store-bought hammocks that cost about US$12, or one-fifth of the price of the Cashinahua ones. Most women also sewed their own dresses and some of the men's clothes. There were several sewing machines in the village during my stay there. Cotton handicrafts were the best means for a woman to make money, although she could also raise and sell pigs and chickens. The sale of handicrafts in Recreio via the village cooperative equalled or surpassed the sale of rubber at that time. As usual, women preferred to limit their contact with the outside. Occasionally they negotiated directly with the Cariú river traders, but on the whole they preferred to deal indirectly by asking one of their kinsmen to negotiate on their behalf. The male leader sold most handicrafts through the village cooperative.

Women usually work alone at home, cooking or weaving. Sometimes they harvest their gardens accompanied only by a child. Even during semi-ceremonial collective expeditions the entire labour process is carried out by each woman on her own. Later she will reciprocate, by inviting the owner of the garden to harvest in her own garden on another such occasion. Thus the female collective domain is characterized by a circulation of the objects of labour (plants in the garden), whereas the male collective domain is characterized by a circulation of labour itself. Where female production is done in cooperation by pairs of women or girls, it might involve an asymmetrical relation of tutelage. The pair could be related in any number of ways: as mother and daughter, maternal grandmother and grandchild, mother-in-law and daughter-in-law, sisters or elder and younger co-wife (usually sisters), or sisters-in-law. However, the hierarchical relation remains very low-key. One rarely hears an order given. Authority is expressed most frequently in the hissed and rapidly spoken reprimands issued by adult women to their children, usually in connection with some task performed sloppily, some mistake in work etiquette. Small cooperative groups are most often made up of mothers and daughters (not married sisters), and one woman generally helps the other do her work. Mothers will help their adult daughters in collaboration rather than in authority. Only young girls perform tasks under the direction of an older woman. In these cases the direction is considered training .

Working Together

Certain activities, both traditional ones, such as planting peanuts or fishing with poison, and innovatory ones, such as making manioc flour on a metal sheet, require a combination of male and female collective labour. All Cashinahua plant *puikama* fish 'poison'. The pounded leaves of this bush (*Paullinia pinnata* (Lat.)) are formed into a ball and then dissolved in shallow streams and in the still pools of the smaller rivers, causing the fish to rise to the surface gasping for oxygen, so that they can be easily caught. There are four forms of fishing expedition involving *puikama*. Small 'in-family' trips involve a couple and their children. Small groups of women and children often fish with poison in small streams. The classic form of fishing with *puikama* involves large collective expeditions – all the residents of a village or, in the Jordão, relatives from several neighbouring *colocaçoes* (the small settlements located at the 'mouths' of several rubber-tapping paths). Finally, women sometimes initiate an all-female collective *puikama* fishing expedition when the men are occupied with a collective work task and are unable to spare time for hunting or fishing.

Peanuts are an important part of the Cashinahua diet, and they are famous in the region for the cultivation of this crop. The entire settlement plants peanuts collectively on the beaches laid bare by the receding river in April at the end of the rainy season. Every woman with children and every couple is allocated a carefully measured section of beach. Where beach area is scarce elder couples receive the largest section, since they are responsible for feeding more people. The planting may be preceded by a ritual called *tama kenakinan*, 'calling/naming peanuts'. At dawn on the day of planting the men and women set out for the beach, carrying little enamel or plastic mugs, which the owner of the peanuts will fill up with sprouted seed. Men pound holes with long, sharpened poles, and the women bend over thrusting the sprouted seed into them. The sexual conotations of this style of planting are not lost on the Cashinahua, who lose no opportunity to make approriate jokes to their cross-cousins. This crop ripens in August and September, and is harvested like manioc in collective female expeditions, when women are invited to harvest in each other's plots. When the nuts harden the remainder are usually harvested with male help. A second crop is sometimes planted in the winter months, in a patch of the high-ground garden. This might be harvested collectively, during February or March, by the entire community. In this case, women uproot the plants and the men make bundles and transport them back to the houses.

Some few work processes are carried out by a team of people co-resident in one house, in a configuration that might be called 'household-based production'. These include making *farinha* (P.) (manioc flour), planting sugar cane in a harvested patch of the garden, and weeding beaches for subsequent planting with peanut and watermelon. This same group goes poison-fishing, gathering, or visiting together. Where labour results in an immediate product, each person appropriates his or her own product, except in the case of *farinha*-making (which is made using Cariú technology and organization of production). The *farinha* belongs to the person who initiated the work and from whose garden the manioc is taken.

Usually men perform one kind of task and women another, so that their labour is complementary. However, there is no exclusion of either sex from these tasks. Thus men may sieve manioc flour and women toast it, although they rarely do so. However, there is still a clear distinction between male and female tasks, and even where the same task is performed by both men and women they tend to be done in different styles by each sex. Hence women catch fish with their hands far more often than they spear them; men carry the *kuki* carrying baskets with the strap around their chests, whereas women brace the load against their foreheads.

Male and female agency are clearly differentiated in this system. Whatever a person does is done in a genderized style, serving to reinforce created gender difference symbolically. However, there is no absolute dichotomy between male and female, no prohibition on men performing female work, or women male, for both after all involve forms of human agency. Nevertheless, the Cashinahua emphasize at every opportunity the division and interdependence between the sexes. Man and woman cannot live or work without each other. Male and female personhood is predicated upon the daily enactment of male and female agency in production. Upon marriage, young uxorilocally resident grooms are suddenly faced with responsibility for their parents-in-law. To their mother-in-law, *achi*, they owe certain prestations, such as meat, but no direct service. Rather they work 'on behalf of' their father-in-law. They work in his name, but the labour is not seen as an exchange against rights to a bride, or as payment of any sort. Instead, it takes the form of cooperative work in the name of an adult individual of the same sex. In this way it is like any work done by a young relative on behalf of, or 'helping', *dabe-*, an older kinsperson of the same sex. Such help is predicated on relations of sameness between two people, rather than on relations of difference. The labour establishes the young man as part of the family. Men's unmarried sons are also called upon to help in the same way, and an inmarried son-in-law will develop close cooperative relations with them. As long as the groom has no children of his own, he has no need for his own garden, or his own house. When he has several children, he is directly responsible for them and may assert his own independence if he and his wife so wish. Ideally, though, he should stay on in his wife's parents' house until they die. Although the rhetoric on work is most often employed when talking about marriage and about the duties each partner has towards the other, in fact the most important economic relationship entered into by a young man upon his marriage is with his parents-in-law, and the most important cross-sex economic relationship that with his *achi* (mother-in-law), not his wife. This is why a young woman does not find her working life suddenly changed upon marriage; she simply continues as before, working together with her married sisters, and on behalf of her mother. With children, her responsibilities will become direct, and she will begin to 'own' her own section of her parent's garden. A young woman who lives virilocally after marriage finds herself performing female work on behalf of her same-sex parent-in-law in the same way as a young man uxorilocally resident performs male work for his. She must cooperate with her mother-in-law, and must make certain prestations to her father-in-law, especially cooked food. It cannot be said that by working in this way she is exchanging labour for her spouse, or performing a kind of 'groomservice'.[10]

As these young people assume more responsibility for the work that they do, and their parents and parental affines grow older and weaker, several shifts in 'ownership' of house and garden, and responsibility for them, could occur. Where the son-in-law is taking over from his father-in-law, but the mother-in-law is still strong and active, these two become the central productive figures in the household. The one is responsible for male work, the other for female. This is why it is often said that a son-in-law makes a garden and hunts for his *achi*. His wife or wives are frequently unable to work hard because they are looking after babies. They cannot leave them unattended or take them to the gardens until they are at least about five months old. It is upon the wife's mother that the heaviest burden usually falls. When a woman is still strong but no longer fertile, she works harder and assumes greater responsibility than ever before. She no longer has infants of her own to breastfeed, and her daughters are in need of help. Her daughters have, of course, already spent many years helping her in her own work, and looking after their younger siblings. Those women who are unlucky enough to have no daughters devote themselves to helping their daughters-in law.

Frequently, fathers or mothers allow or even persuade their son-in-law to marry a second daughter; or they arrange a young husband for her. The newcomer joins his 'brother' in the house of their *dais* (parents-in-law). For several years the two young men might work together, helping their *kuka* (father-in-law, MB); but eventually the older moves out with his wife and children to set up his own house and garden. If the couple remains in the same settlement as the wife's parents, their house is built close by the old house and their garden is an extension of the old garden. If they move out of the settlement, the relation of cooperation is curtailed except during periods of visiting, or if the son-in-law is called to help his *dais* for a major task such as garden clearing.

Spouses help each other in tasks normally performed by one or other sex. For example, women help their husbands to hunt paca and agouti with dogs, to go cast net fishing, to weed the gardens and so on. I came across several cases of women who collected the latex that their husbands had tapped. In the same way men help women to harvest manioc and banana, with some of the tasks involved in the preparation of cotton, in butchering meat and so on. People go along with their spouses to help in these tasks, but as far as I could tell the help was always peripheral. Tasks strongly linked to gender, like the actual killing of a game animal, or the uprooting of manioc, are rarely performed by the opposite sex if someone appropriate is there. The complementary nature of male and female production is dependent upon the gender-linking of activities and styles of doing them. It is merely assumed that the person of the appropriate age and sex will perform the activity in question. On more than one occasion, for example, when I was travelling with Cashinahua men I was handed a catch of young caiman or fish and endured the ensuing hilarity as I attempted to clean and cook it. Yet women occasionally kill animals or clear scrub and men sometimes cook (as often as not my onlookers would grow irritated at my feeble attempts and take over the preparation of the meal). Gender does not emerge within a rigid code or bound by restrictive rules, but rather follows the logic of Cashinahua epistemology. Both sexes are fully human; that is, complex persons whose bodies bear the imprint of the myriad experiences that form their capacity to act, to know and to be gendered. Through these fragile bodies they are able to work together and to thus to produce not just the food and goods that survival requires, but also the morally informed if imperfect form of sociality that shapes their world. The inside is a place which must always be constructed by human workers and is created from the transformed outside in a never-ending process. The outside itself is thought of as the outward manifestation of other 'insides', the male face of other social domains, and as the source of things useful to the progress of their own social world. What is at stake is the transformation of the products of those domains into Cashinahua products and people.

Notes

1. Obviously, this point is subject to very different interpretations, depending on theoretical orientation of the author, but I believe that, stated thus, most Amazonianists would agree with it.
2. The literature on Amazonian perspectivism is discussed in greater detail in Chapter 7.
3. For example, Overing (1982) argues against use of the distinctions nature/culture or humanity/animality. She prefers 'domesticated/ undomesticated' and 'the untamed forces of culture/the tamed forces of culture within society'. Descola's study analyses 'the relations between humans and their environment from the standpoint of the dynamic interactions between the techniques used in socializing nature and the symbolic systems that organize them' (Descola 1994:3). Descola's book concentrates on the relations that humans develop with beings in the 'natural world', which for the Achuar is an extension in large part of the 'domestic domain' and the sphere of intra-human sociability. Thus women make garden plants their 'consanguines', while men treat forest beings such as game animals as affines. Viveiros de Castro (1992, 1993) argues that in Amazonia Nature, Culture and Supernature are encompassed in the sphere of possible sociabilities.
4. The logic of swallowing a fieldmouse is that boa constrictors swallow them, so the would-be hunter imitates the action of the source of hunting skill.
5. The *chana*, according to Montag (1981), is a yellow-tailed cacique or oropendola bird (*Cacicus cela* (Lat.)). Its capacity to imitate the sounds made by other species gives it an iconic status. It gives rise to the term for chant-leader, *chana xanen ibu*.
6. See especially Viveiros de Castro 1993, 1996; Vilaça 2000; Taylor 1996.
7. Lagrou (1998) discusses the concept *yuxibu*. They are hierarchically organized and linked to the moieties.
8. Men make many items, such as women's carrying baskets, the shafts of metal tools like axes, hoes and scythes, feather and bamboo headresses, bows and arrows, fishing nets, and toys for their children (Dwyer 1975).
9. For recipes see McCallum 1989.
10. See references to critiques of the literature on brideservice in Amazonia in the Introduction.

—4—

Consumptive Production

Appropriation and the Circulation of Labour

How does a person come to own things? This question must be answered before discussing the distribution, consumption and exchange of the products of labour. Underlying all appropriation is the idea that the maker owns his or her product, seen most clearly in the case of immediate products such as cooked food. The labour involved in the preparation of a single product might come from several people, but nevertheless the product belongs to only one person. The Cashinahua describe this quite clearly in talking about labour processes. A woman may ask: '*Medabe vapa? Atsadan mia chukaxunaitsa?*' ('May I help? Perhaps I could wash the manioc on your behalf?'). The first question contains the morpheme -*dabe*, which here means 'help', but also signifies 'double'. The verbal phrase *medabe va-*, which means 'to help (in some task)', suggests that one person is identified with another, since it implies that the speaker is identical to the person to whom the question is addressed. The morpheme also has a verbal form, and from the usage of this we may find further evidence supporting this analysis. Thus, to the question 'What are you doing?' a Cashinahua might reply, using the verb *dabe-* (to help), '*En dabeaii*' (I am helping). *Dabe-* also means to 'help to form a foetus', as does a pregnant woman's lover, who 'helps' her husband in the work of making the child. These usages reflect the particularly Amazonian approach to personhood that underlies the Cashinahua process of appropriation.

In Melanesia, persons may be understood as processually formed 'dividuals' who transact gendered aspects of themselves in the constitution of sociality (Strathern 1988). In Amazonia personhood is similarly processual and relational (Conklin and Morgan 1996). But Amazon persons are not so much dividual as accumulative and encompassing. They blend into others or cut off sharply from them, but do not transact with parts of themselves in the constitution of a more global social sphere (McCallum 1999). In this sense the Cashinahua conception of the person assumes an integrity of the self, though not within the confines of one body. One example of this is the relation between people and their possessions, which may only have one owner. People do not have relative rights in things – they either own them or not. This is why it is better to understand the relationship between people and their gardens or houses in terms of responsibility, rather than in terms of ownership *per se*. Strictly speaking, food and things may be owned absolutely, and everything else (land, hunting territories, lakes, gardens) may have connotations of ownership - but that is all. Something of this attitude spills over into the relation between parents and children; but relations between people are in no way comparable to relations between persons and things.

Things are aspects of the person who owns them. By this I mean that possessions are closely identified with their owners. When the person dies they must be destroyed or thrown away, not inherited. If a person gives away or sells a thing, its alienability or non-alienability depends upon the relationship between the transactors, upon whether or not they are co-resident kin. Conversely, the form of prestation or transaction defines and redefines relationships. To return to the discussion of the morpheme *dabe-*, we have seen that a person may help a 'double' with whom he or she identifies. Such work acts to 'transfer', as it were, selfhood from one person to another of the correct category, in the sense that working often involves a lending of personal powers or effort to another person. The integrity of the self is not damaged when one person works for another. Helping another person means behaving like that person, or giving one's energies to that person as if they were the other's own energies. Usually that other person is of the same gender, though in practice this rule is not absolute. In moments of symbolic elaboration, however, the separateness is crystal-clear.

The morpheme *dabe-*, to recapitulate, implies relations of identification between two subjects, between helper and helped. Such identification in the context of production nearly always occurs between persons of the same gender, and it informs same-sex relations of production. The form of cross-sex relations of production, on the other hand, obeys a different logic. The second question in the example given above – *atsa mia chukaxunaitsa?* – contains the morpheme *xun-* , which means 'on behalf of, for'. It occurs in speech describing labour processes aimed at giving the product to either sex. It is always used in a transitive mode, attached to a verb of action. One person does something for someone, makes something for him or her, contributes labour to an object that will be for another's use or become his or her possession. It implies a different kind of relationship to that implied by *dabe-*. A person may ask: '*Min java vai, Evan?*' ('What are you doing, Mother?') and the woman may answer:

'*En dais disi timaxunyuaii, inankatsidan*' ('I am weaving a hammock *for* my son-in-law, so that I may give it to him.') This second form of relation, implied by the morpheme -*xun*-, is one of differentiation between persons. While it is rare for men to help (*dabe*-) women, and vice versa, people do things on behalf of (-*xun*-) either sex. This is important because it means that strictly speaking labour is only exchangeable between people of the same sex. The limited sphere of reciprocity involving the circulation of labour is based upon people lending each other their personal powers, their skills and strength. With time each will receive a return of labour. It is inconceivable that such a debt between kin can be cancelled by material reward. Where labour is exchanged against things, the relationship between transactors is one of non-kin, of strangers or even enemies. Rather than producing sociality, it constructs its opposite.

This non-exchangeability of labour for thing between kin is related to the conception of the product. Labour that results immediately in a tangible product invests the worker with individual ownership. Objects are 'aspects of the person', whether this person be the maker of the object or someone who receives it as a present. Possessions are therefore to be destroyed at the person's death. Personal possessions are not related to the owner in terms of a subject–object dichotomy, and on the contrary, the relationship may be thought of as taking one of two distinct but compatible forms: firstly, when the product or item has been made by the owner, a relation between aspects of the self; and secondly, when the product or item has been given to the owner, as a relation between subjects. In the first case the relationship is a simple metonymical one and can be understood in a literal sense: the thing 'is' the person. It should be noted that this is an inversion of the situation in Western models of the relation between persons, where a person can come to be an object like a thing (Strathern 1984). In the second case the item stands for the relationship between giver and receiver. The mother-in-law is making an item that stands for her relationship with her son-in-law. Things can relate to their owner, then, either as extensions of self, like a man's bow or a woman's hammock, or, alternatively, as symbols of a person's relationships with specific kin, like a man's hammock, made by his wife, or a woman's carrying basket, made by her husband.

Those products that people make for their own use are in fact always used in the production of relationships. A man's bow is used to hunt game for his wife or mother-in-law, and not for himself. It is an extension of himself, but the self is defined in terms of the actions, the work that the body does, and the work is done for others, especially kin. A woman's pots (which she has made herself) are used in the cooking of food for others, especially her husband and children. Likewise, the consumables that men and women make or bring back – such as women's manioc and men's game animals – are possessed only to be given away in the social process. The distinction between things related to the person metonymically and things related as separated subjects frequently encompasses the distinction between genders. The perfect transaction between separate subjects is one between a man and a woman. The distinction between the morphemes *-xun-* and *dabe-* is indicative of this set of concepts, since the former can be used in cross-sex transactions (a man does something for his wife), while the latter is ideally exclusive to single-sex transactions (a woman does something with her mother).

Distribution and Consumption of Things

A Cashinahua's possessions are considered aspects of him or her in a very real sense. When people die, their *yuxin* are said to long for their possessions just as they 'long for' (*manu-*) their living kin. This is a good motive to place a deceased person's things (*mabu*) upon the grave, or destroy and otherwise dispose of them. Once I found an enamel bowl in the scrub at the edge of a house's patio. I brought it back to the woman of the house, thinking that a child must have thrown it away. She looked appalled, and told me to throw it back. It had belonged to her dead father, she said, and it was of no use to anyone anymore.

There is a rough division between the kinds of things that men and women own. An average man owns a suitcase filled with clothes, some ammunition, a comb, photos, documents (such as baptismal certificates for himself and his children) and assorted odds and ends. In the rafters he might keep some feathers and monkey or squirrel fur for making headresses and sometimes some arrow cane and a bow. He also owns a knife, worn in his belt, a machete, a shotgun, some of the bowls, plates, mugs and spoons used by his wife, an axe and perhaps other storebought tools such as a hoe. Most men own or scheme about owning a wristwatch and occasionally a radio. Some men own a canoe, and a very few an outboard engine. Everyone owns a hammock, and often a cotton mosquito-tent accommodating several hammocks. Livestock are individually owned, although they are not classified as *mabu* and are not slaughtered at the death of the owner. People may also own kerosene, diesel and petrol and other store-bought consumables such as salt and soap. Women have a cardboard suitcase filled with clothes and odds and ends, such as hair oil, lipstick, thread and needles, toilet soap and photos. They usually own a knife, a machete and a number of aluminium pots and pans, as well as basketry and pottery that they have made or been given. Among the things made for them by their husbands are a *kuki* carrying basket, spindles and weaving implements and a *binti* stirring paddle. A few women own sewing machines, watches and radios.

It is no exaggeration to say that most Cashinahua dream of owning bigger, better and more things and of eating more exotic sweet food such as sugar, biscuits or sweets. They invariably covet other people's things. Visitors are often astounded by their importunate behaviour. With the exception of a few more aloof people, nearly every Cashinahua I met initiated our relationship by asking for an object seen to be in my possession or suspected to be located in my bags. '*Ea inanve!*' – 'Give it to me!' – seemed to be at some stages the most repeated phrase in the Cashinahua language. Yet this immensely trying behaviour, which diminishes the longer a visitor stays, is a mark of acceptance. Unwanted strangers are preferably ignored. Their generosity is not thus tested. Visitors are also struck by the quantity of possessions that a Cashinahua person owns. Although they are pitifully few by city standards, the amount and quality contrast with the meagre and unkempt possessions of other indigenous peoples in the area. Sharing is ideal behaviour, and it seems that it is precisely for this reason that the Cashinahua have developed a series of strategies to avoid sharing whilst appearing, they hope, to be generous.

People's *mabu* are identified with them, and in this sense are inalienable and cannot be passed down as inheritance. Their owners may however give them away while alive, and when they do so they create or reinforce bonds of sameness and kinship. Stress is placed upon the virtues of the generous, or *duapa*, and scorn poured upon those who are miserly, or *yauxi*. In fact it is very hard to be *yauxi*, for the more possessions a person owns, the more she or he is fair game for begging. Possessions should neither be hoarded nor used privately. Instead, they should either be given away to others or used to create things to give away to other people in kinship-forming prestations. Of course, this is not always possible or desirable, since the generous would end up propertyless and the mean and importunate would accumulate at their expense. There are many techniques whereby people avoid having to make such prestations and manage to retain prized possessions.

If things are not given away in kinship-forming prestations, they may be exchanged outside the sphere of kinship. This 'exchange' takes several forms, but is typified by transactions with Cariú traders. Something that creates kinship when it is given away as a present, confirms difference if it is sold as a commodity. Furthermore, somebody who demands something openly, expressing a claim to common kinship with its owner, would express a lack of kinship if she or he were to steal the object. Theft, refusal to give and commodity transactions make people into strangers or even enemies, whereas giving and receiving presents make them into kin. The contrast between transactions that create kinship and transactions that reinforce difference is paralleled by the spatial opposition between inside and outside. Enemies and strangers come from the outside, from the deep forest and the city, from far upriver and far downriver. They are entirely necessary for social reproduction because they are the source of the many good things and the powerful knowledge that 'Real People' need. Forest beings are the source of game; river beings are the source of fish. The *Nawa* are the source of many kinds of manufactured goods and consumables that are indispensable to social and economic life. This creates a dangerous dependence that can be painful at times for the Cashinahua. The *aviamento* system and other forms of commercial relations engender relationships with the Cariú that are considered to be necessary and often unpleasant. Most men have experienced the effects of the negative value attached to *caboclo* identity, and have been humiliated and exploited at some stage in their lives. Nevertheless, during the 1980s these interactions were also considered manageable, and the Cashinahua felt able to cope with foreigners, making use of them for their own needs – that is, primarily, for the construction and reproduction of the inside. As well as the production, distribution, exchange and appropriation of things, an essential aspect of this process is the distribution and consumption of food, to which topic I now turn.

Distribution and Consumption of Food

Upon return from the forest, a man turns over his meat and fish to a woman, usually his wife or, if he is recently married, or if she is nursing a very young baby, to her co-resident mother. Occasionally the young man personally gives part of his catch to his mother-in-law when she lives in another household; but more often he leaves this essential present to his wife's care. Women always give part of their game and fish to their mothers, and such transactions go unremarked. It is only when a hunter brings home a pair of animals, or a big kill like a deer, that the ensuing prestation to his mother-in-law is made in the name of both. As the woman sits butchering the animal, dividing it up into carefully considered pieces, she must calculate what pieces she will send and to whom she will give them. Distribution is effected by sending younger people with messages or sometimes with the piece of meat. On receipt of a message the recipient either comes by to pick up the gift of meat in person or else sends a child to fetch it. When the animal is small, pieces are sent in disguise, inside an aluminium pot, or in a carrying basket under a few manioc roots. When there is enough to give to everybody, there is a sudden flurry of activity as women or their representatives converge on the kitchen to which they have been called.

If someone fancies a particular part of the animal, they might pre-empt the decision of the owner by asking for it; in this case it is impossible to refuse. When the game caught is small, this 'begging' (*buse*) can be the cause of much resentment, especially when the coveted meat (or fish) is part of a lop-sided flow. This is because the amount of game coming into different households differs considerably, depending on the number of active men and skilled hunters residing there. The possession of a good hunting dog can also mean that a particular woman always has a supply of meat. Such women are in the minority. On the whole people will not beg unless they consider that they can do so without being considered *daketape* - 'importunate, shameless' – that is, someone who always begs and forces others to part with their possessions. It is safest to beg from one's closest relatives and affines, secure in the knowledge that you have given fairly in the past and will be able to do so again in the future. People are less likely to complain about the *buse* activities of their closest relatives. Even when a woman and her children are hungry pride often prohibits a *buse* sortie. More frequently, the person who wanted something sits resentfully in her house, complaining about the stinginess of her relative. One hears the comment 'so-and-so is miserly' – *'yauxiki'* – more often than the comment 'she is generous' – *'duapaki'*.

As a corollary of this complex of desire, possession and pride all Cashinahua and especially women, are extremely skilled in the arts of hiding their belongings and of barefaced lying. Once meat has been preserved, it will be hidden inside the bedroom or in a basket hanging from the kitchen rafters. Only if the woman who owns it feels that there is enough for all comers will she merely place it out of reach of dogs and small children. If she has hidden it, the arrival of visitors from another settlement or a distant house will not cause undue strain upon her resources. She can say as she serves the standard bowl of manioc that she is very sorry not to be able to offer meat. However, if the meat is on display it would be very rude not to offer it. Most visitors are too proud to ask for what they know or suspect is there, preferring to gossip about the miserly nature of their hosts after they have dined on what is offered and then safely left the house.

Within a populous village like Recreio, it was often impossible to hide the small catches that men brought in, even though every attempt was made to do so. Even if the hunter succeeded, the proximity of the houses meant that the sight and smells of a meal's preparation gave away the nature of the neighbours' suppers. With the exception of a few notoriously importunate and shameless people, generally those with worst access to foods, it was an established convention to avoid those houses where cooking or eating of meat was in progress, but from which no invitations had been forthcoming. People would pass by silently, and if a polite invitation to enter was muttered by the man or woman of the house, would reply that they were on their way somewhere. This restraint was a reciprocal convention between neighbours and between kin. People knew that soon enough they would be in the same situation and would not want to share their meal with friends from other households. If, however, somebody wanted to be fed, she or he would simply arrive at a house when everyone was sitting down to eat. In this case an invitation to partake was forthcoming, no matter how secretly annoyed the hosts felt. Likewise, if a woman wanted a piece of meat from another woman, she would not have to beg if she visited her at the correct moment, when the meat was being prepared for cooking.

In general, those people who are forced into giving still have considerable ability to control what it is they give away. If someone hides all her meat, she is a terrible miser. If she gives a small piece of a less-valued part of the body to someone, she has avoided appearing a miser while at the same time expressing her scant regard for the recipient. If she gives generously, no-one can fault her. The meanings of these transactions are thus graded according to the quality and size of the present, within the context in which it is given. The distribution of fish follows a similar pattern, except on those occasions (relatively frequent in the dry summer months) when collective fish-poisoning expeditions result in an abundance of fish in every household. When this is the case, there is a small amount of giving, especially between mothers and daughters; but since everyone has access to more than enough fish, the emotional overtones attaching to who receives what are virtually absent.

Gifts between women during gardening expeditions are either prompted by the knowledge that a kinswoman is short of the particular vegetable or fruit given, or perhaps represent the donor's showing her friendship to the recipient. These gifts are not the subject of the same anxieties and grievances as the prestations of meat or fish, and no woman will accuse another of miserliness merely because she has never been her beneficiary. Often a woman who is hosting a collective expedition to harvest manioc in her garden will tell all the others with her to cut cane or knock down papayas.

One way that a woman who is unlucky in her supply of meat can express her generosity is by participating in wild fruit- and nut-gathering expeditions or by cooking a large batch of some kind of special food and then giving much of it away. Expeditions set out to gather *inga, cacau, assai, massandaroba, uricuri* (all Portuguese terms) and other such delicacies, and much is consumed on the spot in the forest or on the riverbank as gathering proceeds.[1] Oranges, mangoes, avocados and other cultivated fruit obtained as a present in another settlement are consumed and distributed in the same way as wild nuts and fruits. The gatherers come into the village laden down, walk to their house and dump the contents of the basket on the floor. They immediately begin sorting the fruit or nuts into piles. The biggest piles go to immediate kin; if the recipient is temporarily away the fruit will be stored for him or her. Messages are sent out to those women from other houses who will receive, and on these occasions adolescent girls are also recipients of the gifts (which is rarely the case with meat or fish). All children who happen to be around will get at least a mouthful of fruit by begging it from the collector or from her children, who always receive generous portions. Any men who happen to be around at the time also get a share, often a generous one.

Within minutes of the gatherers' arrival, the floors are covered with the discarded skins and seed of the fruit. Some of those women who have been called to receive a share eat it on the spot; others take their basin or basket of fruit back home to share it with their families. The recipients sit consuming a vast quantity very fast, perhaps so as to give away less to latecomers. Often there is a common pile from which the least favoured eat. Those who eat fastest eat most. Little children deal with the anxiety this causes by grabbing a handful and making for a private spot, where they eat alone and unhappily. Usually they are thoroughly scolded for such behaviour by mother or elder sister, and then lectured on the value of eating peacefully from a common pile with their siblings. No matter how much fruit is brought into the village, it will be gone within a day or so, and often at the first sitting.

Even if a large amount of fruit is consumed during the afternoon, a proper meal will still be served when the hunter or the fisherman returns. There are a two basic kinds of meals – ordinary proper meals shared by the residents of one house and consumed in the *sala* (P.) – the open living area; and collective meals shared by a number of households or the whole village in the leader's *sala*. Sometimes when meat or fish are very scarce a man eats informally with his wife and children in the kitchen. Meals are usually served immediately game or fish is brought in, as soon as it is cooked (often within twenty minutes or so). If the men of a house have been engaged in work until dusk, or have been unlucky in their late afternoon sortie for meat and fish, some semblance of a meal is still served. Meals usually take place after sundown, when people have bathed and finished late afternoon visiting. All the residents of a house then sit down to eat.

A proper first course consists of meat or fish, accompanied by boiled manioc or green banana. When hungry (*buni*) one may eat vegetables by themselves; but it is not considered correct to eat meat or fish unaccompanied with a vegetable dish. The act of consuming the two together is termed *nai-*; this means taking a bite of one and then of the other and chewing them together. Children are constantly admonished with the imperative *'Naive!'* on the rare occasions that they have access to plentiful meat. However, as long as children are seen to be eating their fair share of vegetables, they are not made literally to chew both foods together. People do not like to eat unaccompanied vegetables, and unless they are very hungry will refuse the food, saying '*En pintsiaii*' (I am hungry for meat). But unless a wife or wilful child wants to make a point, people generally eat some substitute for the unavailable meat, such as peanuts roasted in their shells or wild fungi wrapped in leaves and barbecued over the embers. Often, on bad days, boiled sweet manioc is simply dipped in salt, perhaps mixed with a little chili pepper and lemon.

It would be erroneous to interpret the Cashinahua passion for meat as an indicator of relative value ascribed to gendered foods. In some studies of Amazonian societies it is stated that food produced by men, and above all meat, is considered superior to vegetable food produced by women. If an analysis of gender amongst the Cashinahua were to base itself upon such an evaluation, it would miss the extraordinary value attributed to female agency and fail to note the renown earned by women who can always serve a complete and well-prepared meal. Serving food is a prestigious activity that defines a woman's status as a proper person. It also reflects well on her husband's abilities. Plentiful food shows that each spouse is a hard worker and successful producer. Not all women achieve this reputation. It is thought to require years of practice for a woman to become a good cook – and even so, some women 'never learn'. Their food is said to be cooked and served carelessly. The act of serving well conveys a message to those who are being fed about the woman's capacities. She knows how to work in the gardens and how to cook, *bava-*. If cooking and serving are treated as vital steps in the economic process, rather than passed over as 'mere domestic activities', then an appropriate analysis of gender and sociality is possible.

The woman serves the men first. She carefully places whole manioc roots or green bananas in a plate or basin and carries it to where her husband (or whoever she is serving) is sitting. Men sit in the *chintunti* hammock, which is kept strung up in the living room for daytime use, or else on little *kena* stools (child's initiation stools), or on any available object, such as logs or old tortoise shells. They never sit on the floor, preferring to squat if they must. The next plateful is for the women, who sit apart in a separate group or in another room - usually the kitchen. Their communal bowlful is normally smaller. Then the cook will serve her own children separately. If any of the other women have children, they will bring a plate and will serve their own children from the common bowl. However, in these cases they also will have cooked on a separate fire and will also serve first the men, then the women, with plates of vegetables. Very old women may be given separate plates and sit a little apart whilst they eat.

Next the meat-dish is served. A common bowl is set out for the men and another for the women. Very often a woman will also give a personal plate of meat or fish to her husband, and if one of her brothers is eating in her house, another for him. This only happens when meat or fish is plentiful. Otherwise all men eat from the common bowls. If a large game animal has been killed the head is usually served to the men. The cook thus both demonstrates her own generosity and underlines the skill of the hunter. The woman who is serving keeps a piece of meat for herself and makes sure each of her children have a share. If she wants to favour a particular woman, she gives her a piece of meat, which the recipient is not obliged to share with anyone. However, it is often the case that she does share with someone, and this may be what is intended by the original donor, who merely shares the responsibility for the final distribution of the meat by favouring one woman and giving her the opportunity to be generous.

The male style of eating contrasts with the female. Men move forward from their benches or stools to pick up a piece of meat and a piece of manioc and then sit back again to eat it. Eaters must always calculate how much they can take, since they must leave enough for everyone else. The youngest men sit well back, or even stand at the edges of the group respectfully, whilst the senior men lounge in their hammocks and hold forth about the day's events. Sometimes a man holds and feeds a young child. Occasionally a man may call to his wife and hand her a choice portion of meat from the men's share, especially if he knows she is going without. Women sit on the floor, politely cross-legged, their babies in their laps and their youngest children around them. All women accompanied by young children bring their own plates for their children's food and either eat from these plates or from the common plate. Childless women may only eat from the latter unless specially honoured. The woman's group thus spreads out in little groups of mothers and children, while the men's group is ranged around an open space in the centre of which are ranged the plates and basins of food. All except the most senior men move back and forth from plates to seats as the meal progresses. Seniority is thus clearly delineated in the male pattern of eating, but not in the female.

These differing male and female styles of eating also characterize collective meals. Sharing of food between households depends upon the quantity that is available. In Recreio, which was a comparatively a large settlement, men brought in some meat or fish nearly every day. It was unusual not to hear successful hunters calling out invitations to their neighbours to eat. Each guest would bring his own plate of food, prepared for him by his wife (usually a base of manioc or banana topped with a few pieces of meat or fish). Those without meat at home would just bring vegetables or a bowl of *caissuma*. The food was added to the communal collection in the centre of the floor. The communal group thus formed varied in size. But when a hunter had made a large kill, perhaps of deer, peccary, or tapir or several howler monkeys, or when many people had been on a successful fish-poisoning expedition, the village would come together to feast.

In a Cashinahua village settlement, the male leader calls daily from his house inviting the men to eat with him, just as Elias described (Chapter 3), but not everyone comes regularly. Sometimes people stay away, from pride, because they have nothing to contribute to the meal. Sometimes they only go if they know that a big kill has been made. When game or fish are plentiful, most men eat in the leader's house, and the food they bring with them adds up to an impressive variety of dishes. Such collective meals are also common in the mornings before a male collective work party is to set out, even if there is little meat or fish. The male leaders' wives serve the food that they have prepared to the men. In doing so, they behave as *ainbu xanen ibu* (the female leaders to whom Elias referred). Often other women will also serve the men with food - a woman comes across from her own house to where the men are eating, bearing a bowl of *caissuma* or some other dish, which she presents to a male relative. Sisters frequently remember their brothers in this way, but a woman can also give to the other categories of male kin. A woman may also invite

Figure 9. Drinking *caissuma*

her male relatives to meals, though usually a male co-resident (and especially her husband) makes the invitation.

Women eat together frequently, but not in such large collective groups as the men. Women's collective meals tend to be held at different times from the men's, since when the men are eating the women are often engaged in cooking, serving them and feeding the children. When this is done, they are able to sit down to their own meals. However, midday meals are frequently all-women affairs, for men are often away from the settlement at this time. When the sun is high and after the morning's chores are done, a woman will bring down her last package of roast fish from the day before and signal to her sister-in-law to come over and share it with her. If her maternal aunt is at home, she too might come, accompanied by grandchildren and bearing a bowl of food. Someone brings *caissuma*, someone else banana, and the range of food is complete. Lunch consists of a proper meal. These all-female meals have a more informal atmosphere to them than the evening meals when the men sit in a group and their wives serve them. If a man is also at home he sits only a little apart and joins happily in the conversation. It is only when men are in a group exceeding two or three, or if some visitors have come from afar, that an air of ceremony pervades the occasion.

After a collective fishing expedition, all the men and all the women eat collectively, but nearly always in separate houses. Depending upon the convenience of the location, the house of a senior woman will regularly be used as the women's collective dining hall. The site for these meals is liable to change from time to time, whereas the men always eat major collective meals in the male leader's house, except when they go to a particular hunter's house at his invitation after he has made a big kill. On these occasions the hunter's wife will invite all the women too, and they will eat in the kitchen, while the men eat in the living area. The final course of any meal, if it is to be proper and satisfying, is the *caissuma* that one or two of the women participating are sure to bring. The sense of well-being after a good meal topped by a creamy bowlful of *caissuma* is apparent in the contented faces and relaxed bodies of the eaters. Nothing is more conducive to a feeling of friendly sociability.

On all these occasions the sharing of food seems to express and create contrastive male and female identities. The many subtleties of serving, distribution and observance of the rules regarding self-restraint and proper etiquette whilst eating also speak of many shades of difference within each group. But if gender difference is clearly delimited during meals, there is an overriding sense in which men and women also share identity – as kin and as real human beings. Perhaps it is when they are visiting or being visited that the Cashinahua most clearly express their conception of shared being, for the language of the meal is used to create links crossing the spatial barriers between settlements.

If someone in another settlement kills a tapir or several peccary, news travels fast. People drop their work and set out on a visit. Of course there are many other reasons to go visiting. For example, if someone has a good supply of *puikama* leaf poison, he or she might invite relatives to come for a day's fishing. Longer-term visits are occasioned by the desire to see relatives who live far away. Whatever the cause, the guests are always treated according to a set formula, one that it is extremely rude to ignore. Visiting is described as *bai ka-* (to go visit) or as *uin ka-* (to go see), and it is especially common in the dry season. Travel is easiest at this time, and visitors often come from far afield to spend several months with their kin. In the AIAP people frequently went on day trips from Fronteira to Recreio, or one of the smaller settlements, or vice versa. Sunday was a favoured day for such an outing. A typical visit would proceed as follows: Setting out early in the morning on empty stomachs, carrying babies, empty baskets and bundles of clean new clothes, the visitors arrive at their destination after a few hours canoeing or walking. On the outskirts they pause at a stream to wash off the sweat and dust of the trip, perfume themselves and put on their fresh clothes. As the day-trippers come up to the first dwelling, one of them addresses the man or woman of the house by kin appellation, for example, '*Chain!*', and announces: 'I have come wishing to see you' (*En miki uinkatsi huaii*). The 'brother-in-law cousin' then bids all of them enter. Subsequently each of the residents who happens to be at home asks each of the visitors in turn 'Have you arrived, my So-and-so? (kin address term)' (*Min ma huai, ...?*). And the guests reply individually, addressing each relative one by one with the appropriate kin appellation, for example saying 'I have arrived indeed, Mother-in law (etc.)' (*En ma huai, Achin*). Then the visitors sit down in a cluster, men and women together if they are few, separately if they are many. They are immediately served with boiled manioc, which is usually immediately available. If not the woman of the house sits down and begins peeling any tubers she has left over from the last visit to the garden. A bowl of *caissuma* might also be put out, but the visitors do not touch it when they know there is a proper meal in the offing. *Caissuma* is the last course in the meal; and it is common for people to linger for hours chatting and drinking it, when they have finished eating.

The visitors eat their meal on their own. If the hosts have not yet eaten that day, they will eat a little apart. If the woman serving wishes to mark a special relationship with one of the guests, she can favour her or him with a special morsel, or a personal plate of food. In some houses the Cariú custom of serving each person with a separate enamel plate containing a personal portion of meat has been adopted (but in Recreio and Fronteira in the 1980s this was relatively rare). Finally, the owner of the house should make a present of uncooked foods or even smoke-roasted meat and fish to her guests. When the food is good and the atmosphere friendly, visitors linger chatting and might spend hours at the first house they climb up into. Otherwise, they eat quickly and move on to the next house, taking their presents with them. In every house they visit the same process is gone through. As the visitors eat more and more, they begin refusing offers of manioc alone, but never refuse meat or fish. As always the food is eaten *nai*, vegetable and meat together. Gifts to women visitors of fresh game and fish, sweet ripe bananas, peanuts, *farinha*, manioc tubers and so on are stashed in the baskets or bags they have brought with them. It often happens that in one house there is meat, in another fish, in another *caissuma*, in another sweet bananas. By the afternoon, when it is time to go, the visitors should be satiated and the women loaded down with presents. On their way home they might stop to pick up some fruit that was spotted on the outward journey, or if game is sighted one of the men might set off in pursuit.

People who visit too often are treated more casually, although always according to the proper formulae. A woman who feels she is being exploited might decide to withhold the meat she has hidden in the house. Hosts treat close relatives better than distant kin or non-kin unless they have been co-residents recently, in which case the serving of food is less tense and more informal. Visitors who are totally unrelated but understand the rules or are in the process of learning them could be treated exceptionally well, depending upon the proclivities of the hosts. This group includes anthropologists, political workers, missionaries, the few Cariú neighbours who accept the Cashinahua on equal terms, and also Yaminahua and unrelated Cashinahua from other areas. On the other hand, some foreigners, especially Cariú, are treated as if they were invisible and ignored.

Longer-term guests do not join in any work that is planned until a day or two after arriving in the host settlement. Hosts are expected to drop any work they are doing, though if they have no meat or fish it is acceptable if they go looking for it. When leaving, the guests ought to address everyone they have encountered during their visit, saying: 'I am already going, Elder Brother (etc.)' (*En ma kaii, Huchin* (etc.)). The usual response is: 'Go now!' (*Kadive!*). This signals that the formalities are over, and the visitors hasten home before the dangerous hour of dusk falls.

When visitors are fed generously and given presents, they are inducted into the sphere of sociality. The woman who serves the food makes a statement about the shared humanity of herself, her guests and her own kin, on behalf of all members of her household. When she withholds food, she effectively denies a close social tie, and stresses the difference between her own people and the visitors.

As a woman sets out a meal containing the three constituents - meat, manioc, *caissuma* - she sets out three processed substances that sum up the relationships underlying their production. These relationships are not simple ones. The Cashinahua stress marriage as a shorthand for the complex of creative processes based upon the male-female opposition. But the meal is more than a metaphor for these productive processes. It is itself directly efficacious, because the food consumed produces the body that consumes it and the strength and health that is required for production. Together husband and wife make the food that their children need in order to have strength, to live and to grow. This process of feeding is paralleled by the process of sexual reproduction, where men's and women's blood combine with much work (sex) to form a foetus. 'True food' (*piti kuin*) is a combination of both kinds of food, male and female, meat and vegetable, just as human babies are made of a combination of male and female blood.

The corporeal processes of making babies and making bodies are paralleled by the socio-economic processes. Both are powered by male and female agencies. The male collectivity produces and maintains domestic space out of the forest and brings the products of the forest into the domesticity they have created. The female collectivity works within the domesticated space to make the products of the forest consumable. If love-making brings the dual agency of the couple to the work of forming a child, the dual agency of the genders is required in the process of manufacturing the 'community'. Male agency is concerned with trans-formation through destruction and involves a direct confrontation between humans and the denizens of the outside. In understanding why men consume the tongue of a certain boa constrictor, we should think of the snake as both a substantial source of this agency and also as a symbol of the male relation with animals and wild plants – the living things that men must destroy as they hunt or weed their gardens. Male confrontation with live forest animals is mostly a solitary affair, but their dealings with with live forest plants are usually collective. Women, by contrast deal with dead forest animals and river fish and with garden plants, in a process that particularizes female action. Yet the female domain of productive action is not relegated to a hidden or 'domestic' slot in economic organization. Women's production is celebrated by women themselves in semi-ceremonial collective expeditions that female leaders organize; and women are instrumental in the distribution of male and female products, in prestations that strengthen their and their husband's ties with kin and affines. Female agency directly creates sociality in this way. Furthermore, by transforming raw food into real meals, women enable all people, men and women, to come together in its consumption. We may say that the meal they serve stands for the making of social life itself.

The meal is not only valuable because it makes the body; it also stands for the making of this world, inhabited by living kin, people who are really human. When men eat the food a woman serves them, or when visitors eat the food their hosts provide, their hunger and desire are satisfied. They have been respected, treated as kin should properly be treated. The selflessness and generosity of feeding the visitors is only paralleled in the feeding of their children. This is why leaders must feed the village as 'parents' of the villagers. Feeding is the ideal work of kinship and most especially of parenthood. When a male leader addresses his people as 'My Children' (*En Bakebu*), he should not only be speaking metaphorically. As Elias told me, he should also be speaking the truth.

Notes

1. Various species of the fruit genus *Inga* are common throughout Amazonia. The trees bear long pods resembling giant broadbeans, and once stripped open the sweet, fluffy woollen fruit inside them surrounding the seeds is eaten raw. *Cacau* is the cocoa tree (*Theobroma* (Lat.)). *Açai* is a palm that bears clusters of shiny dark berries (*Euterpe oleracea* (Lat.)). Soaked in water for half an hour, the berries are rubbed by hand and a thick, oily, deep-purple juice is obtained, which is delicious mixed with sugar and *farinha*. *Maçaranduba* is a huge tree whose red fruits contain a sweet white pulp. Several varieties are well-known throughout Brazil for their high-quality wood. *Uricuri* is a palm whose nutty elliptical fruits contain a dark-yellow layer of oily meat that may be stripped off with one's teeth. When they fall to the forest floor, peccary eat them, so that hunters who have spent several unsuccessful hours hiding behind a blind bring them back to the village as a (poor) substitute.

–5–

Making Community

In 1985 I accompanied Pancho, the leader of Recreio, on a visit to his relatives living on the Peruvian side of the border. He had not been back there since he had migrated downriver eight years earlier. As we travelled upriver, we stopped and spent some time at every Cashinahua settlement and village encountered on the way. In each one Pancho called a meeting to speak of the benefits of life on the Brazilian side of the border and to persuade his listeners to return to Brazil with us. There, he would say, there was easier access to goods, better health care, a freedom from the excesses of the Peruvian bosses and a virtually guaranteed legal claim to a large tract of land. He appealed to the desirability of relatives' living together. By the end of our stay, he managed to persuade sixty people to move downriver to Recreio with us. These people included his mother's sister, her unmarried and married children and their spouses and children; his half-brother, with his wives and married and unmarried children; two half-sisters, their husband and daughters; and his mother's full brother and wife. In addition, during our stay in Peru he arranged the marriage of his teenage daughter and secured a promise from his future brother-in-law and affines to come and live with him the following year.

A 'true leader' (*xanen ibu kaya*) gathers people together, using his ties to siblings and other kin, as do male leaders all over lowland South America (Kaplan 1975; Price 1981). By responding to a kinsman's call, people choose whether or not to live with a leader at all, for not all Cashinahua live in settlements with a leader – often they simply live with a few of their siblings and siblings-in-law. Shifting settlement patterns can be explained in terms of these two ways of forming settlements. The movement of people into villages occurs in response to the call of such male leaders, while the movement out may be a reaction to the difficulties of living together in larger communities. The term *jake-*, which means 'to live around a leader', reflects the centripetal force exercised by such a figure. It implies living with many of one's kin, instead of just a few. If the principal ties that generate the formation of communities are those of kinship and especially siblingship, affinal bonds are also important. In fact male leaders form new communities by bringing together people who are kin, affinal kin or unrelated affines. But the leader does not use the creation of affinal ties as a primary strategy in the formation of his community, unlike Piaroa or Achuar leaders (Taylor 1983; Kaplan 1975). Rather, he calls those he has a legitimate right to gather together, his kin, to whom living apart is always painful. People often lament that distant brothers and sisters and their children might die before they could ever be with them again. They say that they miss (*manu-*) their kin, and complain about feeling lonely and unhappy. When a powerful relative comes and 'calls' (*kena-*), then they must make the difficult decision of whether to uproot themselves and follow him. Very often they do.

During the second week of our trip to Peru we drew up our canoe at Bufeo, a small settlement a few hours upriver from Conta. This was a typical visit to 'call' kin. Pancho was led up the steep riverbank by his young 'sisters' (MZDs) and their mother, Chiquiana, who was his MZ and FW (her husband had been one of his three fathers). Ritually crying and saying '*En bake juaii!*' (My child is come!) his aunt took him by the arm and sat him in the hammock. She served him with boiled manioc and *caissuma*. After everyone had eaten the tortoise he had brought as a gift for her, the plates were cleared away and he began to speak. On this occasion, unlike a formal public meeting, men and women did not sit separately. His young sisters sat at his feet, touching him from time to time. He spoke very seriously, though briefly, saying that he had come to help them, for he was concerned about their well-being. When he had finished he asked his aunt and then his sisters to speak and to respond to his preoccupation. His widowed aunt Chiquiana spoke first, lamenting how she and her family had been forced to leave the upriver village of Balta because no one had cared for them there. Although she had six young children and a baby, the only person hunting and working for them was her son-in-law, who also had very young children to look after. Then his 'sisters' spoke, echoing their mother. When they had finished, Pancho replied. He then told them that they should come and live with him, that he had come to get them because he had heard of the recent widowhood of his aunt. He emphasized that those who came to live with him would be expected to work hard and live well and not to drink sugarcane rum.

Pancho persuaded Chiquiana and her family easily, but others were not convinced that returning to Brazil with us was a good idea. For instance, his youngest sister Isabel suffered several weeks of tormented indecision, but finally refused, because it would have meant leaving her husband behind. She was, she told me, still very much in love with him. Other people who considered a move finally decided against it, because certain recent visitors to Recreio had been spreading stories about the village that contradicted Pancho's version. Even those people who made the decision to uproot themselves and travel ten days downriver to Recreio only did so with the proviso that they might be back again the next year if they did not like it. In dealing with other human beings, especially leaders, the Cashinahua know that a good dose of scepticism is always wise.

Pancho's gathering of his kinspeople was a deliberate political manoeuvre aimed at increasing his personal power and also at strengthening the Cashinahua claim to land on the Brazilian side of the border. During the 1980s and 1990s, the Purus Cashinahua were busy expanding the territorial boundaries of their land and consolidating their settlements. An increase in population was fundamental to these processes. At the time they had to deal with a number of other political actors involved in indigenous affairs, amongst whom were pro-Indian NGOs such as CIMI and the CPI, their indigenous neighbours the Kulina, government agencies (principally FUNAI) and the local Cariú bosses, traders and rubber tappers. The larger political and economic context of the events I witnessed on the Peruvian Purus, then, was the unfolding relationship between the Cashinahua and these different actors in the process of creating, maintaining and strengthening Pancho's family's community in Brazil. The role of the leader was fundamental in this struggle and in the development of these relationships. A Cashinahua leader like Pancho has a double burden to bear. On the one hand he is a key figure in the internal, day-to-day workings of the community. On the other, he is the outstanding player in the negotiations and political play-offs that must take place with these outsiders. Caught in the middle, his role becomes an ambiguous one, and only a skilful politician can manage to be both the *ibu* (parent, owner) of the community in his followers'eyes, and also the 'chief' that the outsiders expect to find.

Male and Female Leaders

From an external point of view, Cashinahua communities are led by one man, known in Portuguese as the *tuxaua* ('chief'). He is normally the man designated, from the internal point of view, as the main *xanen ibu*, the male leader acknowledged by all members of the community, to whom I refer as the 'main' or 'chief leader'. He is responsible for the production and protection of the community. His wife is nominally at least the 'woman leader' (*ainbu xanen ibu*). The *tuxaua* both represents the community in dealings with outsiders and organizes the collective activities of its members. He is in theory the most '*xanen ibu*' of all the men in the community, the most successful husband, worker and hunter. There are two kinds of *xanen ibu*, the *xanen ibu kaya* – the 'true' or 'big' leader – and the chant-leader (*chana xanen ibu*) who leads rituals such as *Nixpo Pima*, and whose female partner is the *ainbu chana xanen ibu* (though I met no young women training for this role). The chief leader is a true leader and not a chant-leader. Female leadership is less marked than male, and women are never (as far as I know) chief leaders. Their main functions are to lead the women in work activities, to organize collective meals and to feed visitors – thus inducting them into the realm of sociality. Female leadership is recognized as formally complementary to male, and the women are seen as men's partners in political and economic contexts.

A man successfully imbued with male agency is ready to become a leader, a notion closely allied to that of *ibu*. An ideal father catches game and fish, and works hard, so that his spouse can harvest, cook, distribute food, and 'make her kin consume' (*javen nabu pimai*). All such men are classified as *xanen ibu kaya*. Often there are several in each village, but in all communities there is only one chief leader. He has special qualities, such as a capacity to think, to plan and to speak effectively. He usually organizes the men and women in collective productive activities. The chief male leader spends time trading with anti-social outsiders, which is considered a male form of interaction (though not thereby exclusive to men). His house, more imposing than its neighbours, is located in the centre of the settlement and is the focus around which the community is formed. From an outsider's point of view, it is identifiable by its function of receiving new visitors to the village. Usually the leader's oldest wife is in charge of the visitors (although if they are strange men and there is an adult man in the village they might be taken to his house instead). She invites them into her house and makes some gesture towards hospitality, depending on who they are and how she evaluates the relationship. As the place where most community events take place and, when the spirit of community is strong in the village, where collective meals are held daily, her house is a focus of sociality for insiders as well as outsiders. Therefore the central role of the male and female leaders in making community is an extension as well as a development of the role of parents in producing kinship.

The Cashinahua sometimes use the Yaminahua term for leader that may be glossed as 'standing still person' (*nai ibu*). Its popularity is perhaps explained by the way it sums up the centripetal and parental role of the Cashinahua leader. In the same vein, the term *bata ibu*, literally 'sweet

Figure 10. Village meeting – Recreio 1984

parent', someone endowed with the virtues of generosity and kindness, may also be used. In oratory, leaders sometimes address their people as 'My Children' (*En Bakebu*) as they did at the start of the century (Abreu 1941). Main leaders are always married, usually polygynously, and always parents. A polygynous man is by implication a *xanen ibu* man, for an ability to have much responsibility and many children suggests an ability to lead communities. A leader is able to take on the added responsibility of more wives and children than other men could bear. Neither men nor women see polygyny as disadvantageous to women. Where one man marries sisters, their mother is more likely to enjoy continued co-residence with both. The wives themselves can depend upon each other for help in all kinds of ways. Jealousy, described as being 'miserly' (*yauxi*) with one's spouse, is condemned or found laughable. Co-wives cooperate in the responsibilities of female leadership, although only the eldest is formally the female leader. In this system, the leading couple legitimately differentiate themselves from their co-resident kin as metaphorical parents, appealing to their authority to guide and teach others (McCallum 1990).

Disruptions to the smooth progress of social life are many. Some of these have outside orgins, but anti-social behaviour on the part of the village people themselves is a common cause of such upsets. Both male and female leaders are expected to play their part in countering such behaviour by their actions upon the bodies of fellow villagers. Perhaps uncontrolled anger is the most thoroughly antisocial form of behaviour for the Cashinahua. Like other personal traits and capacities, its source lies in the the individual history of each body as it was built up and formed over the years. A tendency to anger may be controlled by external intervention, through the use of plant medicines and also with words. Constantly repeated criticisms of anger and other immoral behaviour – miserliness, laziness, vindictiveness and so on – and injunctions to act morally penetrate the body in a material sense and help correct personal behaviour that disrupts the community. Anger may have consequences worse than direct verbal or physical violence, stimulating people to become sorcerers or poisoners. Indeed, a real fear of sorcery persists, despite claims that it has died out.[1] This adds piquancy and pertinence to the homiletic speeches that leaders proffer in their capacity as parents of the village exercising legitimate authority (McCallum 1989, 1990). In their speeches, they inveigh against all forms of anti-social behaviour. It is because danger is all around, even present in those people who classify each other as close kin, that the Cashinahua vision of sociality is expressed on these occasions in such clear and moralistic tones.

Certain forms of anti-social behaviour are gendered. When I asked informants to compare men to women I was told that women are inveterate liers. In political speeches, too, leaders inveighed against lying in a general sense, but sometimes addressed their oratory specifically at the women. A man is said to be 'like a woman' if he lies. Doubtless the fact that girls and women usually work together in pairs and small groups, with ample time for chatting, contributes to this assessment of the effects of female gender upon a person's capacity for anti-social action. But it is counter-balanced by the emphasis given to personal difference between people with different histories and personalities. Some women I knew were regarded as inveterate gossips and liars, whereas others were much admired for their honesty and generosity. From the Cashinahua point of view women are not 'naturally' liars or gossips, but rather female patterns of social interaction may imbue them with a propensity to be so.

The formation of male gender and agency also stimulates a capacity for anti-social behaviour, though it takes a different form. Men disrupt the community by absences that at times are prolonged over several months, especially on trips to the city. They need to learn a certain aggressiveness and self-sufficiency to be able to hold their own in interactions with the Nawa. Such interaction inevitably forms their personalities in a corporeal sense, as outside knowledge and capacities become engrained into their bodies. A vivid example of this is their enjoyment of modish Portuguese phrases and Cariú styles of interaction. In joking with his *chai*, a man might choose to imitate Cariú male bravado, boasting of his own strength and virility in denigration of his cross-cousin's. During male collective work such bantering mixes in with sexual joking of a more traditional kind and functions to produce both a strong sense of male identity and also a feeling of male solidarity. However, while men use a Cashinahua adaptation of the idioms of Brazilian *machismo* to reinforce collectivity, any display of aggressive behaviour against others is unthinkable. Boys learn to be violent when necessary in the hunt, and the physical knowledge that makes striking and killing possible presents a particular danger if it is turned against co-residents.

Men's acquired fierceness is disruptive of community harmony when it manifests itself in such violence, for example, in the physical mistreatment of wives or daughters. In my experience this was extremely rare, and this is true for many peoples in Amazonia (Overing 1986b). One must be careful not to apply a 'butterfly collecting' mentality to the question of male violence against women in the region, since its occurrence differs both within and across groups and changes over time. Among some peoples of lowland South America, women are portrayed as constantly at risk of men's aggression, for example, the Yanomami (Lizot 1985), the Achuar (Taylor 1983), or the Amahuaca (Dole 1974a). Yet different situations are found amongst distinct groups of the same people, emerging from specific local histories. For example, the tenor of gender relations is more difficult for women amongst the Western Parakanã than the Eastern, even though both share a common origin not one hundred years ago in the same small group of people (Fausto 1997). Cashinahua people are well aware of the possibility that men may be violent against women, and have developed particular strategies against it. In homiletic oratory, for example, both male and female leaders stress its immorality (McCallum 1990). When I lived in Recreio, a young man once struck his wife in a drunken rage. As a consequence, Pancho, the main leader, called a meeting. Then his parents-in-law, helped by other villagers, subjected the thoroughly shamed and now sober aggressor to a barrage of criticism and homiletic speech. Obliged to move back into their house, there he remained, under their supervision, for the next few years.

The Cashinahua think of the 'good' behaviour of a community's residents, which they describe as 'living well' (*jive pe*), as basic to sociality. Since persons are imperfect, sociality is never achieved completely, and it must be constantly striven towards. There is a sense in which degrees of moral personhood are measured along a scale of kinship, so that the closer a person is in terms of reckoning a relationship, theoretically the better behaved and the better person he or she should be. Thus a complete stranger is *a priori* considered a bad person and unworthy of compassion. This logic lies behind the treatment that may be meted out to certain strangers. For example, a young Yaminahua man from the Iaco river came to stay at the village. Pancho paid him to clear a garden thus discarding the possibility of constructing a kin relationship with him. The unfortunate outsider began to look around for a wife in the village, much to the amusement of the unmarried adolescent girls. He became the butt of many loud jokes, pitilessly uttered in his presence, until finally he departed upriver, driven out by the villagers' disdain. It seems that male violence against women (or men) in other parts of Amazonia follows a similar logic: men are able to mistreat women who have no kin to defend them and who come from other settlements and communities. Since among the Cashinahua husbands and wives are normally closely related, situations propitious to male violence rarely arise. Perhaps this was not the case in some situations in the past, for example, when the Cashinahua men working for a Brazilian boss on the Jordão at the start of the twentieth century married captured Yaminahua women.

Female leaders play a vital part in the process of making community. Female leadership has been little discussed in the literature on Lowland South America.[2] Anthropologists have tended to write as if politics is a male domain and as if women are confined to a 'domestic sphere', although it now seems wrong to attribute a distinction between domestic and supra-domestic domains to Amazonian societies.[3] Since Goldman (1963) first described the Cubeo headman's relation to his wife, the mutually dependent relationship between male leaders and their wives has often been noted. It would be surprising if the Cashinahua elaboration of a notion of female leadership were as rare as might appear. Clearly there is wide variation between different groups, as well as within groups and across time. At this stage it is impossible to make a wide comparative statement. The 'invisibility' of female leaders could be attributed to a number of factors, among them the gender of the anthropologist and possible male bias. Another might be the changes taking place within indigenous political systems as a result of the political-economic processes structuring interethnic systems. Male leaders deal directly with outsiders, so on the whole only men gain experience of the national political scenario. As far as the non-indigenous players are concerned, female leadership does not exist, and local political systems based on gender complementarity do not gain recognition. When Cashinahua male leaders become powerful, their political strength is partly based on the relationships they can construct with outsiders, particularily those who engineer access to funds and social services. Internally, however, male leaders may not work without the cooperation of women. Some Cashinahua affirm that female leaders are not as strong as they were in the past. Nevertheless, their position continues to play a vital function in political organization, despite the greater prominence of the male role.

Nowadays it is extremely hard for male leaders to conjugate their duties as *ibu* of the village and husbands to their wives with the activities and forms of interaction imposed by the role of *tuxaua*. Certain male leaders exercising legitimate authority as the former strain at the bounds of their mandates and attempt to cross over into a relatively coercive form of leadership within the community as the latter. Ironically, when they do this they behave like strangers to their kin, a fact taken to demonstrate an embodied condition of difference that, when taken too far, undermines their right to exercise authority. These two styles of leadership are summed up by the Cashinahua in the terms *xanen ibu*, on the one hand, and the Portuguese *patrão* ('boss') on the other. They each emerge from social relationships constructed on the basis of two conceptually opposed forms of transaction.

Exchange and True Giving

As bosses, modern male leaders maintain a high level of interaction with the outside, so as to obtain basic 'necessities' (*necessidades*) such as salt, tools, pans, cloth, clothes, kerosene, gasoline, mechanical parts and many smaller items for the community. The leader enters into 'relations of exchange' with Nawa to obtain these things, to then distribute them to his kinspeople. Objects from outside are crucial to the making of community, but the transition from exchange to kin-forming prestation is a difficult one. There is no simple way for a leader to trade with his close kin. Relations of exchange with outsiders involve a property logic contrary to that which underpins 'relations of caring' between kin.[4] This difference is the source of most social tensions for the Cashinahua. The same object can be transacted in two different ways, and depending on how it is treated the relation between people is defined in its transaction. When leaders try to make the Cashinahuas' cooperatives function, they are bound by the constraints of market trade to attempt to enforce reciprocity upon kin. This constraint binds the least self-seeking and most honest of leaders into a situation where they can be called misers, bosses, foreigners and thieves. They must engage in economic forms that are alien to the social ethic, yet are essential to maintaining the community.

From one point of view the property logic that informs 'relations of exchange' is a commodity logic. Things circulate against things, and may ideally be alienated from their source. Exchange does not imply an ongoing social relationship and the objects transacted do not stand for a social link once the transaction has been completed. Although the *aviamento* system involves debt, Cashinahua traders seek to pay off debts and be free of obigation, to shake off the relationship that the debts impose. Most Cashinahua debtors see continuity in these relationships as a burden and not an advantage, unlike labourers in some other patron-client systems in Amazonia, such as the *habilitación* system on the Bajo Urubamba described by Gow (1991). In a few cases debtors gather bosses and with them unpaid bills, in an effort to avoid payment altogether. This rejection of close ties to the outside is undoubtedly both a product of years of political campaigning by Cashinahua eager to establish economic autonomy and also a response to the exploitative attitude of many Cariú bosses. Like most local people, the Cashinahua would prefer to have 'good bosses', and they do periodically enter into *compadrazgo* relationships with Cariú in the hope of establishing useful ties. Yet these efforts hardly ever come to anything, since the most friendly Cariú are usually the poorest. For the Cashinahua, in the end, a completed cycle of commodity exchange is ideal. Debts are a nuisance.

The question 'When is a thing to be a gift, and when a sale?' is a source of continual preoccupation. Types of transactions must always be defined, so that relationships are always being redefined too. The Cashinahua term for 'giving a present not expecting a return' is *inankuin-* (real giving); the term for 'giving in expectation of a return' and 'selling' is *inan-*. The latter transaction involves exchange and bilaterality; the former an absence of reciprocity and unilaterality. How gifts are made defines the nature of a relationship. Transactions of an *inan-* nature are ambiguous and dependent on context. For example, I was subject to a barrage of requests for real gifts, 'proof' (when I gave) of my generosity; but true gifts to me were far fewer. However, I could console myself with the fact that few are asked for gifts in this way, since most foreigners are known to be 'angry' (*sinata*) and miserly. Sometimes women would make friends with me by giving me (unilaterally) bead bracelets or necklaces, or cotton wristbands, as they do to visiting kin (and especially namesakes) from other communities. More than once, I was given a 'present' and then asked to reciprocate almost immediately, shattering my temporary delusion that I was the object of pure affection. Anthropologists' reports of such loaded gifts and the ensuing series of impossible demands for returns are common in the literature on lowland South America. Despite this attitude to myself and my things, in all cases I was treated with true generosity as far as food was concerned, in contrast to those Nawa considered beyond the sphere of sociality.

The transformation between exchange and true giving, between *inan-* and *inankuin-*, is especially problematic in the case of cooperatives. The coop manager cannot unilaterally give to all those who demand that he does so, and for their benefit as much as his own he must demand a return. Yet by so doing he distances himself from them. He behaves like a boss and becomes like a Nawa, so how coop transactions are defined directly affects the leader's relations with its members. The possibility of a hostile relationship and the ubiquitous presence of avarice characterizes the system of riverine trade in the Cashinahua view. As far as they are concerned, traders and bosses try to cheat and enslave them, rejecting the possibility of kinship. The bosses comment that 'Indians' (*caboclos*) are liable to be thieves, either not paying their debts because of laziness or else because of their natural immorality. Indians are regarded as more animal than human, and this justifies treating them as a source of profit, through the exploitation of their labour, or through unfair trading. The indigenous people of Acre were aware of this Cariú attitude to them. With the help of aid agencies they were trying to organize an alternative source of goods and supplies, through the cooperatives. However, there were many problems. Sometimes it was difficult not to view the leaders, in their guise as *ibu* or 'owners' of the cooperatives, as if they were *Nawa* dressed in the clothing of kin – that is, as miserly, selfish and inclined to be coercive.

The Cooperative and the *Comunidade*

Next to the leader's house in Recreio, in Fronteira and on the *seringais* of the Jordão, stands the coop building, known as the *cantina*. It is the only building in the settlement that is entirely walled, and has a door and a chain and a padlock securing it. Inside, like any Cariú *barracão*, it should have a stored quantity of rubber and stockpiles of trade goods and supplies obtained downriver in the nearest town. The account books are stored there, a heavy-duty scales, fuel containers and spare parts for the village outboard engine. Usually the stock of medicines is kept there too. It is one of a modern leader's responsibilities to ensure that both produce and supplies are always available. Mostly, however, they are not.

The coops run according to the principles of the *aviamento* system. The coop manager provides workers with supplies on a credit basis and they are expected to pay off their debts before they obtain more. Attempts to institute a cash-down exchange system meet stiff opposition, and if a leader tries to withhold supplies from his clients, he is angrily criticized, albeit in private. Although the *aviamento* system is the basic form of the cooperatives' economic organization, not all of the practices of the Cariu bosses are adhered to. The leaders say that they attempt to make sure that the prices of goods are lower and those of rubber higher than in neighbouring *barracões*, or in the rivertraders' boats. They do not charge rent for the *estradas*, nor *quebra* on the rubber.[5] Consequently, the profit margin is very low even when the tappers and artefact producers actually do pay their debts. During the 1980s the coop managers saw non-payment of debt as the principal cause for the general failure of the coops to be financially self-sufficient. They continued to survive because outside agencies injected capital periodically.

Behind the counter in the *cantina*, the coop leader looks for all the world like a Cariú boss. His kinspeople come in one by one and hand over their product or deposit it on the scales. Everyone observes the form, learnt from many encounters with river-traders and other bosses. The leader notes down the details and the credit in his book. He normally distributes what he can afford to his 'client' (*freguês* (P.)) irrespective of payment of previous debts – so many grams of powder and ounces of shot, fifteen caps, a knife, four litres of kerosene, five kilos of salt, a new shirt, a kilo of sugar, two needles, a button. Each item is listed and the prices are calculated in the right-hand margin. He informs the client of the total debt as she or he bundles up the things to carry home. Onlookers crowd around the counter, taking note of everything that goes on. Sometimes, the leader allows his own children in behind. Normally, only his wife or another trusted associate will be allowed to enter the inner recesses of the shop.

The definition of ownership of the coop stock is a matter of disagreement and ambivalence. Several interpretations govern the way distribution is handled or understood. In one common view, coop stock is regarded as the unfairly acquired property of the leader. It is treated in the same way as the property of any person who owns more than another, any *hiku* (from the Portuguese *rico*, 'rich man'). From this perspective, the leader is a bad relative, since he does not give freely of what he has not worked for in the first place. He is pressured by his closer relations to give them more than their fair share of the supplies. Later they complain that he has been miserly and unfair because he favoured someone else. Often leaders give preference to their own family's needs, and in their houses one finds a greater quantity of newer cooking pots, mosquito nets, clothes, shotguns and other items, though this wealth is not comparable to that of Cariú bosses. It marks the leaders out as being particularly subject to the predatory begging of their relations, at least in their own eyes. Certainly leaders are compelled to stealth if they want to preserve their own good reputation and a personal supply of some bought *necessidade*. A second attitude to coop stock treats it as without an owner. This is used as justification for not paying back debts. Since the leader has not worked to achieve the stock of goods, they are not 'his' but rather a gift, a windfall from benevolent foreigners (such as OXFAM, FUNAI, or the Canadian Embassy) to each person in the 'community'. The stock is then thought of rather like gathered fruits from the forest, and is subject to similar rules of appropriation: those who gather fastest and most furiously get more. Finally, villagers might view the objects that are brought back for them by the leader as already their property. This happens when the coop's stock is purchased independently of any loan or gift from an outside agency. Rubber, handicrafts, or livestock are accumulated and sold by the leader in the towns downriver. As a relative, he ought to behave as an intermediary between maker and buyer, so that the products continue to be thought of as belonging to the producer until the moment they are sold. Then the leader should fetch individual commissions (*encomendas* (P.)) from the city with the proceeds, rather than acting as a merchant who buys goods and resells them to his kin at marked-up prices. The money used to buy goods is not his, the thinking goes, but instead belongs to the person who produced the product. It ought to come back again to the maker as the thing s/he asked for, with no profit being creamed off in the process.

Once during late May 1984, Pancho came back from a trip downriver bringing enough supplies for everyone. He had been absent for several months and the village was out of salt, kerosene, and ammunition. Some had exchanged a few kilos of rubber with passing traders, or at the *barracão* in Mamoeira, for a little shot or some kerosene. Only one of the eight *estradas* had been opened up that year, and very little rubber was being produced. Instead, male collective work had been focused on making a new house for Pancho, clearing the village of scrub and, together with the women, planting the beach gardens with peanuts and watermelon. Otherwise people were engaged in small-group activities such as marking out new gardens. A flu epidemic had just swept the river, and in most households production had come to a standstill. On arrival, Pancho expressed his anger to me. He said that nothing got done when he was away and that his people were irresponsible and lazy. (He was speaking in the huge veranda of his new house at the time). He therefore decided that he would not distribute any ammunition to the villagers until they had cleared every single rubber estrada and begun regular production. He communicated this decision to everyone. His brother-in-law, Zé, was disgusted with this behaviour. Had he not looked after the village, organized the collective clearing of village scrub and the building of Pancho's house and planted his peanut garden? Hadn't everyone been afflicted with a terrible flu and hadn't he himself nearly died? Pancho's withholding of the ammunition, in the name of forcing people to produce and pay their debts to the coop, was no different from the high-handed behaviour of the Cariú bosses. At this time Zé constantly referred to his brother-in-law as *o patrão* (the boss), rather than *en chai* (my brother-in-law). Few leaders behave in such a high-handed fashion, and when they do it is only a temporary phenomenon. When Pancho's ammunition ran out, he had no more hold on the coop's clients than any one else. Control over material things is not self-perpetuating, for distribution is eventually effected willy-nilly. The leader's real monopoly is his knowledge of how to deal with city people, the foreigners who give donations, organize healthcare, or sell goods and buy rubber. People who go to the city to hospital, to sign up for a pension, or to study are often dependent on the superior knowledge of the leader during their stay. The stories they later tell only back up his position of power in his community. It is not temporary ownership of goods that gives him power, but rather his ability to get them.

The coop leader knows how to engage more or less successfully in relations of exchange with the Nawa. But then he is afflicted with the problem of transforming the commodities obtained according to anti-social principles into things that can be transacted according to social ones. The logic of commodity transaction dictates that he distribute them in expectation of reciprocity. But the sleight-of-hand involved in making a commodity appear to be a present is difficult, and the ability that leaders have to manage it defines the tenor of their relations with their 'clients' and the extent to which they are defined as bosses (one of them) or as kinsmen (one of us). If the male leader has tried to act in a coercive manner, coop members criticize him: 'He is not a boss, he does not own the land,' they say, 'so he cannot ask us to pay rent for the *estradas*. The coop is not his property, it is ours. It belongs to the *comunidade* (P. = community).'

To understand this use of the Portuguese term *comunidade*, it is necessary to dwell further upon Cashinahua notions of property. The Cashinahua do not have well-defined concepts of commonly held property, communal ownership, or unitary corporate action upon the basis of which they might organize stable and self-perpetuating corporations or social groups. At issue here are concepts relating to movable goods on the one hand and to land ownership on the other. Things are owned by separate persons and relationships are constructed on the basis of transactions between two individuals rather than between groups or between a leader and a group.[6] When outside agencies treat what they also term the 'community' as if it were corporately based, for example, making a loan of capital to the cooperative, they come up against this singularizing vision of personhood and social action and competing definitions of who owns the coop stock. This is also true of 'communal' property – Recreio's one outboard engine, for example. The villagers treated such objects either as Pancho's property or as ownerless and according to him this was why community machines were always broken. If no one owns them, then no one takes care of them.

When land is at issue, it is clear that no one individual owns land; but then neither does a collection of individuals. Once, when discussing the illegal incursions by Nawa fishermen on lakes located on indigenous land, my informant exclaimed that since God had made the earth and the lakes, no individual could own it. If the Cashinahua understood this, he explained, the Cariú did not – so when they were expelled it was with complete justification. They were trying to appropriate the land as well as its products. The problem remains of explaining how certain people have equal claims upon the use of defined tracts of land such as that within the village bounds. This is solved by designating the main leader as *ibu*. Here it is best to not to gloss the term as 'owner' but rather, following the sense of 'parent', as 'responsible one'. The main leader himself does not own the village, its land and *estradas*, then, he is merely responsible for them. He should organize the maintenance of the settlement and the major paths that run through it and connect it to the gardens. This meaning governs certain uses of the term *comunidade*. When village paths are in need of clearing, for example, people say that the work to be done is on behalf of the *comunidade* and that the main leader, as a parental *ibu*, should initiate and organize the collective work required. So every few months he calls all the men to spend one day cutting down the undergrowth with their machetes. On the morning of the appointed day, often a Saturday, he shouts out in the formal manner for the men to assemble in his house to eat. They come bearing plates of food or bowls of *caissuma* to be shared in the collective meal. The female leader should serve them with the meat or fish that her husband has caught and the *caissuma* she has prepared. After the meal, machetes are sharpened and the work party, slashing down the brush in close formation, makes its way steadily through the designated area. The atmosphere is one of excitement and the workers let out whoops from time to time. Between bouts of intense work they stand joking and smoking cigarettes, the sweat pouring down their bodies. There is a pervasive feeling of male solidarity. Only the leader refrains from entering into the group, instead performing smaller tasks on his own at the periphery. Usually the majority of the village's adult men and older boys take part in the main work group. Younger boys aged between nine and thirteen clear some smaller area separately, in a style imitating the adults. Only old men and those currently at odds with the leader keep away on such occasions. The absence of any able-bodied man is conspicuous, and indicates a dispute between the two men.

This work can be seen as 'helping' (*dabe-*) the leader as a son helps his father. Labour is 'lent' to him, and since he is the 'principal labourer', the final product is legitimately attributed to him as its main author. Workers and the leader are identified. In this specific sense, *comunidade* encompasses all the workers including the leader. Other meanings of the term emerge in other contexts and from other points of view. For example, a man who refuses to work is rejecting the leader in his guise as *ibu* of the village. Viewed from his perspective, the collective work may be interpreted as if it is for the benefit of the leader alone. The villagers may say that when they cleared the scrub they were 'working on his behalf' (*dayaxun-*) rather than helping (*dabe-*) him. The implication is of separation between them, and stress is placed on difference rather than identity. In this second sense, then, the term *comunidade* refers to the leader and his faction alone. The people of Recreio sometimes used the term in a third sense that denied that the leader was part of the community. For example, when Zé left Recreio to make a new settlement down river in Santa Vitória in 1985 he told me bitterly: 'It was us who did all this; there was nothing when we arrived, just jungle and that's all. We cut down trees, planted gardens, cleared the scrub from the field. The boss says it is his, but he's not the owner, no Missus. It was with our work that all this was done, we really struggled. It's ours, the *comunidade*'s, not his!' Used thus the term *comunidade* no longer indicates 'belonging to the leader our kinsman'. Instead, it means 'belonging to us and not the boss', who is thereby excluded from the group. The village space belongs only to those who created it by physical labour. The 'boss' did not work on it, so it is not his.

The semantic flexibility that characterizes use of the term *comunidade* allows the Cashinahua to capture something of the ambiguities inherent in personal action in the context of modern social life. To recapitulate: It may signify a kinship-based group whose members share a common interest in 'helping' their more senior kinsman and where individual action takes place in relation to him as part of and at the forefront of the *comunidade*. Here the underlying sense is of temporary unity between autonomous workers and the male leader who is 'the same' as them. Secondly, the term is also used placing emphasis on separation and difference, where individual action is done 'on behalf of' (-*xun*-) another person. Nevertheless, this separation is encompassed by the 'inside' – the domain where sociality is produced – and a spirit of friendly cooperation governs the relationship. The worker's personal autonomy is not threatened. Thirdly, other factors may cause the relation to veer into antisociality when the main leader tries to coerce or otherwise mistreat the workers, thus threatening their autonomy. The relationship is then interpreted as constituting the interface between the inside and the outside. Thus 'community' (if we can adopt this term from the Cashinahua usage) is never stable, but rather grows or fades in the tension between the assertion of personal autonomy and the centripetal pressures that make autonomous people work together

As a responsible kinsman, a male leader must use his special attachment to things or to the settlement land to engender sociality and thereby make community. When he fails he is destructive of it, as when Pancho tried to restrict access to the coop's ammunition, after which episode several people left the village. Such disputes about things lead to the breakup of settlements. In the case of organizing collective work and meals, the leader is usually successful in working harmoniously with the village men for the benefit of all. In these moments the leader is not 'boss' but 'one of us', and the interest of one is the interest of all. Such idyllic moments are essential to the progress of particular communities. The healthy and harmonious state of social life is concretely manifested in the physical state of the village and its paths and gardens. A beautiful, well-tended settlement indicates that the male leader stands for community more often than he stands against it. He manages to be 'one of us' more often than 'one of them'. Those who live in an ugly, overgrown settlement might well be at greater odds with their own leader. Like the Cubeo headman, the male leader is often the one blamed if a feeling of social harmony is not maintained, and, like Cubeo local groups, the Cashinahua 'community' is always on the move, either growing stronger and more unified, or weaker and less coordinated (Goldman 1963). In the ambiguous meaning of the term *comunidade* one may discern the difficulties inherent in this progress. On the other hand, the Cashinahua term that can sometimes be glossed as 'community' is more directly suggestive of the constant work required in making a community as well as this organizational volatility. *Mae* is a term that is used to describe any settlement, whether it be a rubber-tapper's *colocação*, a pre-colonial *maloca*, or a modern village or hamlet. *Mae evapa* (big *mae*) means a 'town' or a 'city'. The term implies, in its most common usage as a single settlement, a space of land cleared of trees and scrub upon which houses stand. Such land is constantly reinvaded by vegetation, and the idea of *mae* contains the assumption that the physical space is not fixed but constantly created. In verb form, *mae-* means 'to move house', suggesting both the constant movement that pits the living environment against human agency and also the process whereby communities are formed from the moving bodies of autonomous people.

In this chapter I have described some of the most important facets of the formation of larger-scale settlements or villages amongst the Cashinahua during the 1980s and 1990s. I showed how the main leader is a central figure in the making of these modern communities and how he must juggle his dual role as internal leader and external representative. Instead of discussing this juggling as occurring at a historical transition-point between 'traditional' and 'modern' social forms, I was careful to demonstrate that the successive innovations that have been imposed upon or made available to these people during the twentieth century (enslavement in the *aviamento* system, renewed independence in Indigenous Areas, the cooperative movement) are, whenever possible, adapted to the internal dynamic of day-to-day village life. Although some innovations are problematic, causing such difficulties as the contemporary lack of self-sufficiency in production and dependence upon commodities, they are used as a positive force for the defence of rights to community land or within a process of ethnogenesis. Adaptation to the day-to-day dynamic of life is achieved through the relationship between male and female leaders who are the *ibu* of the village. The role they play in maintaining the bodies of its people through activities constitutive of sociality is fundamental. The constant tension between the production of sociality and the swings into anti-sociality results in the permanent instability of the communities that are formed. This is exemplified in the struggle for the definition of transactions with the main leader, who is caught between the need to 'make true gifts' and the necessity to 'make reciprocal exchanges', that is, to navigate the treacherous semantic waters between *inan-* and *inankuin-* as he manages the economic and political aspects of the Cashinahua engagement with the capitalist world system. Such struggles over meaning as this – or those over the cooperative or the imported term 'community' – can be seen as emerging from the classic dilemma that Amazonian societies created for themselves, in their fundamental need to plunder or milk that which is different and dangerous in order to regenerate and create that which is similar and safe (Overing 1981, 1983–4). In this chapter I have shown that this same dilemma informs the making of Cashinahua communities historically. In the next chapter, I return to a cosmological dimension and discuss the making of community from the perspective of ritual. But before I do so, one last point is important here. This concerns the place of embodied personhood in these processes. In the end it is difficult to abstract a notion of 'community' at all with respect to Cashinahua modes of social organization, where everything is transitional and what is one thing at one moment may become its opposite at another. Without the sort of weight and clarity that a notion of communal property would give them, communities form and break up with remarkable speed. A 'village' or *mae* may be portrayed as just a temporary spatial location for Cashinahua individuals caught in the flux of history. But to make this analysis would be to ignore the historical weight and substance that these people see themselves as carrying in their own bodies. If male leaders bring them together, as Pancho did when he visited his relatives in Peru, he may do so because of this, the fruit of past 'good living', and upon the promise of continuing to constitute sociality in the future.

Notes

1. Kensinger 1973, 1974, 1995, discusses sorcery and shamanism. See also McCallum (1996a) and Lagrou (1991).
2. There are some exceptions. For example, Basso (1973) describes the Xinguano ceremonial statuses that both men and women inherit, mentioned also by Gregor (1985) and Viveiros de Castro (1977). Basso writes that Kalapalo women and men become leaders, and mentions 'senior women'.
3. This argument is put strongly by Lea (1986, 2000) in relation to the Gê.
4. Gow (1991) coined the phrase 'relations of caring'.
5. *Quebra* is the percentage of weight deducted by the purchaser of rubber in order to compensate for future weight loss due to water loss.
6. The difficulties in applying the notion of 'corporate group' in Amazonia are discussed in Overing Kaplan (ed.) (1977) and Seeger *et al.* (1979).

It is worth summarizing some of the issues at stake. Lévi-Strauss (1969) argues that Amazonian political structure is founded on the balanced exchange of the 'values' 'women, words and things' between leader and 'group'. Clastres argues, in contrast, that the supreme 'value' — women — are 'pure and simple gifts from the group to its leader, a gift with no reciprocity' and that the relation between leader and 'group' is not one of 'balanced reciprocity' (Clastres 1977:31). Such non-exchange ejects power outside society, because the leader is the eternal debtor or 'servant' of the 'group' rather than its ruler. At issue here are the notions of group, on the one hand, and exchange, on the other. Gow (1991:227) points out that Clastres uses a mistaken notion of group that ill suits the ethnographic context. Often the most important function of leaders in Amazonian societies is to create rather than 'lead' local groups (Kaplan 1975; Rivière 1984; Kracke 1978). This creation of groups is a continuous process, not a single event. The proponents of both views — reciprocity's centrality, or else its absence — may be criticized for using a false dichotomy between leader and group, that reifies the notion of 'group', making it at times a subject (the giver of women) and at times an object (the receiver of words and things). The kindreds out of which communities draw their residents are in no sense a bounded group (Overing Kaplan 1977; Seeger et al. 1979; Rivière 1984).

6

Ritual and Regeneration

A 'community' is the spatial and corporeal dimension of sociality, and the visible manifestation of the myriad processes and actions that go into its making. It bears witness to the micro-historical processes that have produced true persons as well as to larger historical events and developments. Both the little quotidian acts that compose the subsistence economy and the transactions taking place within institutions shaped by national or international forces (such as the cooperative movement) deal in some measure with transformations from the outside to the inside. Both are 'historical' in nature. This is so whether one takes the Cashinahua perspective, seeing micro-histories sedimented into the bodies of active living persons as knowledge and power, or whether one takes an external perspective, seeking trends and structures in the modern political economy of the region. Transformation from the outside to the inside is the dominant movement in these historical processes, and may be distinguished as the constructive element *par excellence* in the 'making of community'. But there is another dimension to this manufacture, the ritual one. It is described in this chapter.

Kachanaua is a part of this never-ending process of making community. When I asked informants to tell me the purpose of this ritual complex, they invariably said that it is held to ensure that gardens produce abundantly. They explained that it works by humans 'calling' or 'naming' (*kena-*) the plants in the gardens during the ritual, which has an impact on them analogous to that upon the bodies of children made to grow through naming in *Nixpo Pima*. *Kachanaua* is therefore appropriately described as an increase ritual. However, the ritual is efficacious in multiple ways, and a close examination of the cycle of events involved allows not only an appreciation of this complexity but also a deeper understanding of the relation between gender, personhood and the social process. Through a discussion of the meanings constituted and actions performed in different moments of *Kachanaua*, this chapter and the next brings, to a close our analysis of gender and sociality amongst the Cashinahua, and through the prism they allow, amongst Amazonian peoples.

The Cashinahua distinguish between 'small' and 'real' *Kachanaua*. Small *Kachanaua* run one or two nights and are described as 'mere games' (*só brincadeira* (P.)). Full-scale 'real' *Kachanaua* take two weeks to a month to perform and involve a series of lesser festivals of the same type as the small *Kachanaua*, building up to ceremonial giving of food between moieties. If one of the village leaders feels that there is a scarcity of meat, he might arrange a small *Kachanaua*. It begins with an evening dance, during which garden-plant naming songs are sung. Afterwards most of the men of the village spend several days away hunting and fishing. Most people view *Kachanaua* as a means to satisfy their desire to eat meat and fish to the point of satiation. One way of describing *Kachanaua* is to say that it is 'head-making' (*buxka vai*). An abundance of heads of game animals is a synonym for the abundance of meat. *Kachanaua* is thus a means both of fostering vegetable life and of achieving large quantities of meat. In the past the large *Kachanaua* was also a means of stimulating the production of fermented corn *caissuma*, but this practice has been abandoned. Nowadays women make ordinary unfermented *caissuma* as well as boiled manioc and banana for the food prestations and feasts that follow the hunts. After describing the ritual events, I will show how an analysis of deeper meanings and metaphorical references reveals the connection between the death of the game animals and fish and the propagation of the garden fruits and vegetables. The Cashinahua themselves offered me no explanation of this connection.

Kachanaua is also viewed as a means of improving community morale. Smaller *Kachanaua* are explicitly held 'to liven up' (*pra animar* (P.)) the village, or to create a mood of animation after a particularily unhappy period. A sense of buoyancy is an integral aspect of the feeling of community, of the sense that the *mae* is a living and growing entity. Thus a real *Kachanaua* may be held after a minor epidemic, a period of scarcity, or, when a year or so has passed, a death. People are enthusiastic about the ritual because they have fun. They say that it is a game, that they are 'playing' (*beyus-*), the same term used to describe children's games, or sports such as football. Such rituals are termed in regional Portuguese *mariri*. Visitors from the city consider *mariri* as a kind of carnival, and this portrayal seems to have its counterpart in the Cashinahua description of it as *beyus-*. But in fact the carnival aspect and the fun have a serious religious purpose that the Cashinahua do not stress when describing the festival to most outsiders. Informants told me that the songs that name plants are 'prayers', using the Portuguese term *reza* as a translation for the Cashinahua *deve*. Thus a religious weight is necessary for making community, requiring an atmosphere of happiness and a mood of animation.

When for any reason the people of the community are depressed and activity is slack, then a leader might decide to initiate such a festival, just as Cubeo headmen do with drinking parties (Goldman 1963:202). Thus, when the vegetables of the garden are made plentiful, the people of the village are assured a means of strength and growth.

Another function we may attribute to *Kachanaua* is that of defining indigenous identity. When a visitor from one of the pro-Indian NGOs is about to arrive, leaders think about calling a *Kachanaua* in order to entertain them and show 'how Indians play' (*como os índios brincam* (P.)). This may be looked upon as part of a process of 'ethnogenesis'. In Brazilian areas during the twentieth century it became logistically difficult to organize *Kachanaua* because of the physical dispersal of the Cashinahua on *colocaçoes*. In some areas, such as the Énvira, people stopped organizing the ritual and even forgot how to perform it, perhaps in an effort to escape negative evaluation as *caboclo* by the local *Cariú*. Even the oldest inhabitants of Fronteira, who were born and brought up on the Énvira, told me that they had not seen a *Kachanaua* festival until their relatives from Peru arrved in the village. In other areas, notably on the Tarauacá river, it was never forgotten, but rarely performed. This situation has now been reversed. The Cashinahua now have a justification for turning the negative evaluation of such markers of Indian identity on its head. In NGO workers and anthropologists, they have found admiring external witnesses from the cities. More important, perhaps, they have the political and logistic means to perform rituals of this type, now that they have regrouped in the Indigenous Areas. During the 1980s and 1990s they made full use of this opportunity. However, it would be wrong to overstress this 'ethnic self-affirmation' aspect of *Kachanaua*. The major rituals are not conducted from this point-of-view and take place with or without external stimulation such as the presence of anthropologists or political rights workers.

Kachanaua can be held during any time of the year, but is most likely to be held during the months of the rainy season around December to February when the main ridge-garden corn crop ripens, the time of year called *xekitian*, corn-time, when it may be combined with *Nixpo Pima*. Both men and women participate in *Kachanaua*. The gender of the leading protagonists at the high point, when the food prestations are made, is always male, whether the givers be men, or women playing the male role. People distinguish not only between real and play *Kachanaua*, but also between women's (*ainbunaki*) and men's (*junibunaki*) *Kachanaua*. During the women's *Kachanaua* a central aspect of the culminating day is gender-role reversal. In all *Kachanaua* both men and women take part.

Between 1984 and 1990 I participated in one woman's real *Kachanaua*, one man's real one and seven lesser men's ones. The man's real one was held in Recreio on the Brazilian side of the frontier and the woman's real one was held in Conta on the Peruvian side. Four of the lesser *Kachanaua* I witnessed were held in settlements on the Brazilian Purus and three on the Jordão river. The following description is based on these experiences, on analysis of the songs, prayers and myths that play a part in the proceedings, and on interviews and conversations with Cashinahua people.

The *Kachanaua* Ritual

Kachanaua may be initiated by any leading man in the village, either as his own idea or in response to a suggestion from someone in his family. He ought to inspire village-wide collaboration, which is not always the case, especially in the larger settlements. The real *Kachanaua* I witnessed in Recreio was initiated by the main leader with the support of Zé Augusto, his father-in-law, who was the principal chant-leader of the village. It was held during the first two weeks of November 1984 just after the planting of the new gardens. It was intended, Pancho told me, to end a period of unhappiness during which several important people had died, including his first wife Luisa, Zé Augusto's daughter, and Sampaio, the father of his second. Various others disasters had befallen the village, such as a month-long influenza epidemic and a period of meat and trade-good shortage. Pancho explained to me that the *Kachanaua* would cheer everyone up. It would also celebrate the end of a period of hard work by the young men, who had cleared a demarcation path around the AIAP.

In order to announce and discuss his decision to initiate a large *Kachanaua*, Pancho called a meeting. He began the proceedings by asking his mother-in-law, who had lost both husband and eldest daughter, if she wanted a *Kachanaua*; and after she agreed to the idea, several other women added their support. The leader then asked again, this time addressing the assembled women. They responded with a cry of '*Heeeee!*', which is an expression of happiness. He then turned to the men, who as usual were sitting apart, and asked: 'Since there are many beautiful women, do you want to liven yourselves up?' The men shouted '*Heeeee!*', indicating their approval. That same afternoon several young men went to the forest close to the village and a Dua man felled a bottle palm tree (*Iriartea ventricosa* (Lat.)) (Figure 11), so that the *Kachanaua* belonged to the Dua moiety. A section about three metres long was cut, hollowed

Figure 11. The bottle palm (from H.W. Bates *The Naturalist on the River Amazons*, London: John Murray, Albemarle Street, w. 1910)

out and attached to a pole by means of bark strips. This was the *kacha*. It was carried back to the village slung on the shoulders of two Inu men, to the accompaniment of rhythmic shouts of '*He He He!*'. No-one paid much attention, except for small children, who began playing with the *kacha* as soon as it was dumped on the patio in front of the leader's house, where the dancing was to be held. Over the next two weeks it was progressively destroyed by children and the village cow, until it was actually broken up by young men on the final night. Early that evening people began to gather in the leader's house and on the patio in front of it and then the female chant-leader began to sing *Hu Hu* songs. With the chant-leader at the front, about ten women linked arms and began walking in a circle around the *kacha*, repeating each short verse in unison after her. After half an hour the women stopped and everyone went home. Someone commented that things only get really lively when the men take part.

The Cashinahua call this genre of song *Hu Hu* after the rhythmic sound that is used to punctuate each verse. Following them, I use the phrase 'Ho Ho song' to refer to the genre. There are male and female types of Ho Ho songs, and these are considered the most important 'prayers' (*deve*) to be sung during the various nights of the ritual. Their rhythm marks the step of the dance, which picks up soon after the participants begin walking in a circle. People dance according to gendered styles. Women link arms with the person in front, hold hands with the one behind and step sideways, crossing their feet with a gentle swing at the end of each beat. Men put their arms over each other's shoulders and dance more vigorously and uniformly. Some women merely walk to the rhythm. The word for dance of any kind is *nava*; thus *kachanaua* means 'the dance of the *kacha*'. It will be recalled that the substantive *Nava* (or, in my adaptation for English text, 'Nawa') may be glossed as 'Foreigner' and sometimes as 'Spirit', meanings that are of direct significance to the interpretation of the ritual developed below.

Several nights after the women's gentle start, a similar dance was held, but this time men participated from the beginning and a male chant-leader (*chana xanen ibu*), led the singing. The formation was typical: The dancers made a circle around the *kacha*, men on one side and women on the other, eldest women walking in front of the younger. Children tagged on at the end of the women during moments when the circle was not closed, or else held on to the adult's clothing, forming appendages in clumps of twos and threes on the outside. Otherwise they played in the centre of the circle of chanting dancers, darting at intervals through their legs. Participation in *Kachanaua* is entirely voluntary. On this occasion as on many others most of the male dancers were young and most of the female dancers did not have to care for very young children, so their group was composed of adolescents or elder women. A large crowd, outnumbering the participants, sat on logs, benches, or upturned tortoise shells around the edges of the patio. Sometimes family groups formed, but mostly men and women sat separately. The front of the leader's house was taken over by women, who held sleeping babies in their laps or swung them in the hammocks that they had brought with them. There was no moon and the kerosene lamps threw a weak yellow light, forming pools in the blackness.

The first line of the song is sung by the chant-leader and then it is repeated by the dancers. Men repeat in the same gentle tone as the chant-leader, whereas the women use a harsher pitch, that rises at the end, creating a contrast with the smooth and melodious male voices. The following is a typical women's Ho Ho song:

Ho ho ho ho, ho ho ho ho
Its juice dripping
Maize juice dripping
Dripping, dripping
Ho ho ho ho, ho ho ho ho,
Peanut juice dripping
Dripping, dripping
Ho ho ho ho, ho ho ho ho,
Manioc juice dripping
Dripping, dripping
Ho ho ho ho, ho ho ho ho,
Banana juice dripping
etc.

Men's Ho Ho chants share this repetitive structure and also refer to garden products. While the limited set of meaningless rhythmic punctuation marks such as Ho Ho are constantly repeated, the referent is changed, so that all the products of the garden are named. The songs are in 'Old One's language' (*Xenipabu Hancha*) and are only partially intelligible to most people. Most of the older persons who lead the chanting do understand them, however. Everybody is aware that the song's purpose is to summon and name the vegetables; indeed, the names of the plants in the songs are their everyday names, not esoteric terms. The following is the first song that Perreirinha and his son Nilo sang in a mini-*Kachanaua* performed on the Jordão during my visit to Seringal Boa Esperanza in 1985:

Ho ho ho, ho ho ho,
Chai came to get me
Chai came to get me
The *chai*s came
The way the fish go upriver
The way they go downriver
Chai came to get me
Make *caissuma* for me
Hua maize *caissuma*
Give me to drink
Drink it with *chai*
Drink it with Inka
With the Inka people
Give me to drink
Drink the swirling liquid
Drink it with our *chai*
Ho ho ho, ho ho ho,
Ho ho ho, ho ho ho, [etc.]

The song indicates the presence of visiting Nawa, spirits who address the residents as *Chai*. Therefore the relationship between outsiders and insiders is one of affinity. The spirits name themselves as the Inka people. They describe how they came to get the real people, took them back to their village and gave them maize *caissuma* to drink.[1] The song continues and in each verse the same lines are repeated, but the name of the food that the insiders are invited to consume is changed. The singer mentions all the different kinds of vegetable foods. In the next song, the rhythm changes to a four beat. The song refers to each of the plants that are cultivated on high land or on the beach in turn and to their maturation (*kani-*). All the songs I recorded are about vegetables and fruits that are cultivated in the gardens. None of them are about game animals or fish.

Whilst the singers circled around the *kacha*, the onlookers talked in low voices, or sat watching in silence; but soon the calm mood began to give way to one of excitement, as the dance-leader changed the tempo, responding to increased trumpet-blowing and shouts of *Heee!* from the men. The dancers began to leap at speed around the patio (*ixchubain-*), a dangerous operation on a moonless night. The fast rhythm contrasted with the more stately sway of the earlier dancing to the beat of the Ho Ho songs. If the chant-leader decides to skip this part, when the dancing takes a more energetic turn, or if particiapants preempt him, the conclusion of the first phase of Ho Ho singing and dancing could be signalled by the start of sexual taunting without any jumping. On this particular night in Recreio, the taunting began within an hour of the start. This is an exchange of insults between men and women that has a competitive flavour. It is referred to as *Kaxin* (Vampire Bat) or *Hina Ichaka* (Penis Insulting). At the instigation of the chant-leader, the men began taunting the women with cries of '*kaxin!*', which is a perjorative euphemism for 'vagina'. The cries obey a staccato rhythm that increases as the men begin adding other references such as *hue* (a frog), *heu* (a large toad) and other mainly inedible and unpleasant animals. Before long one of the elder women began the plaintive first bars of the *Hina Ichaka* song. Its melody contrasts strongly with the men's shouting. Each woman sings her insults independently, but extending the last sound out so that there is a continuous hum at the same pitch as that of the other women. Yet their insults can be heard clearly, and provoke more and more hilarity as the women become inspired and invent new and increasingly hilarious comparisons for male sexual organs. 'Just like a huge tortoise neck. Same as a big tapir penis', they sing, as they lean close to their victims. Women are instigated to flirt directly and publicly with their husbands, lovers or intended sexual partners.

After a while several women slipped off into the darkness to collect bundles of palm-straw from the roofs of abandoned houses or old chicken huts. All the women and most of the older men left the circle of male dancers, who continued their taunts in a taut tempo, punctuated by staccato shouts of '*He!*'. Then the women lit the straw bundles in the embers of cooking fires and came running towards the circle of men. Holding out the flames they swept them at their legs, taking aim for particular men, usually their husbands, but in fact any woman can attack any man. In order to avoid their fast-moving pursuers (even great-grandmothers are capable of great bursts of speed) the still chanting dancers were leaping and running and the circle itself no longer kept to its course around the *kacha*, but zipped all over the patio and into the edges of the darkness. By this time the bodies of the men were glistening with sweat, so that they were not actually burnt by the flames. If they had been, I was told, it would mean that they would be protected from snakebite. The women shouted rather than sang phrases from the taunting song between gasps for breath, as they went in to attack. All of a sudden they succeeded in breaking up the circle and various women set off after particular men around and through the houses. Even some spectators found themselves obliged to take to their heels. The flames quickly die out and the attackers return often to relight them or to make new bundles. During one of these lulls the men managed to regroup, and when they were attacked again succeeded in catching hold of several women and dragged them, struggling with all their might, into the circle of dancing men.

There were another three such sessions before the grand finale. An interval of five days preceded this final day, during which time the men intensified their hunting and fishing in order to be able to amass plenty of surplus game. They set out in small groups of twos and threes. One group slashed a path into a little-hunted area where certain kinds of game were said to abound. They built a shelter and stayed there hunting for a week. Others went on family camping trips to nearby lakes for three or four days, after fish and caiman. Some men decided not to participate, or limited their hunting to the day before the finale. The hunters brought back the meat and fish, preserved by daily smoke-roasting over a low fire, to the village. Their arrival was carefully coordinated. They waited for each other outside the village so as to enter it in a group. As the men walked in among the houses their catches were prominently displayed for all to see. Unmarried men handed over the catch to their mothers and married men gave it to their wives or mothers-in-law. The women safely stored it. There was much excitement and each house was buzzing with talk about which hunter had made what kill. The women then began intensifying their preparations for the finale. In the early morning of the following day one of the older women invited the others to harvest manioc in her garden. An adult woman from every house in the village, accompanied perhaps by a girl, joined the crowd gathering in one of the houses, bringing her basket and a machete. As always, the hostess served boiled manioc and a little meat to the waiting group before they set out. This particular collective harvest was very festive, and the women laughed and joked more than usual.

The men had also brought back genipapo fruit for their women, and that afternoon, after the cooking was done, they set about painting designs on each other's faces and bodies. First, brick-red urucu was smeared on the face and rubbed in to form a pale orangey layer. This is the only occasion when urucu is used as a base for genipapo. It is never used to excess, and when I applied too much on myself, the women laughed and said I looked like a Kulina. After this the design, *kene*, is drawn by one of the older women using the preparation of genipapo juice. A variety of designs are used. The colourless genipapo paint turns black within an hour of application. That evening some of the men were also painted.

The *kacha* was prepared. Two poles were erected at each end of it and a cord strung between them. A few manioc tubers and bananas dangled from it over the hollow (Figure 12). The following dawn a trumpet blast

Figure 12. The *kacha*

summoned people to the leader's house for the *Kachanaua Chanikinan*, the official announcement that the ceremony is to be held. After breakfast in the leader's house, a group of Dua men, but not Pancho himself, walked into the forest on the downriver side of the settlement as far as a clump of palm trees and began cutting down the fronds to make their ornaments (*dau*). From the village we could hear clearly the frequent trumpet blasts and shouts of *Heee* that they sent up. Suddenly the noise began to increase in volume and frequency, and everyone knew that the 'visitors' were approaching the village, in the guise of the Dua men transformed into *yuxin* (spirits). Several Inani women (the wives and mothers of the Dua men) had already joined them. They were indistinguishable under the palm fronds as the group came into sight at the edge of the village, arms linked and in close formation, two or three abreast. Chanting, jumping forward and letting out trumpet blasts, the group gathered momentum as it neared the patio and the *kacha*. From either side of the path a 'reception committee' of Inu moiety men, brandishing guns, machetes and other instruments, leapt out of hiding in a mock ambush. Shouting out, they rushed up to the *yuxin* and grabbed their arms, thus joining into the procession as it swept into the patio (Figure 13). Several men let off their guns, the explosions echoing through the length of the village and causing young mothers to cover their babies' ears.

Figure 13. Women's *Kachanaua* in Conta – Jumping into the village

The men of the receiving moiety greeted their affines with the formula *'Aniwa Chain!'* signifying 'Welcome Brother-in-law Cousin'. This is the equivalent in 'Old One's Speech' (*Xenipabu Hancha*) of the modern greeting *Min ma huai?* (Are you arriving?). The group circled the *kacha* once before throwing off their palm leaf decorations and taking their places on stools and benches placed in a semi-circle around the patio. All the Dua men and boys sat down, whether or not they had come in disguised as spirits, except those who had not been hunting or fishing. The Inani women, dressed in their best, hair combed and oiled, faces carefully painted with lipstick or urucu over the genipapo designs, took their places behind their Dua husbands. The Banu women (the sisters and mothers-in-law of the Dua) made ready to prepare plates of food for their Inu husbands or sons to give to their *chais*. While the Dua had been decorating themselves in the forest their sisters and mothers-in-law, the Banu, had been bringing baskets of cooked meat and pans of manioc, banana and *caissuma* and setting them up close to the patio. Following their Inu sons' or husbands' instructions, they had already divided the meat according to the number of presents required. One man, for example, calculated that he and his two eldest sons would give away thirty-two pieces of meat and fish.

Figure 14. Men's *Kachanaua* – Food prestation between *chais*

Pancho was the first to receive a present, from one of his wife's two brothers, who offered him a howler-monkey head decorated with a pair of red macaw feathers and flanked with a few pieces of boiled manioc. (Heads are an especially prized animal part.) Pancho's *chai* handed the enamel plate to him saying '*Aniwa Chain!*' and crying '*Hii-ii-iii!*' in a high-pitched tone. Pancho then handed the plate to his wife Anisa, who tipped the contents into a waiting pan and handed it back to her brother.

Other men and boys began taking their gifts to their *chais*, offering the best pieces to their actual brother-in-law, or to the eldest and most senior, but not omitting very young boys. Inu fathers directed their young sons to the latter's *chais*, thus indirectly giving to their sons-in-law. The givers returned each time to the women, who made up the plates for them, or handed them pans and buckets of corn *caissuma* or banana drink. Thus, in effect, women hand the food to men in an affinal relation to them, who formally give to men who are their own actual or categorical affines, who hand the food to their own spouses, who will shortly serve their husbands with what food they take to the communal meal. The marked prestation amidst all this is that between the men who call each other 'brother-in-law' or *chai*. But the women take charge of the food again once it has been given.

Once the flurry of giving was over, about twenty minutes after it started, Pancho arranged some of the discarded palm decorations to form a mat and each man brought a plate of food and a pan of *caissuma*, placing them in the centre. The feast began. The men proceeded by diving in to retrieve a chunk of meat and a piece of manioc, before sitting back on stools and benches to eat and chat. Nearly all the women and children retired to the leaders' house, where they too ate collectively, sitting on the floor around the bowls and plates each had contributed from the food received by their husbands. Each mother fed her own children from separate plates. Some women ate in their own houses, because their husbands had not taken part in the hunting and meat-giving preparations. The remaining meat was taken back to the houses and stored or hidden by the women. This same meat cannot be given back during the afternoon session when the Dua make return prestations to the Inu. By 10.00 a.m. the feast was over and everyone dispersed to work or rest as they pleased. Some visitors from Fronteira went fishing, in order to be able to make prestations during the afternoon. Most families enjoyed a large lunch as soon as their appetites returned, sitting in their own houses.

In the afternoon a group of Inu men went into the forest at the opposite or upstream end of the village to prepare their *dau*. As is usual these were more elaborate than the morning visitors' palm-leaf decorations, and the preparations took appreciably longer, involving toing and froing as helpers fetched feather headdresses, bamboo crowns, beads and so on. The decorations consist of chest-straps, palm-leaf half-skirts hanging down at the back, crowns of long trailing fronds and wound-in leaves, worn over bamboo or feather crowns and everyday Western-style clothes. Tall palm fronds are held up in front of each dancer's face. When they were ready the Inu entered the village in the same noisy style as had the Dua in the morning. The Dua ambushed them in turn and escorted them to the *kacha* with greetings of '*Aniwa Chain!*'. Once again they were accompanied by a few women of the opposite moiety (Banu). The circle did not break up, however, but fell to dancing around the *kacha* to a Ho Ho chant behind the chant-leader (an Inu man). They danced for about twenty minutes until the sun was low over the horizon and the chant-leader's wife told him it was time to give the presents of food. The chant-leader supervised the Inu feast, as the leader had arranged the Dua one that morning, and it followed the same sequence of events.

There was a short interval after the meal, when people took back their pots and pans, collected hammocks for their babies and came back in time to watch or take part in the dancing. This began at dusk and continued until one o'clock, when the remaining dancers dispersed. Chanters sang both Ho Ho songs and sexual taunts, but there was no fire-play, which is only supposed to take place at the beginning of the series of dances. Ideally the dancers should continue until dawn, and there should be such an abundance of *caissuma* that it is vomited up into the *kacha* hollow (a practice that has apparently been abandoned). During the night the *kacha* was broken up and the pieces carried off by young men to be placed stealthily in the hammocks of those who had not resisted the desire to go to sleep. This is described as *'nexman-'* (to submerge; to grope for fish underwater) and here signifies 'to enter the mosquito-net of a member of the opposite sex with seductive intentions'. I was unable to discover if any of the young men actually seduced their victims. In the morning the remains of the *kacha* were broken up and thrown into the forest.

I have described the Recreio ritual as a typical example of *Kachanaua*. But before bringing this section to a close it is useful to make a few comparisons with the Conta women's *Kachanaua* and the other small dances I saw in Recreio and along the Jordão river. In Conta the men spent just two or three days hunting – less time than in Recreio. There was only one small dance prior to the hunt and another on the night before the giving. Only a minority of the men and women of the village took part. In the morning Inani women collected at a downriver part of the village by a Dua man's house, where their husbands made them *dau* and dressed them. As they waited they painted their teeth black with *nixpo* and painted designs with lipstick on top of the genipapo painted on the day before. The women played their husbands and vice versa. Thus each addressed the other by their own real name for the day, husband transformed into wife and vice versa. Because of the gender-role reversal, the Inani 'become' Dua. In the other two entrances I observed on the Jordão, it was also the Dua who arrived in the morning and, as in Conta, they came from downriver.

As the Inani or 'Dua' *yuxin* entered the village, their husbands following behind with carrying baskets and holding babies, they were 'surprised' by Banu women ('Inu') holding weapons and greeting them with *'Aniwa Chain'*. After the food-giving the fifteen receivers shared a hasty feast before dispersing to their own houses to feed their families. In the afternoon the Banu's costumes were again more elaborate than their sisters-in-laws' had been and the entrance was followed by a short period of dancing around the *kacha*. Each of those who had given food in the morning received a present in return. Only those who had meat or fish as well as vegetable foods participated. Only women danced during the first two hours, after which they called to onlooking men to help them. It was explained to me that the elderly woman chant-leader was too tired to continue all night. During one of the following intervals a group of young men and boys, dressed in palm-leaves to represent *yuxin*, entered the patio and gave a performance that can best be described as a parody of *Kachanaua* dancing. Their movements were exaggerated and they sang in hoarse, disguised voices to great comic effect. There was much hilarity among the spectators. After about ten minutes the boy-spirits ended by kicking the *kacha*, and the women and their male helpers began to dance again. During the next interval two unnamed *yuxin*, one male and one female, both well-disguised young men wearing masks and comic clothes, arrived and began clowning. They pretended to scare the spectators and the female spirit dropped a bundle from under her skirt in an apparent imitation of birth. The two clowns were enacting *damiain* (McCallum in press). Shortly after this the leader, who had been observing the proceedings from his hammock, participating only by blowing his trumpet from time to time and shouting, gave directions for the younger men to break up the *kacha*. This was done and the dancing continued until dawn (Figure 12).

Kachanaua and the History of Sociality

Rivière mentions a Trio ritual that seems very similar to the Cashinahua *Kachanaua*. He says that '. . . while the Trio dance festival is an institutionalized way of bringing the outside inside, it also contains the means of restoring things to their normal if repatterned state' (1969:240). *Kachanaua* is certainly an institutionalized means of bringing the outside inside. In the Trio case the 'visitors' came from other, socially distant, settlements, unlike those in the Cashinahua case, where it is enough that members of one moiety make visible their embodied outsider aspect in the guise of spirits. Rivière goes on to say that the Trio dance festival represents '. . . . . social intercourse rather than isolation, friendship rather than suspicion, community rather than individual interest. It is a period during which mythical unity is achieved and during which the empirical diversity and contradictions of everyday life disappear' (1969:258). In what follows, I show that *Kachanaua* works much as did the Trio dance festival. But as an expression of 'unity' it is not one that overcomes empirical diversity and contradictions, if we understand these as embodied in living persons and expressed on a day-to-day basis in the tension between their capacities for making sociality or anti-sociality. The processes of everyday life are not expressed in the form and sequence of the ritual to be transcended, but rather to be renewed, or as Rivière puts it 'repatterned'. The Cashinahua ritual is concerned with the re-establishment of the mundane (not its interruption) within a context of ensuring the abundance of natural resources as the basis for the strengthening of sociality. More than this, it is steeped in hidden allusions to the very history of proper social intercourse, as we shall see here. Views differed as to the purpose and powers of the rites. Converts to evangelical Christianity (like Pancho) prefer to call them 'games', *brincadeira* (P.), but do not contest the exegesis of others, such as the *chana xanen ibu*, who stress the instrumentality of the rites in assuring healthy and productive gardens. Even the sceptical people of Fronteira, who are inclined to be derogatory about the old-fashioned way of life of the people of Recreio, recognized the rite's efficacy. Villagers readily explained to me that the purpose of the ritual is to liven things up, to play, to enjoy oneself and to put an end to a bad period in the life of the community. Everyone also insisted that it works by putting humans in contact with forest spirits. But who are these *yuxin?* My informants did not give me precise answers. I came to realize, for reasons I shall set out shortly, that they are wild plant spirits who give asexual reproductive power to the domesticated plants of the garden on behalf of their human affines, through the Ho Ho naming songs.

Kachanaua may be portrayed as a transformation of other Amazonian rituals that participants explain by direct reference to a corpus of myths. Stephen Hugh-Jones says of the Tukanoan Yurupari ritual complex that '. . . through ritual . . . the elaborate mythological systems of these people acquire their meaning as an active force and organizing principle in daily life' (1979:3). The Cashinahua did not explain *Kachanaua* to me in these terms; but mythology provides answers to many questions. For example, though I asked repeatedly what the *kacha* symbolized and what it was for, I received only the vaguest of answers, and it was only when I came across the story of *Yukan* – which I summarize below – that I began to understand its significance. Hugh-Jones's informants, unlike mine, provided him with considerable exegesis. The silence of the Cashinahua in comparison to the Barasana can perhaps be explained by the different emphasis that each people places upon its ritual. The Barasana are concerned with detail, with naming each of the 'spirits' or mythical figures who come to their house. The Cashinahua are not so concerned with detail. For example, the spirits who enter the village are just referred to as generic *yuxin*. Nevertheless, *Kachanaua* can be seen as the acting out of one particular mythic cycle, that of the original and subsequent creations of the world. The two most important myths of this cycle, in terms of the interpretation of this ritual, are given below. One concerns an original creation of humanity; the other is the story of the great flood and its re-creation. These myths chart the passage from a time when generalized sexuality with siblings was practised, to the present age, when people marry properly into another moiety and into a category including their cross-cousins.

Yukan

At the beginning of the world Real People were created in a hole in a tree. When the people came out, they lived together in one village and there were no restrictions on who had sex with whom. Brothers and sisters lived together in the same house, and when a sister was old enough, her elder brother would marry her. The people increased and multiplied, generation after generation, becoming numerous and spreading out over the world. One night a pregnant woman called Ixma felt hungry for meat. She sent her brother-husband Yukan to the riverside to catch *tua* toads for her to eat. Yukan, who is also known as Binkun Chana, or Ni Nawa Dua (Forest Spirit Dua) lit his straw and rubber torch and went down to the river. There the Toad Spirit called and tricked him into visiting his underwater home. He disappeared from this world and went to live with the people of the River Spirit. His wife and her people were distraught and the next day went searching for him, calling and weeping bitterly as they went, as one does for a dead relative. Finally he replied, telling his wife he would visit her, but only if she prepared *caissuma* for all the people of the river.

She did as he bade and the next day they came, a great stream of fish-people all painted with genipapo and decorated with macaw feathers in their nostrils. The Real People were terrified and ran away to hide in their houses and Yukan's wife, instead of offering *caissuma* to the guests, tricked her husband into entering her hammock, where she clung to him with all her might. The leader of the River People was furious because of the way he and his people had been treated. He led them all back to the river. His revenge was dreadful. Since Yukan only wanted to stay with his own people and did not miss or long for his river people friends, he said, he was going to make them all come to him. They would live in the spirit world. So a great flood arose and the waters destroyed the world. Yukan, the Dua Forest Spirit, did not escape the grasp of his wife, but changed into a *pustu* fly, the kind that sucks blood. All the objects in the village of the Real People were transformed into fish. The Real People themselves were also transformed into dolphins, large tortoises, big fish and all kinds of game animals. There was only one survivor of this great flood, an old woman called Nete (Ministerio de Educación 1980).

Nete's story is the next in this cycle of myths. To her is attributed the subsequent re-creation of the world. Swept downriver on a huge tree, weeping in grief, she was blinded by wasp stings. Then she made four children in a gourd. These became the ancestors of the present-day Real People (Cashinahua). Unlike the Real People before the flood, these people married the correct category of person in the opposite moiety, and the origin of the moiety system may be attributed to them. Indeed, in one version of the myth, the four children are called Dua, Inu, Banu and Inani (D'Ans 1975). Their mother, now called Blind Nete (*Netebuekun*), took her offspring upriver, and on the way taught them the names of the cultivated plants that were by then growing on the beaches. Eventually they arrived at a very steep slope and set about climbing it, a feat that took several days. When they reached the top, they encountered Nete's brother *Navapaketanvan* (Immortal Big Foreigner). He tried to kill his sister, but his wife attempted to prevent him. Finally his 'sons-in-law', Netebuekun's sons, shot a poisoned dart into his enormous testicles as he worked in his garden. Thus Navapaketanvan died; but the creation continued and the children made gardens, built houses, and multiplied.

The social history recounted in these two myths is a simple one. They describe the creation of affinity after the destruction of the original world by the river spirits who had been rejected as affines. The River Spirit wanted a man called Dua Forest Spirit, or Yukan, as his affine, but was rejected by all of Yukan's kin including his wife (also Yukan's sister). The myths suggest that all affines, like all strangers, are dangerous. When Navapaketanvan (who seems to embody both an exaggerated outsider status and excessive male sexuality) tried to kill his sister, he had to be killed by his son-in-law (or his son, Netebuekun's son-in-law, in some versions). The relationship between this character and his sister Netebuekun lies at the origin of the contemporary human world. After these adventures humans discovered the correct form of affinity. The myths seem to say that the wrong affines – the river spirits (who are linked to the Dua moiety) – live downriver and underwater. The right affines – Netebuekun's brother and children – live upriver and on top of a steep slope. They are linked to the Inu moiety and the Inkas. Both Netebuekun and her brother die in the myth, and these deaths signal the end of one age – that of mythic time – and the beginning of another – that of historic time. The children of these two 'Ancient Ones' (*Xenipabu*) were proper humans, and their marriages were the start of proper social organization. But their origins as the children of a 'downriver woman' associated with Dua, and an 'upriver male foreigner' associated with Inu, are important.

The world before the flood was a world of pure 'inside'. Only close kin lived together and married together, and contact with the outside in the form of Toad Spirit ended in absolute disaster. When the pregnant woman was hungry for meat, her husband-brother's attempt to hunt was the cause of the downfall of these, the first Real People, who are called Hidabi giants. Tastevin (1925) reports that the huge fossils along the Muru river were thought of by the Cashinahua of that time as the bones of the Hidabi.

The two myths taken together are moral tales and show the fate of those who have not acquired cultural knowledge. From what we know about Cashinahua mores, it is possible to see that the ignorant behaviour of the Hidabi ancestors caused their own destruction. Only when Netebuekun's children began to interact properly and knowledgeably was it possible for creation to resume, this time successfully, since their descendants are still alive today. If we compare the myth to the ritual, these points become clearer. The ritual does not exactly replicate the myth. On the contrary, the participants omit the errors that the Hidabi ancestors made and show that they possess knowledge that their forebears, to their detriment, never had. Nevertheless this is knowledge that their desdendants must forever strive to acquire, as we have seen in preceding chapters. There is always a sense of danger, and an accompanying emphasis on the potential for disaster if the proper way to live were forgotten.

Creation and Procreation in Myth and Ritual

The myth of Yukan tells that the ignorant ancestors were first created in a tree trunk's hollow (*hi xankin*). In Tukanoan symbolism such a hollow can stand for a womb (S. Hugh-Jones 1979; Reichel-Dolmatoff 1971) and in this case the association is clear. The term *xankin* is also used in everyday parlance for 'womb'. There seems to be little doubt that the *kacha*, with its hollowed-out centre, stands both for wombs in general and the mythic tree-trunk in particular. It also explicitly symbolizes the vagina, entrance to the womb (Kensinger 1995:72). By placing the *kacha*, when it is brought in from the forest, beside the chief leader's house, this central point of the village is rendered analogous to the starting-point of human time, deep in the heart of the forest. It is also like the beginning of a single human life in its mother's womb. The systematic comparison between these two myths and the *Kachanaua* ritual reveals how the historical creation of the world recounted in myth and its cyclical re-creation in ritual are analogous, albeit dissimilar in certain key aspects, and that both processes bear close similarities to the process of procreation, during which human bodies are moulded.

The first event in *Kachanaua* involves the sexual taunting and the fire game, when men and women chase each other with burning bundles of straw. This takes place in the dark and is undifferentiated, in that men chase all or any women and vice versa. This part of the ritual cycle corresponds with the period in the myth when people married their siblings, when sex was undifferentiated. The sex was productive – many children were born – but ultimately it proved destructive. The end was brought about through a pregnant woman's desire for meat. She sent out her husband to hunt for her and his subsequent adventures led to the great flood.[2] The same sequence structures *Kachanaua*. After the fire game and the sexual taunting, that can be taken as metaphorical sex, the men go out hunting. This part of the ritual cycle could also be described as hunting magic, since the men who take part are said to be guaranteed success in the hunt as a result. Yet while the unfortunate Yukan is unlucky, tricked by the river spirit and trapped in his underwater home, the young hunters of the present human world are successful. With the help of the spirits they make real kills, in the same way that they do after consuming the *yubexeni* snake's tongue (Chapter 2). It makes sense that, if accidentally burned during the fire game, the hunter is protected from snakebite. It is as if he has not only taken on the snake's skills as a predator, but has also become like the snake itself. The difference between the historic and the ritual sequences is that while Yukan's people were ignorant, contemporary people are not. Finally, returning to the comparison with sexual reproduction, it can be seen that both the women of a village that has a *Kachanaua*, and also pregnant women observing dietary restrictions in general, are usually hungry for meat at this stage, just like Ixma, Yukan's wife.

Yukan is finally rescued by his people and brought back to the village, though empty-handed. In contrast, the hunters engaged in *Kachanaua* return loaded down with smoked meat and fish. They have prepared for the arrival of the visitors, and their women spend considerable time making the food and drink they will need to offer them. Ixma, Yukan's wife, does not. On the dawn of the day that the visitors will come, the men of Dua go downriver to become the spirits, dressing in the ornaments of palm-leaves and feather-headresses that will transform them. The Duabakebu come in with the rising sun and are greeted individually as 'Brother-in-law'. In the late afternoon, the reverse takes place. The Inubakebu come in from upriver dressed as spirits and are also greeted as affines. Both moieties are greeted by the opposite moiety, but also — and this is important — by their own moiety; that is, the affines receive them first and through the help of the women, who are kin to the visitors, they feed them and thus make them kin. As I have already shown, such food prestations are conceived of as turning potentially hostile outsiders (merely potential affines) into affinal kin. When the men feed their affines with their wives' and mothers' help, they are saying that they are bonded together like close kin. And, just as in day-to-day transactions, it is clear that men are able to feed each other only with the help and consent of their wives. When the affines come in in the guise of spirits they are re-enacting an event that took place in ancestral time, the first foreigner's visit. In contrast to the mythic encounter with the River Spirit People, when Real People succumbed to fear and remained hostile, this encounter with the forest plant spirits of *Kachanaua* is successful, and they are incorporated into the social world of humans and thus transformed from potential enemies to kin via the enactment of affinity. The result of this transformation is the creation of the possible conditions for the reproduction of the world.

The ambush expresses forcefully the fear of the other, and underlines the foreign nature of the guests. But immediately afterwards the hosts affirm the humanity of those they have ambushed. They offer the greeting which gives them the status of *chai*, and join them as they rush into the very centre of the village beside the house of the chief leader. When the forest plant spirits throw off their palm-leaf disguises, they reveal their own affinal humanity, offering it so to speak for appropriation and transformation into consubstantial humanity. The revealed affines are the raw material of kin. Via the present of food, the strangers are transformed, created kin. The feeding of one's affines during *Kachanaua*, as well as emphasizing their distinctness, symbolizes as well as it enacts in an embodied sense their integration into 'our kin' (*nukun nabu*). It thus strips away their alien and potentially hostile nature. It is through the consumption of a proper meal, itself a combination of complementary opposites representing male and female, that the kin relationship is ratified.

In the myth, the River Spirit People come in dressed and decorated, just as happens in *Kachanaua*. They come in from downriver, or underwater, like the Duabakebu. When they arrive they are greeted with consternation and fear. Although the moment in *Kachanaua* when the visitors are ambushed represents this hostility, it passes quickly and, taking heart, the people of the village rush up to the visitors and greet them by the term *chai*, which offers the possibility of kinship. Not so in the myth, where the people run away and hide in their houses. Ixma has not cooked for her brother-husband's friends nor prepared *caissuma* as he had bidden. Instead, she catches hold of him in his hammock and will not let him go. It is a woman, for the Cashinahua, who first refused proper affinity by refusing to part with her brother. She would not give him up, although he had already formed close attachments with the River Spirit People, who had come to visit out of a longing for him. He was already their kin in the sense that he had lived with them. Ixma and her kin condemned themselves to death by rejecting the relationship with these outsiders from another social and environmental domain. As a consequence the leader of the river spirits made them all kin by drowning, so drawing them all into his underwater world. This transformation took place after the refusal to feed outsiders and make them insiders. In *Kachanaua* the opposite occurs. After the feeding, the work of creation begins in the form of Ho Ho singing and dancing. In the songs the dancers name/call (*kena-*) the garden plants. Interspersed with the stately Ho Ho chants are the wilder bouts of sexual taunting. It appears that the dancers are emphasizing the role of sex in the process of production. In contrast to the start of the ritual cycle, there is no fire game on the final night, no wild running and chasing through the dark village. The sexual element is instead cooler and more controlled.

From the flotsam and jetsam of the first world, which had been destroyed in the flood, came the seeds of regeneration. Whereas the first people were created in the hollow of a wild tree, the recreated people were made in a hollow gourd – the fruit of a cultivated tree – found floating on the river. Thus as well as living in a world of 'pure inside', the first people also belonged to the 'outside', since they sprang directly from a wild plant body. The recreated people, by contrast, were more properly of the 'inside', since they sprang directly from a cultivated plant body. The first people are 'of the outside' because they belong entirely to the mythic age. The recreated people are 'of the inside' because they belong to historic time and because they are clearly differentiated from the mythic ancestors by not being the offspring of Netebuekun's body. Unlike the first ancestors, Netebuekun's children stumbled into correct affinity by visiting their *kuka* (mother's brother). On their journey back upriver, their mother taught them about the plants and vegetables of the garden, which she named (*kena-*) as they passed by the beaches where they were sprouting. This episode in the myth is analogous to the Ho Ho dancing and singing, which also combines motion and naming or 'plant baptism'.

However, it is not until Netebuekun and her brother Navapaketanvan have died that the Real People, this time marrying their cross-cousins as they ought, really multiply and the last mythic creation can begin. The death of these two ancestors, who are associated with the original birth in the hollow of a tree trunk, finds its parallel in the ritual when the *kacha* is finally destroyed and thrown out of the village. The *kacha* is a symbol of non-affinal creativity, and for this reason is broken up and thrown away, returned to the forest. The people who perform this act are the young men who are as yet not fully adult, either unmarried or just married. Like the spirit-visitors, they are not fully affines, because they have not yet created children, their parents-in-law's grandchildren. When the young men perform a parody of the entrance of the spirits and the initial Ho Ho dancing in the middle of the proper dancing, they seem to be emphasizing their own nature as semi-affines, as potential rather than actual producers of kin. They are the raw material of affinal kin, the outsiders who will make people's daughters able to produce offspring. By destroying the *kacha*, perhaps they affirm their own morally praiseworthy desire to be good affines, good brothers-in-law and sons-in-law. By slipping pieces of the *kacha* into women's mosquito nets, they appear to be distributing sexuality and fertility throughout the village.[3] The remnants of the *kacha* are symbols, it seems, of the beginning of properly controlled sexuality and creativity at the outset of historic time, when Netebuekun's and Navapaketanvan's children began to marry each other, after their parents' deaths. Finally, returning to the comparison with the process of sexual reproduction, the destruction of the *kacha*, that takes place close to dawn, is also analogous to the moment of birth, after the months of gestation, during which sex is the work of procreation.

The archaeology of meanings in myth shows clearly that the *Kachanaua* increase rites may be read as narrating a processual theory of creativity. The events work through a dynamic dualism, where life comes from death, and kinship from affinity, and the inside is the outside incorporated. As elsewhere in Amazonia, reproduction is only possible when the outside is brought in to the inside and the two are properly combined (Overing 1982, 1986a). Human life is based upon the transformation of the outside and its products and beings into the inside. I have shown in preceding chapters how this works in a number of spheres. Thus the social process depends on moiety exogamy and naming. The economic cycle turns upon the relation between male fetching and female transformative skills. The political process involves male acquisition of external knowledge and products. In *Kachanaua* we can see another dimension of this principle. Here, the normally invisible 'dream world' of forest spirits is brought into the circle of living humans. And as in other spheres, the idea of moiety is employed in the expression of this principle. Moiety captures neatly the rootedness of creation in the process whereby the growth, hardening and withering of bodies is brought about by the bringing together of distinct kinds of bodies. For in addition to the engagement between outside and inside, moiety also sums up the interaction between the mortal and material, on the one hand, and the immortal and immaterial, on the other. Within a living body (whether of a human or of a plant or animal) the tension between the two is held in the relationship between *yuxin* and *yuda*, spirit and body.

Plants and beings of the forest have their spirit side, just as humans do. These appear to dreaming or intoxicated humans as humans. To persons in a normal waking state they appear as simple animals and plants. The separation between these dream and waking manifestations was effected in mythical times, and it must be maintained if living people are to prosper. People need the bodies of plants and animals in order to reproduce themselves. *Kachanaua* shows how they need the help of the spirits of wild forest plants if their efforts to make the bodies of garden plants flourish are to bear fruit.

There is an exchange of services between the humans and the forest spirits. The spirits lend asexual fertility to the garden plants for the ultimate benefit of the gardeners, acting like grandparents naming their grandchildren in *Nixpo Pima*. Their naming 'fixes' and immortalizes the reproductive capacity of plants through a seasonal cycle that began with the planting of hard seeds or sections of stems cut from old plants and ends in the green corn harvest. In return, the humans behave towards the spirits as parents by feeding them. In particular, they feed them animals' heads, which may be taken as a symbol of immortal sexual regeneration. The trees and plants of the forest will flourish as a result of this service and the game animals and fish that men kill will eat of their fallen fruits and nuts. *Kachanaua* works, then, to produce the bodies both of domesticated vegetables and also of wild game and fish. Humans thus continue to dispose of these vital resources.

In *Kachanaua* men give their brothers-in-law game animal heads (*yuinaka buxka*), considered the best part of the animal, a gift that is so noteworthy that a common term for the whole ritual cycle is 'Making Heads' (*Buxka Vai*). Heads have more than gastronomic merits, if one considers the myth of Yube, the Dua man who became the moon. A number of variants of the myth are attributed to the Cashinahua, including one in which Moon was originally a girl who would not marry named Yasa (Abreu 1941:5401–2). In the versions I collected, Moon was originally a man.

The Story of Yubenawabuxka

Yube used to visit his sister in the night and make love to her. She did not know who her lover was, so she stained his face with genipapo, and he fled from the village. Together with his *chai* he went to hunt their enemies the Bunkunawa dwarfs. Unfortunately the Bunkunawa killed Yube and decapitated him. His weeping *chai* buried him in the ground, but the head arose from the grave. In hideous fashion it followed after the terrified brother-in-law, bouncing along and pleading all the while for food and drink. All attempts at satisfying the head's thirst failed, for the water poured out of the gaping hole in his neck. Eventually Yube realized that he must transform himself. He asked the women to throw coloured cotton into the sky and by grasping it with his teeth he ascended into the sky and became the moon (*uxe*). 'Look!' a little girl exclaimed, 'There is *Uxe!*'. Furious, Yube's head, who wanted to be known as Yube-Head-Foreigner (Yubenawabuxka) caused all the women to bleed with red macaw tail feathers. After they stopped, they all became pregnant. After this, a rainbow appeared for the first time, transformed from Yube's blood. As a result, humans are able to die, for there is a path from this world to the heavens.

When Yube is killed, his body is buried in the ground and rots, turning into liquid as Dua things do; but his head does not die. Instead, it bounds after its *chai* demanding drink and insisting that it be taken back home. But it cannot stay on this level of the cosmos with its kin, because it is dead, not a real person, and hence unable to produce or to consume. The water that its terrified kinsman pours into its mouth spatters out of its severed neck. Eventually the head's dilemma of longing for its kin in spite of its corporeal unsuitability for kinship is resolved by sending it up into the sky, the proper place for dead souls. Here Yubenawabuxka now fulfils a vital role. He enables Real People to live, reproduce and produce garden crops. As Moon, he lights the night, signals the time when gardens should be planted and causes women to menstruate. He is directly responsible for human fertility, because he causes women to produce the vital substance out of which babies are made. Like Yube himself, moonlight and blood are associated with Dua. Yube's head is immortal and does not rot like his body in the ground. Heads may be thought of as the Inu aspect of a person's or animal's body. Yube's head (*Yube-nava-buxka* or 'Yube-foreigner-head') is detached from his rotted body in a spatial and temporal sense. It is because of this detachment that Yube can continue eternally to give the power of corporeal productivity of mortal bodies to women. His death on this level of the cosmos signalled the start of the eternal process of human living and dying.

Based on this interpretation of the myth, I suggest that when people give their kin animal heads to eat, they feed their temporal bodies a symbol of immortality. Detached from mortal bodies, the heads symbolize a principle of immortal regeneration. In fact, *Kachanaua* feeding inverts the set of events in the Yube myth. There a male affine feeds a head that cannot consume. In *Kachanaua*, male affines feed animal heads to male affines who can consume. The immortal regeneration works like this: Heads symbolize the relationship between life and death. Given to the forest spirits they both 'make body' and thus kinship, and suggest a gift of a principle of regeneration to the spirits, in return for the naming of the garden plants. Yube's spirit gives the power of sexual reproduction to humans. The gift of an animal head to the plant forest spirits suggests the

Figure 15. Group portrait

bestowal of asexual fertility on the wild trees and plants. This results in the flowering and later the fruiting that follows the *Kachanaua* festival. People, animals and fish will consume the fruit and nuts, thus creating strength and health in their bodies. But the real food of humans is not wild forest fruit (the food of game animals) but rather garden produce mixed with the bodies of forest animals and river fish. It is precisely these things that men and women harvest and kill in the historical creation of sociality.

Notes

1. In the past the *kacha* was used as a container for fermenting *caissuma* in preparation for the final night of the ritual. See Chapter 7.
2. It would be possible to argue that the sexual taunting stands for Lévi-Strauss's 'rotten world', indicated by the riotous noise and darkness, signifying a disjunction between sky and earth, a disruption of the process of life by such disasters as eclipse or flood. In this case the

opposition between men and women in their competitive taunting could indicate the disjunction. Lévi-Strauss does make this connection (1970:289). Fire, in the fire game, could stand for the search for mediated conjunction between sky and earth, to avert the danger of total conjunction – the burned world (Lévi-Strauss 1970:293). Lévi-Strauss also argues that there is parallel between the rotten world, eclipse and incest (1970:296), which would fit with my analysis of sexual taunting and the fire game as undifferentiated (incestous) sex. The Ho Ho dances, following his analytic lead, would indicate total conjunction – the burned world – that is associated with chanting. The alternation between taunting (noise) and chanting all night long ends in silence at dawn, which is associated with the desired state, when cooking fire reigns again. See S. Hugh-Jones (1979:227–38) for a discussion of these themes in relation to the Barasana's Yurupari ritual.

3. I am grateful to Stephen Hugh-Jones for suggesting this. Kensinger witnessed men breaking the *kacha* and taking pieces to their mother-in-laws' hammocks, accompanied by sexual repartee between the two (1995:73).

7

Gender and Sociality

In the present, final, chapter I approach the wider issue of gender and sociality in Amazonia through the prism afforded by the Cashinahua ethnography, opening up what has until now been a relatively focused discussion to include a consideration of the contribution that this book makes to gender studies, Amazonian ethnography and related debates in anthropological theory. Thus I explore in greater depth the meaning that we might ascribe to the term 'gender' as we apply it to Cashinahua social life. Critiquing use of the phrases 'gender relations' and 'gender identity' in the literature, I argue that an appropriate approach to gender in Amazonia does not treat it as a fixed attribute or relation (what it 'is'), nor examine it as, in the first instance, personal experience (what it 'feels like'), but rather explores how it informs sociality (what it 'does').

Gender from the Amazonian Perspective

In Amazonian studies it has been commonplace to approach the topic of gender as concerned primarily with social, economic and political structures. The phrase 'gender relations' signified social relations between men and women treated as distinct social groups or as discrete individuals organized by a sexual division of labour. Sometimes authors argued that 'gender relations' in Amazonian societies are hierarchical and that men dominate women. This book does not discuss 'gender relations' as a global issue, and in this it supports the growing consensus in the academy that gender cannot be portrayed as 'a simple structure of fixed relations' (Morris 1995). Increasingly, power is not seen as an intrinsic aspect of social structures but rather as diffusely present in all social relations, waxing and waning as it is reiterated, negotiated and contested.[1] In societies where differences result in significantly differential access to material and symbolic resources, such a view may not capture the way that inequality becomes embedded in structuring processes. But in contexts where the access to the means of material and symbolic production is relatively evenly distributed, it is difficult to find 'hard' structural correlates for the affirmation that 'male domination is universal'. Hence, whatever the theoretical line taken, it is difficult to sustain the positions that in Amazonian societies 'gender relations are egalitarian' or that 'they are hierarchical' (Overing 1986b). This is not simply because Amazonians place a high value on personal autonomy or because sensitive ethnography highlights the subtleties and nuances of power. It is also because it is difficult to give the phrase 'gender relations' analytical force, as I shall explore in this chapter. The fact of the matter is that in Amazonian societies capital is not accumulated and social inequality is not institutionalized in economic or political terms.[2]

Some influential studies of 'gender relations' in the region would have that it *is* institutionalized, precisely within the posited male-female relationship. Before discussing these studies, it is worth making an aside. In making these points, I do not imply that we must not consider the different degrees or kinds of power available to men and women in distinct historical configurations of specific Amazonian societies. Rather, I wish to emphasise that it is necessary to shift from a language of analysis with heavy neo-functionalist implications (Knauft 1997) to one better equipped to deal with indigenous gender constructions and practices. I also hold that it is still necessary to avoid 'gender bias' in fieldwork and in our choice of significant data for analysis. An analysis of social organization that recognizes the full participation of women as well as men in social, political and economic processes and avoids relegating women's activities to a supposed 'domestic domain' is much better placed to illuminate the extent to which female agency is constitutive of political processes and to illustrate how far women have exercised power and enjoyed freedom of movement in Amazonian societies (Harris 1981; Yanagisako 1979). This clearly varies across time and space and within as well as between groups (Chapter 5). Descriptions of daily life, events, ritual games and patterns of relationships that emerge between men and women over time, do give readers a feeling for the varied tonalities of male-female inter-action. A generalizing expression such as 'the tenor of gender relations' may be used to refer to specific historical moments in the life of particular communities. Overall, for example, I would say that the Cashinahua men and women I lived amongst enjoyed generally non-coercive and coopera-tive social relationships. To make this impression explicit is not the same as stating that 'male-female relations in Cashinahua society are egali-tarian'. But it does problematize the idea that in Amazonian societies men dominate women or that an indigenous form of 'masculine identity' is destined to find resonances with a global 'hegemonic masculinity' (Moore 1994:63).

A concept corresponding to 'gender relations' does not emerge from the ethnography of personhood and social life presented in the preceding chapters. But nevertheless it is important to weigh this conclusion against those pioneering discussions of gender in Amazonia and ethnographies focusing on women that used the phrase or its precursor, 'relations between the sexes'. For although a series of authors have critiqued the theoretical and methodological premises that underlie this usage, and despite its tendency to fall into disuse in the literature on other ethnographic areas such as Melanesia, these premises continue to influence thinking on gender and sociality in Amazonia, and therefore it is necessary to give them careful consideration here.[3]

A favourite site for discussing 'relations between the sexes' or 'the genders' is the analysis of ritual. In such contexts, games often pit men against women in encounters replete with sexual language and imagery. In the literature on Amazonia anthropologists have often treated institutions like *Kachanaua* as 'rites of sexual antagonism' exemplifying a hypothetical 'battle between the sexes', much in the way that writers on Melanesian initiation rituals did in the 1970s (Strathern 1988). Claims about the drive towards male dominance in these societies that approach the issue through ritual usually treat it as an ideological mechanism of male control in the context of a much more ambiguous situation in the day-to-day order of things. The first full-length ethnography to treat 'male-female relations' in Amazonia, Robert and Yolanda Murphy's pioneering *Women of the Forest*, is a case in point. Writing about the Mundurucú, they argue that 'the ideology of dominance of male over female runs through rite and myth, but it is not so evident in daily life. . . . the men expressed their maleness, their need for ascendancy, their fears that perhaps their power was not real after all, in the public fantasy of ritual' (Murphy and Murphy 1974:186). During this period Janet Siskind published her book *To Hunt in the Morning*, at once an original analysis of economic organization and a sensitive account of Sharanahua women's and men's lives and engagement in social process. In a chapter subtitled 'Hunting and Collecting, the Battle between the Sexes', she describes a ritual, the 'special hunt', in which a group of women provoke men to hunt for them (Siskind 1973:89-109). In this, the upper Purus, region, communities belonging to other language groups also promote 'special hunts' playfully pitting men against women. (I observed a Kulina special hunt in 1984, so I was able to appreciate the ethnography she presents from a comparative perspective.)[4] In Siskind's description the Sharanahua women tease their 'partners' (who belong to a marriageable category but are not their spouses) and prod them into hunting for them with sarcastic comments and barbed jokes. After the hunters bring meat back and give it to their female 'partners', who cook and distribute it, the villagers eat and then they start to play various games pitting women as a group against men and vice versa. For example, women attack the men with stinging nettles and afterwards men seek to throw the women into the mud.

Siskind sees these games as expressing hostility. But she is careful to qualify this judgement with her ethnography of everyday life. She stresses that 'in most ways in everyday life the sexes are evenly matched . . . against each other in a semi-playful, semi-hostile battle' and that given 'the stability of the male-female relationship, based as it is on mutual social and economic dependence' there is room for an 'open expression of hostility' (Siskind 1973:108-9). Such expression may only take place, in other words, because relations between men and women in everyday life are strong enough to endure any possible strain resulting from the games. But here, as with the Murphys' analysis of the Mundurucú, the emphasis is placed on the separation of the two sexes conceived as enduring 'groups' in ritual and in daily life. The attribution of group membership is assumed and taken as natural rather than problematized. In what sense, we might ask, are the groupings that are formed temporarily in the games so conceived as natural units by the Sharanahua, or as 'solidary', as Siskind affirms? The key problem, as these authors see it, is neither what is meant by 'sexed individual', nor what is meant by 'group', but rather how these units fit into a social structure where power is at issue. It is easy to step from Siskind's emphasis on antagonism and hostility to the view that it derives from or expresses a struggle to subordinate women (though she makes it clear that Sharanahua women are not subordinate). In addition, both books postulate a psychological dimension – a male 'need' to oppose or dominate women and to experience a sensation of male solidarity.[5] For the Murphys, the Mundurukú ritual is a means of male fantasizing about elusive power over women. For Siskind, the Sharanahua 'special hunt' is an open expression of hostility between the sexes that extends their antagonism to its possible limits and creates a beneficial sensation of male group unity.

The theme of sex wars in Amazonia received considerable encouragement in the 1980s with the publication of Thomas Gregor's (1985) book about male sexuality in the Xingu, *Anxious Pleasures*. In the book, which includes excellent ethnography of the Mehinakú people, Gregor devotes a section entitled 'Gender Wars: the Rituals of the Pequi Harvest' to a description of a cycle of rites involving sexual games similar to those played in *Kachanaua* and in *Nixpo Pima*. Like Siskind and the Murphys, Gregor places emphasis on the psychological dimensions of the events.

But while for Siskind the relation between economic organization and male-female relations is of central concern, in this case the problematic constitution of masculinity conceived as male sexual identity is at issue. Using myths as if they were dreams open to a neo-Freudian interpretation, Gregor strongly defends a notion of the universal male, a concept that he constructs out of the Western sexological tradition (McCallum 1994). Men supposedly erect a ritual and mythological complex that allows them to dominate women. They are spurred to do this by sexual anxiety engendered by female physiology and control of reproduction. The principal pillar of male domination is ritual gang rape. The 'gender wars' thus reflect deep-seated male anxiety (held by Gregor to be universal) about women and their vaginas. This anxiety supposedly lies behind the institutionalization of hostility in the men's house and in gang rape. Fear of the latter 'keeps women in their place'. Underlying this logical sequence is the assumption that the act of penetration in sex enacts male domination, which is of course a typical feature of 'Western' thinking on sexuality and long since noted as ubiquitous in much sexual symbolism (Haraway 1989; Gow and Harvey (eds) 1994; Torgovnick 1990). For Gregor, Mehinaku male psychological weakness is transformed into a social structure (male centrality and ultimate domination, female peripherality and ultimate submission), and this turns upon the struggle to maintain a unitary 'gender identity'. One might observe that if such a notion is to be useful in discussing Amazonian peoples, it can *only* be formulated in response to an analysis of the social constitution of gender, not an externally applied psychoanalytical model. But there are other problems with the stress on a unitary and threatened masculine identity.

At least three basic pre-conceptions ground these discussions about the 'sexual antagonism' supposedly expressed in ritual. The first is that men and women are previously 'sexed' and that 'sex' can be read as a natural aspect of individuals understood as bounded biological and psychological units. The problem then becomes to attach social or cultural gender identity to these pre-given bodies. In the most extreme version of this picture, Gregor's account, wholeness can only be guaranteed if (male) gender identity is compatible with the natural characteristics of the sexed body. The second pre-conception is that these individuals come together into collectivities whose differences are ultimately generated by natural attributes such as female reproductive capacity and male sexual vulnerability. These two pre-suppositions then ground the idea that there are two 'sexes' – or in Gregor's more modern version 'genders' – who come together and interrelate, usually antagonistically.[6] Thirdly, the resulting notion of 'sexual antagonism' between two social groups who erect social boundaries of some sort (ritual or psychological) is a pre-condition for the questions 'Are male-female relations egalitarian or are they hierarchical?' and 'Do men control women?' The third basic pre-conception, then, is that gender relations must be either one or the other. The very existence of two 'genders' seems to call for a power structure of some sort. The first two concepts are a pre-condition for this third one, a point that has been made before in other contexts.[7] As Gow puts it, theoretical postulates about Native Amazonian societies, such as that control is at issue in male-female relations when men 'exchange' women in marriage, or when they confront each other in ritual or in daily life, depend upon 'the assumption that gender is constituted *before* issues of exchange or control are mobilized' (Gow 1991:120, my emphasis). The third supposition calls to mind a much more insidious reliance on the view that sexuality is universally an idiom of power, and that the penetrating penis is an instrument of control, as it invades and disrupts the integrity of other selves yet reinforces the superior boundedness of the penetrator. This view emerges from discourse peculiar to Western societies. Its application to Amazonian sexualities disregards alternative understandings, including indigenous ones.[8] In the Cashinahua case, all three suppositions – that gender is added on to previously sexed biological individuals; that sexed individuals form interacting pairs and are members of opposed collectivities internally united by shared biological characteristics; and that relations between groups and individuals concern a dispute for power carried out in the 'natural idiom of sexuality' – are difficult to apply. It is clearly necessary to measure carefully the descriptive terminology and the theoretical apparatus applied to gender and social organization in Amazonian societies, and especially so before attempting to come to general conclusions or to make comparisons with other ethnographic areas (*pace* Knauft 1997).

It is necessary to add some qualifying observations to the above critique. At the time that Siskind and the Murphys were writing, their studies provided a radical and much-needed response to the lack of attention paid to women in anthropology and to the subsequent paucity of information about their lives, problems that feminists had just begun to target (Rosaldo and Lamphere 1974; Reiter 1975). It was normal to speak of 'the sexes' with the implication that *a priori* 'natural difference' was in some sense grounding the socially and culturally elaborated relationships under focus, and that what was at issue was social control. Indeed throughout the 1970s and most of the 1980s the debate that dominated feminist anthropology concerned whether male domination of women is universal or not, and most feminists (and Amazonian anthropologists) simply took it as axiomatic that it was.[9] But by the late

1970s the distinction between sex and gender was in the process of elaboration, in the context of a specifically anthropological critique (with a marked feminist influence) of the nature/culture distinction (MacCormack and Strathern 1980). In parallel, within Amazonianist studies, ethnographers questioned the applicability of a universal category of 'nature' in the region (Descola 1986, 1994; Viveiros de Castro 1984, 1992, 1996). But oddly enough, in the face of the deconstructive work that has taken place in nearly all schools of Amazonian studies, the naturalization of women shows a certain resilience, not so much in the study of 'gender', which is rarely a primary focus of research, but rather in the discussion of the structures and processes of social life itself.[10]

In the context of discussing the light ritual casts on gender, one characteristic noted by Strathern (1988) in her discussion of those Melanesianist interpretations of initation rituals in the 1970s and 1980s that explicitly or implicitly bore the imprint of the 'sexual antagonism model' is a preoccupation with gender seen as a 'sexual identity'. Men are said to find it especially problematic to experience identity as whole and unambiguous, given women's biological superiority in the domain of reproduction. Resolution is achieved 'relationally', so that male culture constructs antagonism with women and asserts a 'social' superiority that outweighs the latter's natural pre-eminence. Strathern says that a focus on gender as identity 'confines gender within the psychodynamics of individual experience' (1988:59); and of course this has unhappy consequences for the theory of 'society' that emerges from or underwrites such a treatment of ritual. The comment is of course entirely apposite in the Amazonian case, as we have seen. The notions of 'gender identity' and 'gendered self' seem to cause more trouble than they do enlightenment.

Gender identity and selfhood are central preoccupations of contemporary gender studies, for example those within the broad frame of what has been called 'performative gender theory' (Butler 1990, 1993; Morris 1995). Rather than one gender identity for each sex, authors stress, we should recognize that within each social and cultural situation there are multiple possible femininities or masculinities that play against each other according to a dialectics of hegemony and counter-hegemony. Masculinities – especially 'hegemonic masculinity' – and the discourses that construct them have pre-occupied many of the writers in this wave of gender studies.[11] Gender identities are constructed in competing discourses that offer alternatives to individuals who 'inhabit' them by identifying themselves – or being made to identify by *force majeur*- with specific subject positions (Moore 1994). Thus personal identities are malleable, evolving, shifting or negotiable (Ginsburg and Tsing 1991;

Gutmann 1996; Bhavnani and Phoenix 1994). They take shape within a field of power and in the wider context of social inequality. The beauty of this approach to gender identity is that it at once overcomes the biological or culturalist reductionism of earlier theories while simultaneously allowing analysis to be open to the dynamic quality and complexity of social life. The earlier functionalist assumption that gender identities are part of a working social or cultural 'system' gives way to a view that they are in fact continually re-elaborated and constructed in historical discourses by interacting subjects. These discourses, in turn, shape and are mutually structured by particular on-the-ground situations that are characterized by inequalities and differences of race, class or gender. Anthropologists unhappy with the term 'culture' defend its replacement with a more dynamic concept of 'intersecting discourses' (Abu-Lughod 1991).

How do these ideas speak to gender and sociality in Amazonia and sit with the Cashinahua ethnography? An initial answer must admit that there are a number of problems in adapting them to this task, deriving from the heavy emphasis on the notion of discourse, the insistence on its embeddedness in situations of institutionalized inequality, and the equally problematic weight given to psycho-social identity. In the first place, in the Cashinahua case, it is difficult to discern 'competing discourses' about possible human masculinities and feminities with which people may identify themselves, even if we compare what men and women say privately about each other or about gender. In practice there were only two hegemonic gendered subject positions considered open to most of the young Cashinahua I knew – proper male (*xanen ibu*) and proper female (*ainbu kuin*). Adolescents are simply not presented with any real choices.

The notion of multiple gender identities was erected as part of the move to deconstruct 'binarism' – and gender binaries are a key target of postmodern and post-structuralist critique of earlier anthropological analytical approaches.[12] One is tempted to say that any search for multiplicity despite indigenous insistence on duality would run the danger of doing violence to the ethnography by ignoring both those discourses that indigenous Amazonians do develop, as well as the rich Amazonianist literature on dualism that they have inspired.[13] Furthermore, it seems to be incompatible with the ethnographic evidence on alterity and corporality, organized most recently under the rubric of 'Amerindian Perspectivism' (Viveiros de Castro 1998; Lima 1995, 1996; Lagrou 1997, 1998; Vilaça 2000; Gow 2001). A theory of gender in indigenous Amazonia must deal with the ubiquitous presence of both dualism and perspectivism in indigenous Amazonian cosmologies and ontologies.

The new gender studies insists that the subject positions open to experiencing persons are multiple, whereas native Amazonians, according to Viveiros de Castro (1998), treat the position of the subject as singular, abstract and genderless.[14] There is only one kind of subject position available to living persons: the human one. Yet every living thing and every spirit sees itself, its fellows, its cultural and social life, as human. Difference emerges when this point of view is not just embodied but also put into action in vision and the other senses. Alterity lies in the *perception* of other bodies ('other species') as different. When other beings are seen as 'same', difference breaks down and bodies die or are transformed.[15] Amerindian perspectivism ascribes points of view not to mind or spirit, but rather to the body (Viveiros de Castro 1998:478). Bodies differ – there are many kinds of animal, plant and person bodies (spirits also have bodies and may inhabit either type). These are distinguished not by appearance, substance, physiology and structure, but rather by their unique sets of dispositions, affects and capacities, akin to a 'habitus' (ibid.) or (I add) to embodied knowledge and 'human agency'. Bodies' appearances suggest dispositions and habituses, but may also hide them. Thus a jaguar body is a good clue to its jaguar habitus (predatory, eater of raw blood); but a human body may also be inhabited by a jaguar. Or, to take a Cashinahua example, a Cashinahua's body is probably inhabited by a Cashinahua habitus – though in what way and how well can differ, depending on the micro-history of its making. A Cashinahua who is brought up by Cariú and lives among them dwells in a Cariú body, despite appearances. A person who looks normal may be a *yuxin*, the term the Cashinahua use to refer to persons with mental disturbances. A Nawa body may also be imbued with a Cashinahua habitus, but (say in the case of my own English body) only weakly, alongside the bodies of real 'real persons'. Viveiros de Castro baptizes this component of perspectivism as 'multinaturalism'. A crucial aspect of it is that difference is in the eye of the outside embodied beholder. For alterity to work it depends upon the healthy embodiment of perspective, which founds the separation of species. The corollary of 'multinaturalism' is the 'subjective equivalence of souls'. Each sees itself as a human subject and perceives others species as Other (animal, enemy or spirit). If this perspective breaks down and, say, I begin to see the Other appearing as human like me, then transformation takes place and I pass over to another perspective. My body dies and I become an animal, an enemy or a spirit. From the 'I' position I pass to the 'You' position, and thereby become other. Rather than 'multiple gender identities' inferred from a set of distinct subject positions available to living humans, we may posit, perhaps, a 'unitary human identity', site of a unique, embodied perspective and created as distinct from that available to the bodies of a myriad of non-subjects – animals, plants, potential affines or enemies. Thus we have 'multiple objects' and just one subject position – the genderless 'I' perspective – located in this world of the living, in opposition to the one available alternative subject position – the 'You' perspective – located in the other world of the spirits (Viveiros de Castro 1998:482–483).

The bodies of most species are gendered. We saw how the Cashinahua conceive gender as embodied knowledge or 'agency'. Gender difference is clearly located in such created corporeal difference throughout Amazonia. Not surprisingly, it is often an idiom in which the theme of alterity more generally is expressed, for example, as a component of dual organization.[16] This casts an interesting perspective on the notion of multiplicity of gender positions or identities. If in Amazonian philosophy and practice multiplicity is a prerogative of 'nature' and is an effect of the perception of other bodies as Other, then in fact an infinity of choice is available, theoretically, to young Cashinahua. Alternative masculinities are contained in the bodies of male animals, and feminities in female ones. Thus a shaman or warrior who becomes a jaguar embodies not just the predatory inclinations of the species, but also the form that this takes in male or (in the case of a shamaness) female animals. There is evidence that this line of reasoning is worth following. For example, in the dietary restrictions practised during critical periods of life, a clear distinction is made between male and female game. A body's dispositions (among which are gendered aspects) do not disappear altogether after death but rather they linger on attached to the flesh. The same logic applies to the path of the spirits of real men and real women as they travel towards absolute this-worldly death. The differential ways of dying of men and women reflect the differences of their ways of living (McCallum 1996b, 1999). Living bodies also transform into other kinds of people. A Cashinahua person can also transform into a Nawa. If such a process is to take place, then obviously he or she may then construct 'self-identity' at the intersections of discourses emanating from Euro-American cultures and social groups – articulated, for example, by Cariú, missionaries, human rights workers or government officials. It would be fair to add that ideally the transforming Cashinahua would actually engage in sex with the foreigners as well as eat their food (McCallum 1997).

This brings one to a fourth problem with the idea that gender is in the first instance an 'identity' that sustains the organization of social relations. There is a danger of suggesting that native Amazonians are involved in a historical process in which a system based on dual identities – male or female – and twinned social roles is giving way to a more complex arrangement where a multiplication of gender identities and a concomitant diversification of social roles emerge from insertion into national society and the world capitalist system. This tempts us to bow to the idea that, in the case of 'simple' ahistorical Amazonian societies, new discourses making available novel gender identities arise principally when modernity impinges on tradition, and when complex cultural forms become accessible to members of 'newly' historical and increasingly unequal social structures.[17] Once again we arrive on extremely rocky terrain, if we begin to imply that history only began for Amazonian peoples when Christopher Colombus arrived in the New World.[18] Of course much of the readily identifiable diversity within and between indigenous cultures in lowland South America can be attributed directly to different histories of 'contact'. This is evident in the largest and geographically most spread out populations, such as the Kaingang.[19] However, history is also generated and internalized as kinship by local communities, not just imposed from outside by colonialist regimes (Gow 1991). Obviously, if alternative gender identities are to be seen as principally made available in the power asymmetries of interethnic systems or colonial encounters, then we run the risk of subscribing to a colonialist psychoanalytical theory that sees indigenous people (or people of African descent) entirely as historical victims and not agents in their own right (Mama 1995).

In short, a stress on gender as identity, even as a temporary and negotiable aspect of a decentred subject, seems to create more difficulties than it solves in the indigenous Amazonian context. Unless wielded with extreme caution, it serves to reinforce the notion that gender is primarily about the psycho-social identity of the individual subject, and only secondarily, as an outgrowth of this condition, a dynamic and generative aspect of specific social processes.[20] Indeed, the theme of unstable, shifting identity proposed by the new gender studies posits a universal psychological process. For example, Kum-Kum Bhavnani defended it as a concept with which to politicize psychology (Bhavnani and Haraway 1994).

The leap from a concern with identity to a concern with 'the self' is pertinent here. A further development in the new gender studies is the idea that multiplicity may be internalized, so that one person may nurture a fractured or partial sense of self (Moore 1994; Haraway 1991).[21] The incompleteness of the self, like identity itself, is an 'effect' of the relational engendering of knowledge as subjects exchange and rework different discourses. Indeed, Haraway wants to stress the relational manufacture of self-identity and proposes that the concepts of discourse and relationality are interchangeable (Bhavnani and Haraway 1994). People participate in each other as they produce and listen to discourse in social interaction, thereby temporarily drawing each other's boundaries. This formula neatly dispenses with the bounded and unitary subject, while allowing for the contingent, situational and historical aspects of the production of knowledge (and 'self-identity'). There are curious parallels between this idea that knowledge is always positioned, partial and constitutive of the self and the Panoan notion that bodies are constantly incorporating knowledge in interaction with others and with animate aspects of their material and spiritual environment. The idea that persons are processual and relational resonates with the Amazonian ethnography. Indeed, some authors have taken this up, though with explicit reference to Melanesian notions of the person rather than performative gender theory.[22] Sometimes in the latter the 'partible self' of this new feminist approach to the psychodynamics of subjectivity is likened to the Melanesian 'dividual' as discussed by Strathern (1988); but the two seem to sit uneasily together. This is because the ethnographic analysis of personhood uses a distinct epistemological angle from that applied to the 'partial self' in the feminist literature. While ethnography treats the biographical elements of social and cultural constructions from the outside, so to speak, the idea of the partial self treats it from the inside – it is infra-biographical (Gell 1998). It is the internal biography of the experiencing self (accessed through reflexive discourse) that is of concern, not the external biography of the gendered person (accessed through the ethnographic method) as he or she is located in the process of generating sociality. Once again, I worry that the 'indigenous point of view', available to us mainly through the written texts produced by anthropologists, is in danger of being lost in the process of analysis.[23]

Feminist criticism of Western assumptions in anthropological analyses encouraged researchers in the 1970s to pay greater attention to women. By the 1980s they were also stimulated to engage in constant self-appraisal at a time when 'reflexivity' came into fashion (Clifford and Marcus 1986; Kulick and Willson 1995). These anthropologists tried to be vigilant in the making of new ethnographies, listening to indigenous people speak, observing practice and resisting the unwitting intrusion of 'Western' conceptions. Feminist-influenced fieldworkers tested paths of interpretation against the 'data' and also against their own embodied understandings and memories, acquired through long-term participation in daily life. These ethnographically oriented anthropological studies of gender of the 1980s and 1990s aimed, therefore, to describe local social and cultural 'constructions' of gender and interpret them without recourse to

Cartesian dualisms or the reductionism characteristic of essentialist thinking.[24] They were very much a development of the Malinowskian ethnographic tradition (and the present book can be said to belong to this genre). Notably, although many authors, such as Vigdis Broch-Due, read and incorporated arguments from 'performative gender theorists', these ethnography-rich studies dispense with the near-exclusive analytical emphasis on 'discourse' and prefer a wider conceptual apparatus that allows much greater space for non-linguistic constitutions of meaning. For example, Broch-Due (1993) relies extensively on the symbolic analysis of non-discursive practices and argues for greater recognition of metonymic reasoning in the constitution of gender. Haraway herself remarks: 'There is no pre-discursive or pre-relational, using discursive as a kind of synonym for relational. One of the problems with using the word discourse is that the metaphor of language can end up carrying too much weight. I'm willing to let it carry a lot of weight, but I'm not willing to let it then finally *be* everything. There are non-language-like processes of encounter. But there is nothing pre-relational, pre-encounter' (Bhavnani and Haraway 1994:32). In a methodological frame developed largely out of the analysis of texts or of interviews, it is natural that the term 'discourse' should come to prominence. It is less natural from the perspective of the anthropologist searching for meaning in an Amazonian village. It is time to return to the ethnography – and the village – once again.

Sexuality and Gender in Ritual

The Sharanahua and Cashinahua are similar in many ways, so whilst I admire Siskind's sophisticated account of life on the Peruvian Purus in the late 1960s, I have always felt bothered by the notion that the games played by men and women were expressions of 'antagonism'. From a subjective point-of-view, when I experienced the Cashinahua fire chase and took part in the women's mock attacks on men after a Kulina special hunt, the principal sensation that I had was that of wild fun and not hostility at all. The games generated laughter and uproarious good spirits as the principal outcome, not a feeling of 'victory' by one side after a hostile competition. Was the tenor of the relations between Sharanahua men and women in the 1960s more aggressive than that of those between Cashinahua men and women in the 1980s? Or was Siskind overstating her case? I do not wish to give an overly 'angelical' impression of social life in the region.[25] In fact hostility between individual Cashinahua men and women may manifest itself on specific ritual occasions and people may take advantage of the games to injure those with whom they are already in conflict, as Kensinger documents carefully in his description of two cases he witnessed in Peru in the 1960s (1995:53–65). Yet these cases were atypical, leading to intervention from others, and provoked considerable anguish among co-residents. The fact is that the rites contain multiple possibilities for social action, and afford opportunities for a variety of postures and styles of participation. For example, it is equally possible and indeed expected that people use the games, which are laden with explicit reference to genitalia and to sexuality in general, to flirt with potential partners and indeed to seduce them.

In fact, it seems to me that if we seek a general characterization of the *Kachanaua* games, they are best described as a celebration of sexuality and an incentive to engage in sexual relations, not a 'war'. This is borne out by a number of experiences. On one occasion, during a *Kachanaua*, I was grabbed by a Cashinahua woman to whom I was related by name as 'sister'. She vigorously encouraged me to shadow her husband (my *chaita* or marriageable cousin) shouting insults to his penis. Pushing me against her husband as he sang and danced *Kaxin*, she sang the words to me and urged me to repeat them loudly into his ear, for all to hear and see. I understood this behaviour as part of my education as an *ainbu kuin* (real woman), since at that stage some of the villagers had decided to take me in hand and teach me everything from spinning cotton, to cooking, to proper sexual insults. Yet in fact some onlookers took my successful display of a capacity to insult my *chaita* as a public statement that my instructor's husband was my lover, something that only came to my attention years later when villagers told another anthropologist that this was the case (Elsje Lagrou, p.c.). It now seems to me that this was my 'sister's' way of telling me that she would approve of such a polygynous arrangement. Part of my training as a proper Cashinahua woman, conceived and treated as a process of physical embodiment of words, sights, sensations and substances, was to have been in real sexual contact with a *huni kuin*.[26]

Several years later, on a return trip to the Purus, during a small *Kachanaua* dance, I was asked to restrain another person's sexuality, not exhibit my own. This came about because I was assigned the task of keeping an eye on a teenage girl who was bent on seducing a highly desirable (in her eyes) young man against her family's wishes. I had become the young girl's special friend, and she nannied me and accompanied me everywhere. That night, after her older sisters tried unsuccessfully to keep her at home by ordering her to look after one of their babies, her family tried an alternative strategy. They knew that she would keep close to me during the fire games and the dancing, so her father asked me to get her to restrain her insults against the man and to pull her back during the heat of the moment, at which task I failed miserably. (Later she became pregnant by him and her father had to treat her with plant-based abortion medicine, since a marital union between the two was out of the question.) In sum, individuals use *Kachanaua* for a variety of purposes, very rarely for 'war between the sexes'. The rites may be experienced as highly erotic, stimulating participants subsequently to engage in sexual relations.

This brings me back to the question of discourse. One may ask whether *Kachanaua* might usefully be seen as discourse, as an indigenous commentary upon different kinds of relationships that men and women enjoy with each other as gendered persons, as well as an arena for the development of specific relationships (as in the cases described above). If this is so, then the outstanding theme of the discourse is sexuality. I suggest that if ritual is to be seen as part of the discursive construction of sexuality, any 'discourse' we seek to isolate should not be seen as 'ideology' imposed upon a contradictory reality, but rather as an elaboration of themes and ideas that are integral to everyday practice, including especially those that describe 'transformative processes' such as sex (Sanders 2000). However, I want to refine the linguistic apparatus of analysis here. As became clear in my exploration of *Kachanaua* in Chapter 6, there is very little in the way of explicit exegesis to go on when searching for deeper meanings of components of the rites. Therefore I had recourse to a rather old-fashioned method of analysis that owes much to the Lévi-Strauss of *Mythologiques*. Inspired by Stephen Hugh-Jones's (1979) investigation of the *He* rituals as practised by the Barasana in Northwest Amazonia, I found ample evidence to show that 'discourse' elaborated in myth, when related to day-to-day meanings and practices, explained not just the Cashinahua's own exegesis but also uncommented practices and characteristics of the ritual complex, such as the *kacha* and the operations performed upon it. Therefore, it is not correct to call the ritual a vehicle of a specific discourse, given that *Kachanaua* tells no stories, but merely alludes to some indirectly. Perhaps to describe ritual as 'discursive practice', in the sense that sets of meanings and values embedded in both ritual and other practices, of a variety of origins, permeate participants' experiences and embodied memories of the rites, would do it better justice.

As people participate in rituals or ordinary everyday activities, or talk to each other, or merely think, they are in a constant process of re-making meaning for themselves. This process is fundamentally social and inter-subjective. To engage in any social relationship, even with one's inner self, is to make meaning (Toren 1990, 1996, 1999, 2000). When making sense of myth and ritual by doing it, participants in *Kachanaua* interact with the structural residue of older semantic projects in the individual constitution of new meanings, ideas and theories, for example about gender and sexuality. When my 'sister' tried to make me more thoroughly her sister by encouraging me to have sex with her husband – and making this public – or when my teenage friend defied her family and seduced the forbidden object of her desire, both women were naturally inhabiting and thus redefining the sets of meanings and ideas encapsulated in *Kachanaua*, bequeathed them by their Panoan-speaking forebears, who originally created and later developed the ritual complex. Our best entry into making sense for ourselves of the bond between these ancient and contemporary projects in making ritual out of meaning (and vice versa), is to delve into it in an archaeological sense, as I did in Chapter 6, and relate the results to exegesis. In this case, the encouragement of proper sexuality (and discouragement of improper sexual unions) is clearly important, within the overall purpose of generating human and plant fertility and fostering community well-being. (Hostility between men and women is not.) This interpretation may cast a different light on rituals that we have been asked to understand according to the sexual antagonism model. In Gregor (1985), for example, the reader's attention is deflected from the Mehinaku affirmation that the Pequi rites are concerned with plant fertility and the health of the children by the insistence that they are above all 'wars'. Perhaps if they were seen as discursive practice in the sense I give this phrase here, the theme of war would simply fade away.

Kachanaua may be seen as the locus where a number of different discourses and other practices concerned with sexuality, gender and sociality intersect. One of these is contemporary sexual practice and exegesis about it. Another, expressed in the mute language of symbolism, with its barely hidden reference to myth, is a specific discourse on gender and sociality. I conclude this section by drawing out the mutual implications of this association.

In Chapter 1 I described how men and women use the term *chutaname* for 'to mutually fornicate', stressing the effect of the particle *–name* in emphasizing the reciprocity of the exchange of sexual substances, seen in the effect on the bodies of the couple, described as a *troca* (P.). Thus sex sometimes weakens a partner and strengthens the other, or vice versa. It is not interpreted as a metaphor for male dominance, nor is the penis an instrument of control. Rather sex is a source of physical and emotional pleasure and a means to make babies, though dangerous for the effects it produces in either men's or women's bodies.[27] Thus, when I suggest that the sexual taunting between men and women during the fire game in *Kachanaua* and in *Nixpo pima* is analogous to penetrative sex, I am most definitely not suggesting that taunting is concerned with an antagonistic competition for power. In the light of the ethnography of the sexual act itself, then, taunting can be seen as suggesting that the *particular* cross-sex relationship mobilized during sex, which encompasses all others during the games, is structured around a competitive reciprocity of action where what are exchanged are male and female agencies (sexual substances).[28] This relation is of course that between *xanu* and *chaita*, and/or husband and wife. What is at stake is male-female affinity, and this is the relationship that governs this moment of the ritual events. As during love-making itself, the mood is one of excitement and wildness, expressed in the rough and rapid physicality of the running and dancing, and in the creative abandon of the taunting, as people invent ever more ludicrous and disgusting metaphors for their companion's sexual organs, and suggest increasingly extraordinary or ridiculous sexual feats. Of course, just as in the real sex that couples enjoy later in the dark of the night, this metaphorical sex is concerned with creation, reproduction, transformation – and pleasure.

So of course the *kacha* is a symbol of the womb. In many of the *Kachanaua* I witnessed, several manioc tubers or plantains hung on a string over the hollowed out interior of the *kacha*. This seems to suggest male sexual organs, especially as women may taunt men by referring to their testicles as 'knobbly sweet potatoes' and their penises as 'minuscule bananas'. When the *kacha* is placed at the centre of the swirling mob of ribald men and women engaged in metaphorical sex, there seems to be a simultaneous stress on sex as both pleasure and reproduction. This association is strengthened when we recall that the growth of a foetus depends upon the man's consumption of *caissuma* and subsequent repetitive injection of it, transformed into semen, into his partner's womb. In the past, women would prepare a considerable quantity of *caissuma* for the last night of the festivities, and it would be vomited up into the *kacha* before the young men broke it up into pieces in the hours before dawn. The regurgitated *caissuma*, transformed orally (rather than genitally) into 'semen' thus accumulates to make a 'body' in the tree hollow cum 'womb'.

Abreu (1941:95–9) reports on the *Kachanaua* or 'Dance of the Pot-bellied *Paxiúba*' that the people of the Iboiçu used to organize at the start of the twentieth century. I summarize Abreu's informant as follows:

One man, the *kacha ibu*, cuts down the pot-bellied *paxiúba* palm and others help him excavate the middle and carry it back to the *maloca*. Meanwhile the women make a huge amount of *caissuma*, which they pour into the *kacha*, previously lined with banana leaves. It is covered over and left. Men and women together dance Ho Ho all night around the filled-up *kacha*. After five days and nights, they summon visitors and together everyone dances around the *kacha* till dawn, when it is finally uncovered and drunk dry. Then they vomit and take tobacco snuff, and the visitors go home. The *kacha* is thrown away.

Abreu's other informant gave a slightly different description of the proceedings. He said that the festival was held upon the *xanen ibu*'s orders when the corn was beginning to ripen and everyone wanted to drink *caissuma*. For the five days that it fermented in the *kacha* they danced at night and slept when the sun was high. On the morning of the final day other households were invited. Dressed in *dau*, they entered the house shouting, were sat upon stools and given food 'that they might eat'. After they had eaten, they danced till dawn, drank the *caissuma*, vomited, snorted tobacco snuff and then went home.

From these descriptions we can see that the association of *caissuma* and the *kacha* is very strong. Ritual *caissuma* is analogous to the transformed semen and menstrual blood that repeated sex shapes in the womb to form a child. The yellow corn, associated with high-ground gardens, stands for semen; the purple-skinned peanuts, associated with riverbanks and beaches, for menstrual blood. In this context, then, corn is male and the peanut female. This also makes sense if one considers that it is men who plant corn, whereas it is women who insert sprouted peanut seeds into the earth. Thus the ritual *caissuma* in its trough is like male and female blood in a womb. The sexual taunting is like sex. So the conjuncture of raucous men and women and the fermenting *caissuma* is analogous to the 'work' of sex, that is, the repeated intercourse that creates the body of the child.

These episodes of 'hot' sexual taunting initiate *Kachanaua*. They alternate with 'cool' Ho Ho dancing and singing in what follows. These shifts in tempo also signal a shift in the social relationships under focus. Ho Ho signals a sequence in which different forms of same-sex alterity rapidly substitute for or overlay each other. At first, the relationship between the two male moieties is one of potential enmity, immediately transformed into potential affinity in the use of the address term '*Chain*' (same-generation male affine). Eventually, these potential affines take the first step in becoming real affines, when they eat the real food ('heads', manioc and *caissuma*) that is served them. Eventually, they will complete the transformation, engaging in metaphorical sex with their *chai*s' sisters. Thus while the 'hot' moment of the games stresses cross-sex reciprocity and complementarity in reproductive work, the 'cool' singing and dancing of Ho Ho plays up the unstable but transformable qualities of same-sex male affinity.

Kachanaua transforms same-sex (male) enmity into affinal cooperation. Dangerous foreigners – the forest plant spirits – are made to become human for the benefit of the continued growth of humanity. They are greeted as affines and then they throw off their plant spirit clothes, materially transforming into humans in the perception of the villagers.[29] The process continues as they then substantialize the condition of affinal kin by eating proper human food. Then, linked together physically, arms over shoulders, hands clasped, visitors and hosts dance together and unite their voices in singing their relationship. Joined by the women, they dance to the gentle steady sway of the Ho Ho songs, around a symbol of a womb and a penis, of the conjunction of men and women in the creative process, of the reciprocity of sex. The focus now shifts away from reciprocity: the *kacha* now stands for complementarity in the economic cycle of the production, circulation and consumption of vegetable foods. At this moment men and women no longer shout out jokes referring to game animals and steeped in the imagery of sex. Instead they join together, singing the same words in different gender-defined styles. If the day began with an emphasis on a male relationship, by its end the focus is once again a male-female one. Taken as a whole, the day's events richly evoke the complex conjunction of distinct same-sex and cross-sex relationships that gives motion and content to the social process.

Other forms of alterity are also at play. The rites can be seen as cooperation between humans and spirits. In Ho Ho, singers name the domesticated plants out of which human life is created, so Ho Ho is an initiation ritual for plants, a vegetable baptism, akin to *Nixpo Pima* for humans. But who are the singers? The humans – the receiving moiety – are like the parents of the plants, the ones who foster the birth and growth of their bodies. The forest spirits – the incoming moiety – are like the affinal grandparents of the plants. They effect the attachment of their names. One need not look far for the origins of this instrumentality in mythic times. As Netebuekun and her children journey upriver after the flood she names the domesticated plants found growing wild on the riverbanks. Netebuekun is associated with forest spirits because she survived the flood by climbing on to the trunk of a huge tree that had been felled to make a garden. Such trees are said to be spirits, or the homes of spirits, and are also said to form connections with the upper layer of the cosmos, like the river itself. Thus the garden plants are named in myth by a figure who is not only an 'outsider' because she belongs to another age, but also because she is associated with the forest and the river. The plants are named in ritual by outsiders who stand in an affinal relationship to the 'parents' of the garden plants, the humans. This is an inversion of the situation in the naming of human children, who receive their names from persons of their own moiety and in a relation of kinship to them. Naming plants is a key step in ensuring their growth and general increase – and thus the health and fertility of the human community.

We may also see complementarity both across generations and between parents encompassed by Ho Ho and projected on to the task of making garden crops grow. The relationship between the incoming and receiving moieties may be cast as mimicking male-female affinity. By virtue of its localization 'inside', the welcoming moiety may be thought of as female. This impression is confirmed if we consider the very visible presence of women in preparing and handling the food that the receiving moiety gives to its spirit guests. Wives hand plates to their husbands, who serve their *chais*, who then hand the plates to their own wives. That this duality of gender in the incoming moiety is important is reinforced in women's *Kachanaua*, when men make a point of dressing as women, complete with babies and carrying baskets, and standing near their 'male' wives. If the wild plant spirits are taken as the fathers of domesticated plants, then they are the mothers. The forest spirits pass on plant fertility to their plant children, subsequently nurtured by the 'mothers'. Ho Ho seems to suggest this complementarity between male and female productive activities, but in material terms adds the reproductive agency of the wild plant 'fathers' to the creative process. This coupling of spirit masculinity and human femininity thus complements the linguistic work of naming led by the male and female chant-leaders, figures who seem to be analogous to name-giving grandparents. Seen in this light, *Kachanaua* suggests a whole set of different relationships, encompassing the spirit-human continuum and the intergenerational divisions of kinship, not just general 'male-female' ones.

In the alternation between Ho Ho and sexual taunting, which continues from dusk till dawn, the singers delineate the dual nature of sexual reproduction, which combines male and female substances, and Dua and Inu names, in the creation of life. They also express the cooperation between the forces of life and death, of mortal and immortal spirits, that underlies this process and the fertility of the garden plants. *Kachanaua* evokes a contrast with the fate of the Hidahi ancestors, who earned their own obliteration under the floodwaters because they did not know that

sexuality should be confined to certain categories of kin and that incestuous sex is wrong (Chapter 6). In *Kachanaua* there is a celebration of this
knowledge: men and women know as they dance and sing that those
whom they address as their *xanus* and *chais* are not at the same time
their sisters and brothers. This is the crucial difference. The existence of
affinal kinship is only possible through the recognition of the opposition
between marriageable and unmarriageable men and women and the
practice of correct sexuality.

There is a sense in which *Kachanaua* can be read as a commentary on
the corporeal fixedness or malleability of different forms of alterity.
Gender, once it is embodied as knowledge, seems to remain relatively
unaltered as a distinguishing condition, simply accumulating and waning
in physical power as life progresses and the body grows feeble. Corporeal
humanity, on the other hand, is considerably more malleable. Humans
become spirits once they have donned the *dau* for the Kachanaua.[30] These
spirits then become humans during the rite, as humans become spirits
when they die. This takes place as the transformation from one kind of
masculine entity to another (perhaps here one finds evidence of 'a
multiplicity of masculinities'). This may be simply because men are
epistemologically best equipped to deal with the outside. But men do not
become women nor women men. And perhaps this gendered distinction
between fixedness and transformability in bodies underwrites the fact
that proper gender is the key operator in the making of sociality among
living human beings.

Sociality in Amazonia

In his book on another Panoan-speaking group, the Matis, Erikson (1996)
seeks to reformulate the question of dualism by giving special emphasis
to the body. He coins the phrase 'dimorphic dualism' to call to attention
the key role of sexual dimorphism in the moiety systems of many Panoan
groups. He says: 'From many standpoints, sexual dimorphism appears
as the key metaphor, furnishing the conceptual model that serves to think
all the other sociological oppositions among the Panoans' (1996:102) (my
translation).[31] Although this emphasis on metaphor and conceptual model
call to mind a brute form of structuralism, wherein 'nature' is a raw
material out of which 'culture' makes itself, in fact Erikson's brilliant
ethnography of Matis body techniques belies this impression. In the
concluding chapters, he says that work on the body (tattoos, piercing,
decorations, etc.) are 'ontological components (*composantes*)' that are
part of the flesh, not just added on. He goes on to ask whether 'the effective

and symbolic work on the body, the famous fabrication of the person, also goes to play a constitutive role comparable to that played elsewhere by lineages and kinship relations more generally' (1996:327 my translation).[32] He is alluding to the view that 'African models' are not applicable to lowland South American social formations and to the perception that the notion of the person operates as a key structuring principle.[33] Erikson has his doubts about abandoning classical kinship analysis for an exclusive focus on the person. Like other, mainly French and Brazilian anthropologists during the 1990s, he adopts a Lévi-Straussian approach, devoting several chapters to the formal aspects of Matis kinship, viewed from the perspective of 'constitutive alterity' ('the will to integrate the outside in order to constitute the self' (1996:90) as a pan-Panoan phenomenon. Yet there is no need to oppose the formal analysis of kinship systems to the analysis of the relationship between personhood and sociality. On the contrary, in the Cashinahua and Matis cases, alterity is doubly constitutive – of the body on the one hand and of the social order on the other – and the language in which constitutive alterity operates is that of kinship. Whether it is the creation of a child's body with real food, names and ritual, or ritual mobilization of the moieties, a number of well-circumscribed social relationships are involved in a sequence of activities and events that result in the constitution of sociality itself. Mothers and daughters, fathers-in-law and sons-in-law, cross-cousins, husbands and wives – all these relationships are encompassed within an idiom of affinal and consanguineal kinship, in a perfect logical fit with moiety and namesake group. Gender is an aspect of these relationships, not so much in a static form as embodied knowledge, but rather when this transforms into energy, that is, when it is put into action in the cycle of economic and political activities.

Social action is infused with the male and female agencies engaged with each other in a complementary fashion (Chapter 3). Gender is embodied in the producer as a capacity for action. The transactions that structure social action operate along a continuum from true prestation to exchange. But the economic process, when it constitutes sociality, exhibits a centripetal logic. Gendered agency may be imagined as an invisible force that colours social relationships and inflects them in certain ways. It takes material shape not just in the flesh and organs of agents themselves, but also as the potential contained in the substances and gifts that pass between them, either on the transformative route towards constituting another human being (centripetal), or away from this and towards making otherness (centrifugal). Social value inheres in the action of giving, as it does in other 'brideservice economies', rather than accumulating in the object transacted.[34] If the object continues to circulate in alienable exchange, it loses its constitutive potential. If sociality is to be produced, value is realized in the act of consumption, rather than further circulation in cycles of exchange. One may interpret this (with some poetic licence) as a variation of Marx's 'consumptive production', where objects consumed are turned into people (Strathern 1988:364).

In this book I have stressed that sociality is best approached by examining social relations in movement and as part of a series of processes. As the book progressed, I analysed the series of links between the distinct forms of social relations between gendered persons in different domains and at different times. In this chapter, I showed that *Kachanaua* can be read as a commentary on such links, treated by the Cashinahua themselves as the foundation of social and economic process. Siskind rightly intended to demonstrate that the basic dynamic of economic organization in Amazonia derives from male-female interaction. These, she argued, were powered by the exchange of male meat for scarce female sex. Discussing the Piro, Gow comments that there 'is no simple exchange of meat for sex but a much more complex set of exchanges between men and women in marriage' (Gow 1991:126). One might add that these transactions are also embedded in or enmeshed with a series of other relationships, informed with gendered agency. More than focusing upon sets of exchanges within specific relationships, and instead of treating artificial constructions such as 'male-female relations', I have tried to approach sociality by describing the dynamic interactions of relationships within the whole set made available to the Cashinahua by their inherited social systems. In understanding sociality one must consider relations between relations, as Lévi-Strauss long since taught us.

There is no one social relationship that defines the making of sociality. Rather, a series of interconnected relationships are in constant motion. The most useful model for thinking this is a processual one that emphasizes the distinct stages in the economic cycles that structure social living (Gow 1991). Production, predation, appropriation, distribution, consumption, reproduction are all linked stages in this cycle. Both cross-sex and same-sex relations of production are brought into play at different moments of the agricultural cycle or at key stages in the life of a community. As Belaunde puts it in the Airo-Pai case 'each stage of the socio-economic process combines individual, conjugal and communal aspects, and, . . . at each stage cross-sex and same-sex ties are played out. For this reason, (. . .) Sahlins (1972) scheme of the domestic mode of production does not fully apply (. . .). and the married pair cannot be seen as an economic atom' (Belaunde 1992:19).

Cross-sex and same-sex relationships are organized by the second conceptual opposition basic to the generation of sociality: between the inside and the outside. This is lived by the Cashinahua in terms that allow for the transformation of extreme outside into the inside, of enemy into potential affine, potential affine into real affine and thereafter into kin. Viveiros de Castro (2001) writes: 'The construction of kinship is the deconstruction of potential affinity'.[35] That is, the dynamic between these two processes is integral to the constitution of human sociality. In an image that captures the spirit of this dynamic precisely, the Cashinahua say that upon death a Real Person goes to marry an Inka (*Inkan benewa-* or *Inkan ainwa-*) at last realizing the potential for affinity with *yuxin* that he or she must refuse during life. Viveiros de Castro notes that the position of gender in relation to the inside/outside opposition shifts in distinct Amazonian contexts; therefore, so too does its role in the constitution of kinship. Following Taylor (1983, 2000) on the Achuar, for example, he writes that only women can attain pure consanguinity; pure affinity is a male condition. In the Barasana case, by contrast, 'the distribution of gender values' is inverted.

In the Cashinahua case, gendered knowledge, when put into action, may be said to encompass the set of operations that converts (virtual) potential affinity into (embodied) actual kinship. Thus the relationships that are set up sequentially in the making of sociality are inflected with gender. Male-male affinity allows men's engagement with male beings of the outside to transform them from supposed enemies into potential male affines. It implies the subsequent activation of male-female affinity, as men turn inwards again towards women. The process continues from here until eventually kinship is produced. Thus the transformation of the external to the internal, or affinity into kinship, is made possible by putting male-male affinity into interaction with male-female affinity. These are vital stages in the processes that work by the logic of 'constituent alterity' to produce, but (differently from bridewealth systems) not transact, persons.

And so we may agree with Erikson – and with him the Panoans who endlessly re-invent moieties – that dualism works through bodies and that it does so by conjuring with the relationship between two oppositions: male/female and inside/outside. In their embodied form these oppositions are distinct. The former (gendered agency) is a condition for social action and also its mode of operation; the latter (true name) is a condition for human existence, for life itself. The Cashinahua term for 'to live', *hive-* is also, in substantive form, the term for 'house'. The house is the focus of sociality and it seems to me that this slippage in meaning between the active and the substantive reflects nicely the phenomenally dynamic view of matter in Amazonian ontologies. A solid house may stand still, but it contains the perpetual motion of life within it. The point here is that 'living the good life' (*hive pe*) depends on the constitutive work of dualism. This 'dynamic dualism' should be understood as generating a 'perpetual disequilibrium' that gives impetus and direction to the system (Lévi-Strauss 1991; Viveiros de Castro 2001).[36] This is equally true of cosmological, sociological and physiological processes, as is most obvious in the case of moieties, which are at once aspects of bodies, of communities and of the cosmos itself. And from the analysis of ritual in this book, it is clear that body processes are infused with and driven by cosmological ones.

Lagrou (1998) emphasizes the unstable chronological dimension of Cashinahua dualism. 'Alterity is produced out of sameness and sameness out of alterity . . . each pair of opposites (Dua moiety/Inu moiety, Snake-water/Inka-fire) participates in its opposite, and form resides in the relatively fixed and stable intersection/mixture of complementary opposites (bone/skin, body/soul, masculine/feminine, parent/affine etc.)' (Lagrou 1998:9, my translation). She emphasizes that all beings are intrinsically double, composed of opposites that depend upon each other for continuity of existence. Thus the body needs *yuxin* to exist, and she writes: 'This dynamic combination, that underlies the apparent stability of form, means that life itself is both precarious and possible' (ibid.). Lagrou's point is well taken. Cashinahua dualism insists that human form arises when the material and the immaterial are joined in the process of living. I would comment, however, that to this formula we must add that gender is not just one of the differences out of which new forms are made, but rather occupies a special place in the overall process whereby sociality is produced.

If I can sum up in a few lines, then, it is as follows: We can safely say, after the Cashinahua, that for Amazonian peoples sociality is rooted in the active gendered body. Social action projects itself into space and time in an endless tapping of difference, without seeking to transform all difference into social inequality. Amazonian gender is not reducible to its embodied form, existing above all as proper social interaction between Real People. This works to transform difference into living humanity. It is how Real People are made.

Notes

1. On gender and power see Moore (1994); Ortner (1996); Sanders (2000).
2. See the discussion of 'brideservice societies' and the 'political economy of control' approach to gender in Amazonia in this book's Introduction.
3. Recent examples include Lorrain (2000); Knauft (1997). For a critical approach see Overing (1986b, 1988); Gow (1989, 1991); Belaunde (1992) and in the Melanesian context, Strathern (1987). For a recent discussion of their continued influence see Lasmar (1999).
4. It seems that the Sharanahua ritual observed by Siskind was borrowed from the Kulina. For example, she notes that they sang in Kulina. Of course, this does *not* make the Sharanahua version any less authentic. See Pollock (1985) and Ruf (1972) for descriptions of the Kulina special hunt.
5. See Strathern's discussion of comparable arguments in the use of the sexual antagonism model in the anthroplogy of experience in Melanesia (1988:56-65). Knauft (1997) makes some apposite criticisms and surveys a wider range of Amazonian ethnographies than I do here, but unfortunately does not follow up his critical points.
6. Used in this way the very notion of culturally constructed 'gender', supposedly free of the biological conotations of 'sex', is in fact inseparable from them. Sex and gender are conflated, and 'culture' stands for or merely overlays 'nature' in an insidious and hidden form (Butler 1990). To say, on the basis of careful ethnography, that bodies are actively 'fabricated' by Xinguanos (Gregor 1985, 1977; Viveiros de Castro 1977, 1987) or other Amazonians, is not the same as making a theoretical claim that gender is 'constructed'.
7. See the discussion of Western notions of 'the self' as bounded and integral in Moore (1994) and Kulick (1995). Kulick cites Nedelsky (1990) and Keller (1986), who critique these ideas about selfhood as 'functions of a sexist apparatus intimately linked to practices of domination' (Kulick 1995:17). Instead, they stress the self's openness and fluidity.
8. The literature on sexuality, gender and power in European and American culture is vast. See for example Moore (1994); Gow and Harvey (1994); Torgovnick (1990).
9. Eleanor B. Leacock was one of the few who took the opposite view. See for example 1981, 1978. In the Amazonian context see Barclay (1985); Buenaventura-Posso and Brown (1980).

10. Perhaps not all authors would see themselves as engaged in 'deconstruction', but rather 'reformulation' of key categories such as 'nature' and 'supernature' in terms of ethnographic analysis. For example see Lima 2000.

11. Recent work on 'masculinities' includes Cornwall and Lindisfarne (eds.) 1994; Kimmel 1996; Gutmann 1996.

12. Hence the fascination with 'third genders' in performative gender theory noted by Morris (1995). For a critical discussion see Kulick (1998).

13. Key studies of dualism in Amazonian societies include Lévi-Strauss 1958, 1991; Carneiro da Cunha 1978; Maybury-Lewis (ed.) 1979; and Viveiros de Castro 1986, 2001.

14. Viveiros de Castro (1998); Vilaça (2000); Lima (1995), (1996) and Gow (2001) assume a genderless subject position. However, the examples that they give are almost exclusively male.

15. Theorists of Amerindian perspectivism have not as yet treated the topic of gender directly. However, Viveiros de Castro (2001) sets out the framework of a 'grand unified theory' or 'GUT' (as he calls it, after an expression coined by physicists) of Amazonian sociality, within which an approach to gender is encompassed. The paper prefigures a book-length study on the topic, entitled *A Imaginação Conceitual na Amazônia Indígena*.

16. For a general discussion see Erikson (1996:89-108)

17. Knauft (1997) does this.

18. On history and ethnography see Gow (1991).

19. Veiga (n.d.) describes considerable religious and social organizational variation among the Kaingang, population over 20,000. But see Fausto (1997) on significant divergences in the small Parakanã population.

20. If 'identity' is seen as constructed relationally, this problem might seem to be solved (Bhavnani and Haraway 1994). However, the outcome depends on the theoretical slant taken on social interaction. To date no in-depth published studies treating these problems with 'multiple gender identities' in the indigenous Amazonian context are available.

21. See the discussion in Kulick (1995).

22. Conklin and Morgan (1996); Pollock (1996); though the 'dividual' or 'partible person' of Melanesian ethnography is significantly different from the 'accumulative person' in Amazonia (McCallum 1999). For a comparative discussion of the dividual see also Busby (1997).

23. I do not mean to suggest that performative gender theorists or others working within the broad field of postmodern gender studies necessarily ignore ethnography. But it does seem that there is a tendency to sidestep the issue of dualist systems. Writers seem to prefer to discuss 'modern' and 'globalized' situations for examples of multiplicity and change and examples drawn from 'pre-capitalist' societies when critiquing anthropologists for binarism.

24. The theoretical basis of the concept 'construction' should not be confused with social constructionism, a methodology that sees actors as socialized into cultural roles. 'Gender construction' here is used in the sense of 'constituted in discourse and practice'. Therefore, it only works as a tool of analysis through ethnographic discussion. For examples of the ethnographic approach see MacCormack and Strathern 1980; Strathern 1988; Broch-Due *et al.* 1993; Kulick 1998.

25. Taylor (1996:206) gently questions what she terms the 'overly angelic accounts' of social relations by the 'English School of Americanism', citing Belaunde 1992; Gow 1991; McCallum 1989; and Santos Granero 1991 (though only one of these anthropologists is English, they were all students of Joanna Overing at the LSE during the 1980s). Viveiros de Castro (1996) also critically discusses the work of these anthropologists, coining the label 'the moral economy of intimacy' to describe their approach and likening it to the Fortesian concept of kinship as 'amity'. He defends an emphasis on exchange and predation over production, which is given higher theoretical value in the publications of this group (Rivière 1993). For a critical response see McCallum 1998; and see Rival (1998), who also questions an exaggerated emphasis on warfare and predation, though from a different angle.

26. Occasionally the Cashinahua encourage or permit sexual contact with 'good outsiders' like myself. In McCallum (1997) I analyse occurrences of this relatively rare phenomenon as part of the two-way sexualization of inter-ethnic relations. The encouragement of sexual relations with a few 'good foreigners', though running against the Cashinahua's strong preference for endogamy, follows the material logic of 'making real people' as described in this book. (For the record, I endured celibacy all my time in the field.)

27. See also Kensinger (1995:31-52 and 75-82).

28. Not meat for sex (Siskind), nor vaginas for men's sons (Kensinger 1995).

29. As elsewhere in Amazonia, ritual should not be interpreted as a 'performance', where 'actors' 'represent' spirits. When the Cashin-

ahua say they *are* spirits it is important to take them seriously (McCallum 1994). The condition is embodied (Erikson 1996). Clothes, masks, headresses and other body decorations alter the material condition of alterity in a person's body. On these issues see Gow 1991, 2001; Viveiros de Castro 1998.

30. A bien des égards, le dimorphisme sexuel apparaît comme la métaphore clef, fournissant le modèle conceptuel servant à penser toutes les autres oppositions sociologiques chez les Pano.

31. . . . le travail symbolique et effectif sur le corps, la fameuse fabrication de la personne, va également jusqu'à jouer un rôle constitutif comparable a celui que tiennent ailleurs les lignages et plus généralement les relations de parenté.

32. Overing Kaplan (1977); Seeger *et al.* (1979)

33. Collier and Rosaldo (1981); Strathern (1985); Belaunde (1992). For a detailed discussion see McCallum (1989).

34. I cannot do justice to Viveiros de Castro's theory here. Suffice it to signal its potential importance for understanding gender in Amazonia.

35. Lévi-Strauss's views on dualism are often misrepresented, so it is worth quoting an expert on his 'structuralism' at length here. Viveiros de Castro (2001) writes: 'The name of Lévi-Strauss usually evokes a strong partiality towards static, reversible and symmetrically binary oppositions. This image, however, corresponds much better to some "British" versions of the structuralist paradigm. Lévi-Strauss (1958) himself had very early pointed up the precarious nature of the symmetry exhibited by socio-cosmological dualities. It is hardly necessary to recall the points made in his famous article on dual organizations: the static quality of diametric dualism as a formal structure; the asymmetric values often attributed to diametric partitions as lived structures; the implicit or explicit combination of diametric and concentric forms of dualism; the derivability of the former from the latter; the triadic origin of concentric dualism, and its dynamic quality; finally and more generally, the derivative status of binary oppositions in relation to ternary structures.' Viveiros de Castro goes on to argue that Lévi Strauss transforms his model of concentric dualism in his discussion of 'dynamic dualism' in *Histoire de Lynx* (1991). Gow (2001) also profits from the capacity of Lévi-Straussian structuralist techniques to understand process and change.

References

Abreu (see Capistrano de Abreu)

Abu-Lughod, L. 1991. 'Writing against Culture'. In *Recapturing Anthropology: Working in the Present*, ed. R. G. Fox, pp. 137–62. Santa Fé, NM: School of American Research Press.

Aquino, T. V. de 1977. 'Kaxinawá: de Seringueiro "Caboclo" a Peão Acreano, MA thesis, Universidade de Brasilia.

Aquino, T. V. de and M. P. Iglesias 1999. *Zoneamento Ecológico, Econômico do Acre: Terras e Populações Indígenas*. Rio Branco: Instituto do Meio-Ambiente.

—— n.d. *Kaxinauá do Rio Jordão: História, Território, Economia e Desenvolvimento Sustentado*. Rio Branco-Acre: CPI-Ac (c. 1994)

Bakx, K. 1986. 'Peasant Formation and Capitalist Development: The Case of Acre, Southwest Amazonia', Ph.D. thesis, Liverpool University.

Barclay, F. 1985. 'Para civilizar-las mejor'. *Shupihui*, p.289–300. (Iquitos).

Basso, E. 1973. *The Kalapalo Indians of Central Brazil*. New York: Holt, Rinehart and Winston.

Belaunde Olschewski, L. E. 1992. 'Gender, Commensality and Community among the Airo-Pai of West Amazonia (Secoya, Western-Tukanoan Speaking)', Ph.D. thesis, London University.

Bhavnani, K. and D. Haraway 1994. 'Shifting the Subject: A Conversation between Kum-Kum Bhavnani and Donna Haraway, 12 April 1993, Santa Cruz, California'. In *Shifting Identities, Shifting Racisms*, ed. K. Bhavnani and A. Phoenix. London, Thousand Oaks, CA, New Delhi: SAGE Publications Ltd.

Bhavnani, K. and Phoenix, A. (eds) 1994. *Shifting Identities, Shifting Racisms: A Feminism and Psychology Reader*. London, Thousand Oaks, CA, New Delhi: SAGE Publications Ltd.

Broch-Due, V. 1993. 'Making Meaning out of Matter: Perceptions of Sex, Gender and Bodies among the Turkana'. In *Carved Flesh, Cast Selves: Gendered Symbols and Social Practices*, ed. V. Broch-Due, I. Rudie and T. Bleie (Cross-Cultural Perspectives on Women Vol. 8). Oxford/ Providence: BERG.

References

Broch-Due, V., I. Rudie and T. Bleie (eds) 1993. *Carved Flesh, Cast Selves: Gendered Symbols and Social Practices*. (Cross-Cultural Perspectives on Women Vol. 8). Oxford/Providence: BERG.

Buenaventura-Posso, E. and S. E. Brown 1980. 'Forced Transition from Egalitarianism to Male Dominance: The Bari of Colombia'. In *Women and Colonization*, ed. M. Étienne and E. Leacock. New York: Praeger.

Busby, C. 1997. 'Permeable and Partible Persons: A Comparative Analysis of Gender and Body in South India and Melanesia'. *Journal of the Royal Anthropological Institute incorporating Man (JRAI)* 3/2:261–78.

Butler, J. 1990. *Gender Trouble: Feminism and the Subversion of Identity*. New York, London: Routledge.

—— 1993. *Bodies that Matter: On the Discursive Limits of "Sex"*. New York, London: Routledge.

Capistrano de Abreu, J. 1941. *Rã-txa Hu-ni Ku-i: Gramática, Textos e Vocabulário dos Caxinauás*. Rio de Janeiro: Edição da Sociedade Capistrano de Abreu. [1914].

Cardoso, F.H. and G. Müller, 1978. *Amazônia: Expansão e Capitalismo*. São Paulo: Ed. Brasiliense.

Carneiro da Cunha, M. 1978. *Os Mortos e os Outros: Uma Análise do Sistéma Funerário e da Noção da Pessoa entre os Índios Krahó*. São Paulo: Ed. Hucitec.

Chandless, W. 1866. 'Ascent of the River Purus'. *Journal of the Royal Geographical Society* 35:86–118.

—— 1869. 'Notes of a Journey up the River Jurua'. *Journal of the Royal Geographical Society* 39:296–311.

Clastres, P. 1977. *Society against the State: The Leader as Servant and the Human Uses of Power among the Indians of the Americas*. Oxford: Basil Blackwell.

Clifford, J. and M. Marcus (eds) 1986. *Writing Culture: The Poetics and Politics of Ethnography*. Berkeley, CA: University of California Press.

Collier, J. and M. Rosaldo 1981. 'Politics and Gender in Simple Societies'. In *Sexual Meanings*, ed. S. Ortner and H. Whitehead. Cambridge: Cambridge University Press.

Conklin, B. A. and L. M. Morgan 1996 'Babies, Bodies, and the Production of Personhood in North America and Native Amazonian Society'. *Ethos* 24(4):657–94.

Cornwall, A. and N. Lindisfarne 1994. *Dislocating Masculinity: Comparative Ethnographies*. London, New York: Routledge.

Crocker, J. C. 1985. *Vital Souls: Bororo Cosmology, Natural Symbolism and Shamanism*. Tucson, AZ: University of Arizona Press.

References

Da Cunha, E. 1966. [1906]. 'O Rio Purus'. In *Obra Completa* Vol. I: 681–734. Rio de Janeiro: J. Aguilar. (Also in *Um Paraíso Perdido – Reunião de Ensaios Amazônicos*. Petrópolis: Vozes, 1976.)

D'Ans, A.-M. 1975. *La Verdadeira Biblia de los Cashinahua*. Lima: Mosca Azul.

—— 1991. *Le Dit des Vrais Hommes*. France: Gallimard.

—— n.d. 'La parenté et le nom: sémantique des denominations interpersonelles des Cashinahua'.

Dean, W. 1987. *Brazil and the Struggle for Rubber: A Study in Environmental History*. Cambridge: Cambridge University Press.

Descola, P. 1986. *La Nature Domestique: Symbolisme et Praxis dans L'Écologie des Achuar*. Paris: Editions des Sciences de l'Homme.

—— 1994. *In the Society of Nature: A Native Ecology of Amazonia*. Cambridge: Cambridge University Press.

Deshayes, P. 1986. 'La Manera de Cazar de los Huni Kuin: Una Domesticación Silvestre'. *Extracta* No.5. Lima: CIPA.

Deshayes, P. and B. Keifenheim 1982. 'La Conception de l'Autre chez les Kashinawa', Doctorat de 3ª. Cycle, Université Paris VII.

Dole, G. 1974a. 'The Marriages of Pacho: A Woman's Life among the Amahuaca'. In *Many Sisters: Women in Cross-Cultural Perspective*, ed. C. J. Matthiasson. New York: Free Press.

—— 1974b. 'Endocannibalism among the Amahuaca Indians'. In *Native South Americans: Ethnology of the Least Known Continent*, ed. J. Lyon. Boston, MA: Little, Brown and Co.

Dwyer, J. P. (ed.) 1975. *The Cashinahua of Eastern Peru*. Boston, MA: Hafenreffer Museum.

Erikson, P. 1996. *La Griffe des Aïeux: Marquage du Corps et Démarquages Ethniques chez les Matis d'Amazonie*. (Collection 'Langues et Sociétés d'Amérique Traditionnelle', 5.) Paris, Louvain: Éditions Peeters.

Fausto, C. 1997. 'A Dialéctica da Predação e Familiarização entre os Parakanã da Amazônia Oriental: Por uma Teoria da Guerra Ameríndia.' Ph.D. thesis, Museu Nacional, Universidade Federal de Rio de Janeiro.

Gell, A. 1998. *Art and Agency: An Anthropological Theory*. Oxford: Clarendon Press.

Ginsburg, F. and A. L. Tsing 1991. *Uncertain Terms: Negotiating Gender in American Culture*. Boston, MA: Beacon Press.

Goldman, I. 1963. *The Cubeo*. Urbana, IL: University of Illinois Press.

Gow, P. 1989. 'The Perverse Child: Desire in a Native Amazonian Subsistence Economy'. *Man*. N. S. 24:299–314.

References

—— 1991. *Of Mixed Blood: Kinship and History in Peruvian Amazonia*. Oxford: Clarendon Press.

—— 2001. *"A Man Who Was Tired of Living": How an Amazonian World Changes in Time*. Oxford: Oxford University Press.

Gow, P. and P. Harvey (eds) *1994. Sex And Violence: Issues in Representation and Experience*. London, New York: Routledge.

Gregor, T. 1977. *Mehinaku*. Chicago: University of Chicago Press.

—— 1985. *Anxious Pleasures: The Sexual Lives of an Amazonian People*. Chicago: University of Chicago Press.

Gutmann, M. 1996. *The Meanings of Macho: Being a Man in Mexico City*. Berkeley, CA: University of California Press.

Haraway, D. 1989. *Primate Visions: Gender, Race and Nature in the World of Modern Science*. London, New York: Routledge.

—— 1991. *Simians, Cyborgs, and Women: The Reinvention of Nature*. London, New York: Routledge.

Harris, O. 1981. 'Households as Natural Units'. In *Of Marriage and the Market*, ed. K. Young, C. Wolkowitz, and R. McCullagh. London: CSE Books.

Hornborg, A. 1988. *Dualism and Hierarchy in Lowland South America: Trajectories of Indigenous Social Organisation*. Uppsala Studies in Cultural Anthropology No. 9, Uppsala.

—— n.d. 'Panoan Marriage Sections: A Comparative Perspective'. Paper presented in the symposium 'Classic Panoan Topics in Light of Recent Research', 47th International Congress of Americanists, New Orleans. 1991.

Hugh-Jones, C. 1979. *From the Milk River: Spatial and Temporal Processes in Northwest Amazonia*. Cambridge: Cambridge University Press.

Hugh-Jones, S. 1979. *The Palm and the Pleiades: Initiation and Cosmology in Northwest Amazonia*. Cambridge: Cambridge University Press.

Ingold, T. 1986. *Evolution and Social Life*. Cambridge: Cambridge University Press.

—— 1987. *The Appropriation of Nature: Essays on Human Ecology and Social Relations*. Iowa City, IA: University of Iowa Press.

—— 1996. 'Introduction', In *Key Debates in Anthropology*, ed. T. Ingold. New York, London: Routledge.

Ingold, T. (ed.) 1996. *Key Debates in Anthropology*. London, New York: Routledge.

Kaplan, J. (See also J. Overing.) 1975. *The Piaroa*. Oxford: Oxford University Press.

References

Keller, C. 1986. *From a Broken Web: Separation, Sexism and Self.* Boston, MA: Beacon Press.

Kensinger, K. 1973. 'Banisteriopsis Usage among the Peruvian Cashinahua'. In *Hallucinogens and Shamanism*, ed. M. Harner. Oxford: Oxford University Press.

—— 1974. 'Cashinahua Medicine and Medicine Men'. In *Native South Americans: The Ethnology of the Least Known Continent*, ed. P. Lyon. Boston, MA: Little, Brown and Co.

—— 1975. 'Studying the Cashinahua'. In *The Cashinahua of Eastern Peru*, ed. J. P. Dwyer. Boston, MA: Hafenreffer Museum.

—— 1981. 'Food Taboos as Markers of Age Categories in Cashinahua Society'. *Working Papers on South American Indians (WPSAI)* 3:157–72.

—— 1984. 'An Emic Model of Cashinahua Marriage'. In *Marriage Practices in Lowland South America*, ed. K. Kensinger. Urbana, IL and Chicago: University of Illinois Press.

—— 1985. 'Cashinahua Siblingship'. *Working Papers on South American Indians (WPSAI)* 7:20–25.

—— 1995. *How Real People Ought to Live: The Cashinahua of Eastern Peru.* Prospect Heights, IL: Waveland Press.

—— n.d. 'Notes on *Nixpu Pima*'. ms.

Kimmel, M. 1996. *Manhood in America: A Cultural History.* New York: The Free Press.

Knauft, B. 1997. 'Gender, Identity, Political Economy and Modernity in Melanesia and Amazonia'. *Journal of the Royal Anthropological Institute incorporating Man (JRAI)* Vol.3, No.2:233–59.

Kracke, W. 1978. *Force and Persuasion.* Chicago: University of Chicago Press.

Kulick, D. 1995. 'Introduction: The Sexual Life of Anthropologists: Erotic Subjectivity and Ethnographic Work. In *Taboo*, ed. D. Kulick and M. Willson. London, New York: Routledge.

—— 1998. *Travesti: Sex, Gender and Culture among Brazilian Transgendered Prostitutes.* Chicago: University of Chicago Press.

Kulick, D. and M. Willson (eds) 1995. *Taboo: Sex, Identity and Erotic Subjectivity in Anthropological Fieldwork.* London, New York: Routledge.

Lagrou, E. M. 1991. 'Uma Etnografia da Cultura Kaxinawa: Entre a Cobra e o Inca', MA thesis, Universidade Federal de Florianopolis.

—— 1997 'Cashinahua Cosmovision: A Perspectival Approach to Identity and Alterity', Ph.D. thesis, University of St. Andrews.

References

—— 1998. 'Caminhos, Duplos e Corpos: Uma Abordagem Perspectivista da Identidade e Alteridade entre os Kaxinawa', Ph.D. thesis, Universidade de São Paulo.

Lasmar, C. 1999. 'Mulheres Indígenas: Representações'. *Estudos Feministas* Vol.7, Nos.1/2:143–56.

Lea, V. 1986. 'Nomes e Nekrets Kayapó: Uma Concepção de Riqueza', Ph.D. thesis, Museu Nacional, Universidade Federal de Rio de Janeiro.

—— 2000. 'Desnaturalizando Gênero na Sociedade Mebengôkre'. *Estudos Feministas* Vol.7, No.1/2:176–94.

Leacock, E.B. 1978. 'Women's Status in Egalitarian Society'. *Current Anthropology* 19:247–75.

—— 1981. *Myths of Male Dominance*. New York: Monthly Review Press.

Leeds, A. 1974. 'The Ideology of the Yaruro Indians in Relation to Socioeconomic Organization'. In *Native South Americans: The Ethnology of the Least Known Continent*, ed. P. Lyon. Boston, MA: Little, Brown and Co.

Lévi-Strauss, C. 1958. [1956] 'Les Organisations Dualistes Existentelles?' In *Anthropologie Structurale*. Paris: Plon.

—— 1969. *The Elementary Structures of Kinship*. Boston, MA: Beacon Press.

—— 1970. *The Raw and the Cooked: Introduction to a Science of Mythology*. New York and Evanston, IL: Harper & Row.

—— 1991. *Histoire de Lynx*. Paris: Plon.

Lima, T. S. 1995. 'A Parte do Cauim: Etnografia Juruna', Ph.D thesis, Museu Nacional, Universidade Federal de Rio de Janeiro.

—— 1996. 'Os Dois e Seu Múltiplo: Reflexões sobre o Perspectivismo em uma Cosmologia Tupi'. *Mana* Vol.2, No.2:21–47.

—— 2000. 'Towards an Ethnographic Theory of the Nature/Culture Distinction in Juruna Cosmology'. *Brazilian Review of Social Sciences* (Special Issue) No.1 ANPOCS.

Lizot, J. 1985. *Tales of the Yanomami: Daily Life in the Venezuelan Forest*. Cambridge: Cambridge University Press.

Lorrain, C. 2000. 'Cosmic Reproduction, Economics and Politics among the Kulina of Southwest Amazonia'. *Journal of the Royal Anthropological Institute incorporating Man (JRAI)* Vol.6, No.2:293–310.

MacCormack, C. and M. Strathern (eds) 1980. *Nature, Culture and Gender*. Cambridge: Cambridge University Press.

Mama, A. *1995. Beyond the Masks: Race, Gender and Subjectivity*. London, New York: Routledge.

Maybury-Lewis, D. (ed.) 1979. *Dialectical Societies*. Cambridge, MA: Harvard University Press.

References

McCallum, C. 1989. 'Gender, Personhood and Social Organization among the Cashinahua of Western Amazonia', Ph.D. thesis, London School of Economics, University of London.

—— 1990. 'Language, Kinship and Politics in Amazonia'. *Man* (N.S.) 25:412–33.

—— 1994. 'Ritual and the Origin of Sexuality in the Alto Xingu'. *Sex and Violence: Issues in Representation and Experience*, ed. P. Gow and P. Harvey. London, New York: Routledge.

—— 1996a. 'The Body that Knows: From Cashinahua Epistemology to a Medical Anthropology of Lowland South America'. *Medical Anthropology Quarterly* 10/3: 347–72.

—— 1996b. 'Morte e Pessoa Kaxinauá'. *Mana* 2/2:49–84.

—— 1997. 'Eating with Txai, Eating like Txai: The Sexualization of Ethnic Relations in Contemporary Amazonia'. *Revista de Antropologia* 40/1:109–47.

—— 1998. 'Alteridade e Sociabilidade Kaxinauá: Perspectivas de uma Antropologia da Vida Diária'. *Revista Brasileira de Ciências Sociais* Vol.13. No.38:127–36.

—— 1999. 'Consuming Pity: The Production of Death among the Cashinahua'. *Cultural Anthropology*. Vol.14. No.3.

—— In Press. 'Incas e Nawas: Produção, Transformação e Transcendência na História Kaxinauá' In *Pacificando o Branco: Cosmologia, História e Política do Contato no Norte da Amazônia*, ed. B. Albert and A. Ramos. Brasilia, Paris: ORSTOM.

—— n.d. 'O Conceito de Socialidade na Teoria Antropológica'. Ms.

Meillassoux, C. 1981. *Maidens, Meal and Money*. Cambridge: Cambridge University Press.

Mentore, G. 1987. 'Waiwai Women: The Basis of Wealth and Power'. *Man* 22:511–27.

Ministério de Educación 1980. 'Ixan: Cuento de los Antepasados'. CLGIS: Cashinahua No.3. Yarinacocha: Republica Peruana and Summer Institute of Linguistics.

Montag, R. 1998. 'A Tale of Pudicho's People: Cashinahua Narrative Accounts of European Contact in the 20th Century', Ph.D. thesis, State University of New York at Albany.

Montag, R., S. Montag and P. Torres 1975. 'Endocanibalismo funebre de los Cashinahua'. (Datos Etno-linguisticos No.45). Yarinacocha: Instituto Linguistico de Verano.

Montag, S. 1981. *Dicionário Cashinahua* (2 Vols.) Yarinacocha: Ministério de Educación Peruano and Instituto Linguistico de Verano.

References

Monte, N. 2000. 'Quém são os Kaxinawá'. In *Shenipabu Miyui: História dos Antigos*. Belo Horizonte: Editora UFMG, pp. 9–22.

Moore, H. 1994. *A Passion for Difference*. Cambridge: Polity Press.

Morris, R. 1995. 'All Made Up: Performance Theory and the New Anthropology of Sex and Gender'. *Annual Review of Anthropology* 24:567–92.

Murphy, Y. and R. F. Murphy 1974. *Women of the Forest*. New York: Columbia University Press.

Nedelsky, J. 1990. 'Law, Boundaries, and the Bounded Self'. *Representations* No.30:162–89.

Ortner, S.B. 1996. *Making Gender: The Politics and Erotics of Culture*. Boston, MA: Beacon Press.

Ortner, S. B. and H. Whitehead (eds) 1981. *Sexual Meanings: The Cultural Construction of Sexuality*. Cambridge: Cambridge University Press.

Overing, J. (See also Overing Kaplan and Kaplan) 1981. 'Review Article: Amazonian Anthropology'. *Journal of Latin American Studies* 13/1:151–64.

—— 1982. 'The Paths of Sacred Words: Shamanism and the Domestication of the Asocial in Piaroa Society'. Paper presented at the 44th International Congress of Americanists, Manchester.

—— 1983–4. 'Elementary Structures of Reciprocity: A Comparative Analysis of Guianese, Central Brazilian, and Northwest Amazon Sociopolitical Thought'. In *Themes in Political Organization: The Caribs and their Neighbours,* ed. A. B. Colson and H. B. Heinen (*Antropológica* Vols.59–62). Caracas: Fundación La Salle.

—— 1986a. 'Images of Cannibalism, Death and Domination in a Nonviolent Society'. In *The Anthropology of Violence*, ed. D. Riches. Oxford: Basil Blackwell.

—— 1986b. 'Men control Women? The Catch-22 in Gender Analysis'. *International Journal of Moral and Social Studies* Vol.1, part 2:135–56.

—— 1988. 'Styles of Manhood: An Amazonian Contrast in Tranquillity and Violence'. In *Society at Peace*, ed. S. Howell and R. Willis. London: Tavistock.

Overing Kaplan, J. (See also Kaplan and Overing.) 1977. 'Orientation'. In *Social Time and Social Space in Lowland South American Societies*, ed. J. Overing Kaplan (Actes du XLIIe. Congrès International des Americanistes (1976), Vol.2.), Paris.

Overing Kaplan, J. (ed) 1977. *Social Time and Social Space in Lowland South American Societies*. (Actes du XLIIe. Congrès International des Americanistes (1976), Vol.2), Paris.

References

Pollock, D. 1985. 'Personhood and Illness among the Culina of Western Brazil', Ph.D. thesis, The University of Rochester, Rochester, New York.

—— 1996. 'Personhood and Illness among the Kulina'. *Medical Anthropology Quarterly* Vol.10 No.3:319–41.

Price, D. 1981. 'Nambiquara Leadership'. *American Ethnologist* 8/4:686–708.

Reichel-Dolmatoff, G. 1971. *Amazonian Cosmos*. Chicago: University of Chicago Press.

Reiter, R. 1975. *Towards an Anthropology of Women*. New York, London: Monthly Review Press.

Rival, L. 1998. 'Androgenous Parents and Guest Children: The Huaorani Couvade'. *Journal of the Royal Anthropological Institute incorporating Man (JRAI)* Vol.4 No.4:619–42.

Rivière, P. 1969. *Marriage among the Trio*. Oxford: Oxford University Press.

—— 1974. 'The Couvade: A Problem Reborn'. *Man* 9:423–35

—— 1984. *Individual and Society in Guiana*. Cambridge: Cambridge University Press.

—— 1993. 'The Amerindianization of Descent and Affinity'. *L'Homme*, XXXIII (2–4)(126–8):507–16.

Rosaldo, M. and L. Lamphere (eds) 1974. *Woman, Culture and Society*. Stanford, CA: Stanford University Press.

Rosengren, D. 1987. *In the Eyes of the Beholder: Leadership and Social Construction of Power and Dominance among the Matsigenka of the Peruvian Amazon*. Goteborg: Goteborgs Etnografiska Museum.

Ruf, I. 1972. 'Le 'Dutsee Tui' chez les Indians Culina de Pérou'. *Bulletin de la Société Suisse des Américanistes* 1972:73–80.

Sacks, K. 1979. *Sisters and Wives: The Past and Future of Sexual Inequality*. London: Greenwood Press.

Sahlins, M. 1972. *Stone Age Economics*. Chicago: University of Chicago Press.

Sanders, T. 2000, 'Rains Gone Bad, Women Gone Mad: Rethinking Gender Rituals of Rebellion and Patriarchy', *Journal of the Royal Anthropological Institute incorporating Man (JRAI)* (N.S.) 6, 469–486.

Santos Granero, F. 1991. *The Power of Love: The Moral Use of Knowledge amongt the Amuesha of Central Peru*. London: Athlone Press.

Seeger, A., R. Da Matta and E. Viveiros de Castro 1979. 'A Construção da Pessoa nas Sociedades Indígenas Brasileiras". *Boletim do Museu Nacional*. NS 32:2–19.

References

Siskind, J. 1973. *To Hunt in the Morning*. Oxford: Oxford University Press.

Strathern, M. 1984. 'Subject or Object? Women and the Circulation of Valuables in Highand New Guinea'. In *Women and Property, Women as Property*, ed. R. Hirschon. London: Croom Helm.

—— 1985. 'Kinship and Economy; Constitutive Orders of a Provisional Kind'. *American Ethnologist* 12/2:191–209.

—— 1987. 'Introduction'. In *Dealing with Inequality*, ed. M. Strathern. Cambridge: Cambridge University Press.

—— 1988. *The Gender of the Gift*. Berkeley, CA: University of California Press.

—— 1999. 'Entrevista: No Limite de uma Certa Linguagem'. *Mana* 5(2):157–75.

Tastevin, C. 1925. 'Le Fleuve Muru'. *La Geographie* 43: 403–22.

—— 1926. 'Le Haut Tarauacá'. *La Geographie* XLV:34–54, 158–75.

Tastevin, C. and P. Rivet 1921. 'Les Tribus Indiennes des Bassins du Purús, du Juruá et des Régions Limitophes'. *La Géographie* XXXV (5):449–482.

Taylor, A.-C. 1983. 'The Marriage Alliance and its Structural Variations in Jivaroan Societies'. *Social Sciences Information* 22(3):331–53.

—— 1996. 'The Soul's Body and its States: An Amazonian Perspective on the Nature of Being Human'. *JRAI* 2/2:201–15.

—— 2000. 'Le Sexe de la Proie: Représentations Jivaro du Lien de Parenté'. *L'Homme* 154–5:309–34.

Tocantins, L. 1979. [1971]. *Formação Histórico do Acre*, Vols. I and II. Rio De Janeiro: Civilização Brasileira.

Toren, C. 1990. *Making Sense of Hierarchy*. London: Athlone Press.

—— 1996. 'For the Motion (2)' in '1989 Debate: The Concept of Society is Theoretically Obsolete'. In *Key Debates in Anthropology*, ed. T. Ingold. London, New York: Routledge.

—— 1999. 'Compassion for One Another: Constituting Kinship as Intentionality in Fiji'. *Journal of the Royal Anthropological Institute incorporating Man (JRAI)* Vol.5/2:265–80.

—— 2000. *Mind, Materiality and History*. London, New York: Routledge.

Torgovnick, M. 1990 *Gone Primitive: Savage Intellects, Modern Lives*. Chicago: University of Chicago Press.

Townsley, G. 1988. 'Ideas of Order and Patterns of Change in Yaminahua Society', Ph.D. thesis, Cambridge University.

Turner, T. 1979a. 'Kinship, household and community structure'. In *Dialectical Societies*, ed. D. Maybury-Lewis. Cambridge, MA: Harvard University Press.

References

—— 1979b. 'The Ge and Bororo societies as dialectical systems: a general model'. In *Dialectical Societies*, ed. D. Maybury-Lewis. Cambridge, MA: Harvard University Press.

Veiga J. n.d. 'Cosmologia Kaingang e suas Práticas Rituais'. Paper presented to the Workshop '*Etnologia Indígena*', XXIV Annual Meeting of ANPOCS, Petrópolis, Brazil, 2000.

Vilaça, A. 2000. 'Relations between Funerary Cannibalism and Warfare Cannibalism: The Question of Predation'. *Ethnos* Vol.65 No.1:83–206.

Viveiros de Castro, E. 1977. 'Indivíduo e Sociedade no Alto Xingu: Os Yawalapiti'. M.A. thesis, Museu Nacional, Universidade Federal de Rio de Janeiro.

—— 1984. 'Araweté: Uma Visão da Cosmologia e da Pessoa Tupi-Guarani', Ph.D. thesis, Museu Nacional, Universidade Federal de Rio de Janeiro.

—— 1986. 'Sociedades Minimalistas: A Propósito de um Livro de Peter Rivière'. *Anuário Antropológico* 85:265–82.

—— 1987. 'A Fabricação do Corpo na Sociedade Xinguana'. In *Sociedades Indígenas e Indigenismo no Brasil*, ed. J. Pacheco de Oliveira Filho. Rio de Janeiro/UFRJ/Editora Marco Zero.

—— 1992. *From the Enemy's Point of View*. Chicago: University of Chicago Press.

—— 1993. 'Alguns Aspectos da Afinidade no Dravidianato Amazônico'. In *Amazônia: Etnologia e História Indígena*, ed. E. Viveiros de Castro and M. Carneiro da Cunha. São Paulo: EDUSP/Núcleo de História Indígena.

—— 1996. 'Images of Nature and Society in Amazonian Ethnology'. *Annual Review of Anthropology* 25:179–200.

—— 1998. 'Cosmological Deixis and Amerindian Perspectivism'. *Journal of the Royal Anthropological Institute incorporating Man (JRAI)* Vol.4 No.3:469–88.

—— 2001. 'GUT Feelings about Amazonia: Potential Affinity and the Construction of Sociality'. In *Beyond the Visible and the Material: The Amerindianization of Society in the Work of Peter Rivière*, ed. L. Rival and N. Whitehead. Oxford: Oxford University Press (in press).

Wagley, C. 1976. [1953]. *Amazon Town: A Study of Man in the Tropics*. Cambridge: Cambridge University Press.

Weinstein, B. 1983. *The Amazon Rubber Boom 1850–1920*. Stanford, CA: Stanford University Press.

Yanagisako, S. J. 1979. 'Family and Household: The Analysis of Domestic Groups'. *Annual Review of Anthropology* 8:161–205.

Glossary

Cashinahua

ain	wife
ainbu	woman
ainbu chana xanen ibu	female chant-leader
ba-	to create, be created, to be cooked
ba	cooked, born
bai	garden
bake	child
bakebu	children
Banu	female moiety name (Dua moiety)
bava-	to cook
bedu	eye, seed
buni	hungry
chai	brother-in-law, male cross-cousin [male speaker]; far away (adj.)
chana	cacique or oropendola bird
chana xanen ibu	chant-leader, male chant-leader
dami	image, drawing, doll, transformation
dami-	to transform
Dua	moiety name, male moiety name
dua	shining
duapa	generous
hancha	tongue, language
hi	tree
huni	person, man
Huni Kuin	Real Persons, Cashinahua, Indians
hunibu	people, men
ibu	parent, owner, responsible one
Inani	female moiety name (Inu moiety)
Inu	moiety name, male moiety name
inu	jaguar
ka-	to go

kacha	ceremonial trough
Kachanaua	increase rites
kena	name
kena-	to call, invite, name
kena kuin	true name, Cashinahua name
kuin	true, real
kuka	father-in-law, MB, [woman's] son.
mae	village, settlement
mae-	to move house
nabu	kin
Nava	Foreigner
navan kena	Christian name
nava-	to dance
nixi pae	hallucinogenic beverage made with *Banisteriopsis caapi* (Lat.)
nixpu kuin	stalk used to blacken and harden teeth (*cordoncillo* (Sp.))
nixpu pima	baptismal rites
nukun	our
pintsi	hungry for meat
tsabe	sister-in-law, female cross-cousin [woman's]
xanen ibu	leader
xankin	womb, hollow
xenipabu	old one, ancient one, ancestor
xeta	tooth
xuta	namesake
yauxi	miserly
yuda	body
yupa	unlucky in hunting
yuxibu	monster, demon
yuxin	soul, spirit, ghost, photo, portrait

Portuguese

alma	soul, spirit
Area Indígena	Indigenous Area [legal term for area recognized under Brazilian law]
aviamento	fitting out
Caboclo	Indian (regional usage in Acre)
Cariú	non-Indian, Brazilian (regional usage in Acre)

Glossary

colocação	hamlet, small settlement, rubber tapper's base. (colocações (pl.))
correria	planned massacre
maloca	indigenous Amazonian dwelling housing several families
parente	relative, kin
patrão	boss, manager
seringa	rubber (*Hevea brasiliensis* (Lat.))
seringalista	rubber boss
seringal	rubber-producing area under control of a seringalista or institution such as a company or cooperative; rubber estate.
seringueiro	rubber tapper
tuxaua	leader, chief

Index

Index

Index

sexual taunting in *Kachanaua* 137, 143, 148, 151, 156n2, 170, 173–6
women's *Kachanaua* 143–4
Kaingang 167
Kalapalo 127n2
Kariera kinship terminology 27–8, 30
Kaxinauá 12
kena stools 43, 101
Kensinger, Ken 8, 27, 170, 156n3, 184n28
kinship 5, 24, 27–30, 32, 115, 178, 180
  cross-cousin marriage 59, 146
  Fortesian concept of kinship as 'amity' 184n25
  humanity and kinship 71, 104, 108, 150, 178
  kinship terminology 29–39
  memory and kinship 7, 67
  moieties and kinship 32, 36–8
  naming and kinship 21–7, 175–6
  relations of caring 32, 71, 75, 117, 127n4
  ritual and kinship 176
  use of kin address terms 30–8, 105
Knauft, B. 182n5
knowledge 46, 48–58, 68, 73, 122, 129, 166, 178, 180
Kulina 12, 21, 30, 111, 138, 159, 169, 182n4

land rights 11, 111, 123, 126
Lea, V. 127n3
Leacock, E.B. 182n9
leaders 68–70, 109, 117–28
  chantleaders (*chana xanen ibu*) 69, 112, 132, 134–6, 142, 144
  chiefs, bosses and *tuxauas* 111, 117–27
  leader's house 68–9, 102, 104, 123, 138
  leaders as parents of the village 108, 111, 117, 123
  male and female leaders 69–70, 102, 104, 108–9, 111–17, 123, 126
  relations with kin 109, 120–3
leadership 68–70, 128
Lévi-Strauss, C. 2, 128, 171, 178–9, 155–6n2, 185n35
Lima, T.S. 66, 183n10

machismo 115
male domination 3, 24, 157–9, 161–2, 172
male violence 115, 116
manioc 17, 47, 79, 81–3, 105
marriage 27, 36, 59–64
marriage sections 18, 24–5, 54
Marx, K. 179
masculinities 163, 177, 183n11
Mastanahua 21
masturbation 16
Matis 177–8
meals
  breakfast 77
  collective meals 102, 104, 123, 138
  eating and sociality 107–8, 112
  feasting in *Kachanaua* 130, 142
  proper meals 99–100, 150
meetings 110, 132
Mehinaku 6, 54, 160–2, 172
Meillassoux, C. 6
Melanesia 91, 159, 163, 168, 182n5, 183n22
memory 49
menstruation 16–17, 52–5
mental illness 165
miserliness 75–7, 95, 113, 120
moieties 24, 37, 31–2, 181
  kinship and moieties 27, 31–2, 36–8
  marriage and moieties 59, 146
  moiety names as address terms 36–7
  moiety principle of social organization 66, 152
  origin of the moieties 146–7
  ritual and moieties 138–43, 149–52, 175, 178
  true names and moieties 24–5, 63
Moore, H. 3, 167, 182n7
multinaturalism 165
Mundurucú 159–60
Murphy, Robert and Yolanda 159–60, 162
Muru river 147
mythology 72–4, 145–56, 171

nabu kuin 28, 32
names
  Christian names 27, 34
  social reproduction and names 27, 63, 178

Index

Index